50 Strategies for Improving Vocabulary, Comprehension, and Fluency

An Active Learning Approach

Second Edition

Adrienne L. Herrell
Educational Partnerships
Panama City, Florida

Michael Jordan
California State University, Fresno
Educational Partnerships
Fresno, California

PEARSON

Merrill
Prentice Hall

Upper Saddle River, New Jersey
Columbus, Ohio

Library of Congress Cataloging-in-Publication Data

Herrell, Adrienne L.

  50 strategies for improving vocabulary, comprehension, and fluency : an active learning approach / Adrienne Herrell, Michael Jordan.--2nd ed.

    p. cm.

  Rev. ed. of: 50 active learning strategies for improving reading comprehension. c2002.

Includes bibliographical references.

ISBN 0-13-171205-5

  1. Reading comprehension. 2. Active learning. I. Title: Fifty strategies for improving vocabulary, comprehension, and fluency. II. Jordan, Michael, 1944– III. Herrell, Adrienne L., 50 active learning strategies for improving reading comprehension. IV. Title.

LB1050.45.H47 2006

428.4'3–dc22

2004064964

Vice President and Executive Publisher: Jeffrey W. Johnston
Senior Editor: Linda Ashe Montgomery
Senior Editorial Assistant: Laura Weaver
Development Editor: Kathryn Terzano
Senior Production Editor: Mary M. Irvin
Design Coordinator: Diane C. Lorenzo
Cover Designer: Terry Rohrbach
Cover Image: Getty Images
Production Manager: Pamela D. Bennett
Director of Marketing: Ann Castel Davis
Marketing Manager: Darcy Betts Prybella
Marketing Coordinator: Brian Mounts

This book was set in Sabon by Carlisle Communications, Ltd. and was printed and bound by Banta Book Group. The cover was printed by Coral Graphic Services, Inc.

Pearson Education Ltd.
Pearson Education Singapore, Pte. Ltd.
Pearson Education Canada, Ltd.
Pearson Education—Japan

Pearson Education Australia PTY, Limited
Pearson Education North Asia Ltd.
Pearson Educacíon de Mexico, S.A. de C.V.
Pearson Education Malaysia, Pte. Ltd.

10 9 8 7 6 5 4 3 2 1
ISBN: 0-13-171205-5

To our friend and colleague Susan McCloskey,
teacher extraordinaire.

ABOUT THE AUTHORS

Adrienne Herrell has recently retired from California State University–Fresno, where she was a professor of reading/language arts and taught classes in early literacy, assessment, and strategies for teaching English language learners. *50 Strategies for Improving Vocabulary, Comprehension, and Fluency: An Active Approach* is Dr. Herrell's eighth book for Merrill/Prentice Hall. Her previous books include *Camcorder in the Classroom* with Joel Fowler, *Fifty Strategies for Teaching English Language Learners* with Michael Jordan, *Reflective Planning, Teaching, and Evaluation: K–12* with Judy Eby and Jim Hicks, and *Teaching Elementary School* with Judy Eby. Dr. Herrell's writing and research are built on her experiences teaching in Florida's public schools for 23 years. She and Dr. Jordan (co-author) are currently engaged in research in public schools in California and Florida. She teaches part-time for her alma mater, Florida State University, in Panama City where she now resides.

Michael Jordan is an associate professor in the Department of Curriculum and Instruction at California State University–Fresno. He has taught primary grades through high school in Georgia, Alabama, Florida, and California. Dr. Jordan is also an actor, education director, and board member of Theatre Three Repertory Company in Fresno, California, and is dedicated to providing access to live theater to children and youth. He and Dr. Herrell incorporate many dramatic reenactment strategies in their joint research working with vocabulary and comprehension development in children learning English in the public schools of California and Florida. This is Dr. Jordan's fourth book for Merrill/Prentice Hall.

PREFACE

Vocabulary, Fluency and Comprehension: The Keys to Understanding

The 2003 Nation's Report Card on Reading, issued by the National Assessment of Educational Progress (NAEP), indicates that 37% of U.S. fourth graders and 26% of eighth graders were reading below the basic level. This means that they could not necessarily demonstrate an understanding of the literal meaning of a text, draw out its main idea, make inferences, and relate their reading to personal experience (http://nces.ed.gov).

Recognizing that nearly one-third of elementary and more than one-fourth of middle school students are having difficulty understanding what they read, this book offers teachers a variety of strategies to assist students with increasing reading fluency and vocabulary, and to advance comprehension. These basic skills provide the opportunity they need to succeed in a constantly changing and challenging society. As students move through grade levels, they are deluged with new and more difficult vocabulary. Required texts have become more intricate and demand greater interpretation and understanding. Failing to give students a foundation for making sense out of the myriad varieties of text they will encounter will only handicap them in a world that expects students to read, analyze, and synthesize greater amounts of information.

Why Did We Write This Text?

All students need the opportunity to become proficient at reading. With increasing pressure to teach the national reading standards, raise test scores, and begin to use performance assessments to measure the competency levels of readers in our schools, teachers are asking for support and assistance in finding ways to teach strategies that actively involve students in processing and understanding text. This book is intended to provide that support. The strategies included in this text are designed to be used to teach comprehension processes used by effective readers. However, they must be accompanied by ongoing teacher assessment in the form of observations and questioning in order to monitor and adjust instruction to benefit the developing reader. Used consistently, the teaching of comprehension, fluency, and vocabulary strategies, and ongoing assessment of their use, work together to improve student success in reading. It is this consistent application that is necessary to move students toward more successful engagement with text and an enjoyment of reading.

Comments from the Field:

"Using strategies from the first edition of this text has enabled me to meet all the language arts standards with my students."

"A timely approach to engaging students."

"It is one of this text's many outstanding features that each strategy is lucidly described and rigorously illustrated."

"One is never bored nor confused when reading this material."

"In my opinion, this book is in the same league as J. Irwin's."

"I think this text has enormous potential to make an important contribution to professional literature in the area of reading instruction. The material is fresh, and the examples are meaningful."

TEACHING THROUGH ACTIVE STRATEGIES: THE PURPOSE OF THE BOOK

This book is designed to assist teachers in actively engaging students to increase their reading vocabulary, fluency, and comprehension. Through an infusion of the best research on the learning of vocabulary, fluency, and comprehension skills, this text shows teachers how to activate the learning process in students; it engages them in the exploration of vocabulary and the development of comprehension skills they need to become enlightened and enthusiastic readers.

- Students are encouraged to become active participants in ongoing vocabulary, fluency, and comprehension development.
- Students are "active learners" in the process, not passive recipients of information.
- Students learn to reflect on and monitor their own comprehension processes and modes of learning, developing more and stronger skills as they progress.
- Teachers are shown to incorporate powerful strategies into their current teaching models without "adding on" more material.
- Teachers are provided with exciting strategies for teaching and assessing the tough topics of reading: inferences, main idea, fluency, and so on.
- "Step by Step" instructions enable teachers to incorporate the strategies quickly and effectively in their own classrooms.
- Classroom examples for different ages are given to assist the teacher in visualizing real-life applications for implementing the strategies.
- Strategies included are classroom-tested and effective with students facing the most difficult challenges in our schools today.

GETTING AROUND: ORGANIZATION OF THE TEXT

This book is organized into six sections related to the five comprehension processes and assessment. Section I relates to word and sentence comprehension and introduces strategies for developing vocabulary and fluency. Section II relates to paragraph-level comprehension and presents many strategies to support a reader's understanding of the connections among sentences and the structure of paragraphs. Section III focuses on strategies for integrating background knowledge into the reading process. Section IV offers a look at holistic comprehension and strategies to strengthen understanding and provide skills in summarization. Section V focuses on self-monitoring strategies and gives suggestions for supporting students in becoming strategic readers. Section VI provides innovative assessment approaches that focus not only on comprehension but also on the assessment of reading-strategy use.

The 50 strategies in this book are designed to support teachers in assessing the strategies currently used by students. The teacher can then use the knowledge gained through assessment to help students:

- learn to process text,
- use the comprehension processes that strong readers use, and
- acquire vocabulary and fluency in a way that will support their comprehension and overall learning in the classroom and in life.

Each chapter defines a strategy, gives step-by-step instructions for implementing the strategy, and provides classroom examples demonstrating ways in which the strategies can be adapted for various grade levels and curricular areas. The focus in each of the strategies is active learning, active involvement of the students, and empowerment of the students to self-monitor, using processes and fix-it strategies as needed.

What Is New in This Second Edition?

Meeting the Needs of English Language Learners

With the increasing diversity in today's classrooms, teachers are concerned about meeting standards with ELL (English Language Learner) students. Because of this need, margin notes are included in each chapter to assist teachers in ensuring they address the needs of English learners in the classroom.

Classroom Examples Illustrate Strategy Use

Two classroom examples are provided for each strategy to illustrate how it has been used in a primary or elementary classroom and how it works for a middle school/secondary classroom. In order to include two classroom examples at different grade levels for each strategy, one example has been included in each chapter and the second one has been included on a CD provided with the text. A variety of grade levels have been used for the examples included in the text, and the CD example for each strategy focuses on a different grade level. Margin notes give the readers an advanced organizer for the second example as well as tell them where to locate the example on the accompanying CD.

Inclusion of Fluency Strategies

In response to requests from teachers across the nation, an increased focus is placed on fluency strategies, an often-overlooked element in proficient reading, throughout this second edition.

Strategies for All Grade Levels

Because we recognize that approaches to teaching reading must be sensitive to the ages and background knowledge of the readers being taught, examples from kindergarten through high school are integrated throughout this second edition. They are clearly marked so the teachers or credential candidates can easily choose the examples most appropriate to their needs.

Acknowledgments

We would like to thank the following reviewers for their insightful guidance and direction: Nancy S. Bailey, Metropolitan State College of Denver; Diane Barone, University of Nevada, Reno; Jennifer Borek, The University of Memphis; Kathleen M. Pierce, Rider University; and Rose Pringle, University of Florida.

CONTENTS

INTRODUCTION

Reading comprehension is an essential part of reading instruction and has been examined in many contexts over the years. Typically, teachers have been taught to employ strategies before, during, and after reading to teach comprehension. For example, before reading, teachers are to support the understanding of vocabulary concepts students will encounter. Processes to use during reading are taught with the notion that students must learn to monitor their understanding and use approaches that help themselves make sense of the text. Activities for use after reading the text to review, discuss, and summarize what has been read are presented to facilitate the memory and integration of the material into the students' schemata. Utilizing schemata before, during, and after activities are still viable ways to develop comprehension. However, Judith Irwin uncovered more explicit processes that provide teachers more in-depth direction for teaching reading comprehension.

What Good Readers Do

In 1991 Judith Irwin published a book entitled *Teaching Reading Comprehension Processes*, which approached the concept of reading comprehension from a different perspective. Irwin, thoroughly examined the processes used by good readers to process text, breaking these processes down into five categories. She explored the microprocesses used by readers as they read vocabulary and gained meaning from the individual sentences they read. Irwin then looked at integrative processes, those used to gain meaning and connections from adjacent sentences. Integrative processes involve the referents of pronouns and other connections between sentences that must be understood in order to make sense of paragraphs in textual material.

Elaborative processes are defined by Irwin as those processes that involve the interaction of past experiences and past readings, called intertexual understandings, with the comprehension of the materials being read. Macroprocesses are those used to gain the overall meaning of the text, such as summarizing or stating main ideas and supporting details. She called the final group of processes metacognitive processes. Metacognitive processes are the strategies used by the reader to monitor his or her understanding and to revisit or reprocess text when understanding is not complete.

Both models of comprehension instruction; before-, during-, and after-reading strategies and the five comprehension processes can and should be integrated into reading instruction. Strategies in this text will provide you before, during, and after active learning experiences that also promote Irwin's reading processes that identify what good readers do. However, strategies that develop reading comprehension should not be taught in isolation. As a teacher you know that some preparation for reading is required with text that is unfamiliar to readers. You realize that readers' background knowledge can be stimulated, if it exists. You may also know that a reader's background knowledge may be insufficient to support comprehension without additional experiences and vocabulary development. Thus, examining the importance of vocabulary development is also useful to learn how to improve your students' reading abilities and comprehension.

The Importance of Vocabulary

Vocabulary development has been widely researched. In the past 20 years there have been a number of research studies examining the impact of vocabulary knowledge on student achievement. As a result of the vocabulary-acquisition research, three main implications for instruction have been recognized:

1. the wide range of vocabulary understood by students,
2. the differences in vocabulary knowledge between low- and high-achieving students,
3. and the importance of a sustained focus on oral and written vocabulary, acquisition within the reading/language arts program.

Several researchers have proposed evidence that strongly links vocabulary deficiencies to academic failure in disadvantaged students in grades 3 through 12. Although there is no evidence that any single method of teaching vocabulary is superior, many comprehensive programs for supporting vocabulary acquisition have produced positive results (Dixon-Krauss, 2002; Lapp, Jacobson, Fisher, & Flood, 2000; Nilsen & Nilsen 2003; Rosenbaum, 2001). For this reason, teachers of reading and language arts are well advised to incorporate daily vocabulary-acquisition strategies into their programs.

Closely related to vocabulary size is the emphasis on vocabulary growth across the grade levels. Research in vocabulary size and growth (Beck & McKeown, 2001; Nagy & Anderson, 1984) estimates that by learning 3,000 new words a year, students will develop vocabularies that will equal those of high-achieving students. Acquiring 3,000 new words a year breaks down to approximately 8 new words per day. However, teachers must be very cautious not confuse *fast-mapping*, the very cursory understanding of words encountered in context, with *extended mapping*, the full understanding of a word's meaning. To accomplish extended mapping, students must have a variety of exposures to words in multiple contexts over time. It is estimated that school-age students are processing approximately 1,600 words in various stages of understanding at any one time. Strategies used in the classroom must support this continuous vocabulary processing and acquisition in order to facilitate optimum vocabulary knowledge in students.

The interdependence between reading achievement and vocabulary knowledge is very strong (Simmons & Kameénui, 1990). Strong readers in 12th grade were found to possess extended mapping of four times the number of words when compared to weak readers at the same grade level. In addition, strong readers at the 3rd-grade level have been found to possess extended mapping of approximately the same number of words as weak readers at the 12th- grade level (Beck & McKeown, 1991). The vocabulary knowledge–reading success relationship is reciprocal; students with rich vocabularies comprehend more fully. Students who read and comprehend well increase their vocabularies through more extensive reading. As a teacher of reading you must find ways to enhance the vocabulary and reading strategies of your students in order to harness this strong relationship.

READING FLUENCY

According to the National Reading Panel one other factor, reading fluency, plays a role in developing good readers. Reading fluency, as defined by the Report of the National Reading Panel, is "the ability to read a text quickly, accurately, and with proper expression" (pp. 3-1). Other definitions of reading fluency include references to reading effortlessly and sounding natural as the words are pronounced (Armbuster, Lehr, & Osborn, 2001). Rasinski (2000) includes references to the importance of prosody in fluent reading and defines prosody to include stress, pitch variations, intonation, rate, and pausing. The research on reading fluency clearly makes a connection between fluency and comprehension and provides a powerful basis for including fluency strategies into any comprehensive reading program (Rasinski, 2000).

Widely accepted approaches to the teaching of fluency are integrated throughout this text and include modeling, repeated oral readings, teacher-assisted reading, reader's theater, and independent silent reading. A very helpful oral-reading fluency scale for assessing fluency and monitoring progress can be found on the NAEP website (*http://nces.ed.gov/pubs95/web/9572.asp*).

READING COMPREHENSION

The research in reading comprehension is extensive and varied. In order to understand what must be done in the classroom to assess and support students' comprehension, this large body of research must be understood and connections must be made to classroom practices that can be easily employed. Before looking at those connections it makes sense to review a definition of reading comprehension.

It is generally recognized that comprehension entails an interaction between the reader and the text. Johnson (1981) states, "Reading comprehension is viewed as the process of using one's own prior knowledge and the writer's cues to infer the author's intended meaning" (p. 16). Note that Johnson uses the word *infer* to imply that we can never be entirely sure of the author's intent. We bring our own thoughts, experiences, and knowledge to the text and these influence our perception of the author's words. Irwin (1991) builds on Johnson's idea, expanding the definition to include the use of the five comprehension processes. Her definition concludes that:

> *These processes work together (interactive hypothesis) and can be controlled and adjusted by the reader as required by the reader's goals (metacognitive processes) and the total situation in which comprehension is occurring (situational context). When the reader consciously selects a process for a specific purpose, that process can be called a* reading strategy *(p. 9).*

One important factor in teaching reading comprehension is that students must be actively involved in the processing and integration of the reading material. Strategies for increasing reading comprehension must support students' understanding of the importance of their self-monitoring and choice of appropriate intervention strategies when text is not being understood. For this reason, the self-monitoring strategies must be introduced early.

SUMMARY

All three aspects of reading instruction—comprehension, vocabulary, and fluency—must be addressed in an integrated manner in effective reading instruction. In this text, some of the strategies focus on one of the three elements but all three must be considered, encouraged, and taught on an ongoing basis in order for the instruction to produce strategic readers. In addition to the three basic elements, teachers must be assessing and adjusting instruction based on their observation and evaluation techniques on a regular basis. Reading is an extremely complex act and attention to the individual reader's approach to text is a vital part of comprehensive instruction.

REFERENCES

Armbuster, B. B., Lehr, F. & Osborn, J. (2001). *Put reading first: The research building blocks for teaching children to read. Kindergarten through grade 3*. Washington, DC: National Institute for Literacy.

Beck, I. L., & McKeown, M. G. (2001). Text talk: Capturing the benefits of read-aloud experiences for young children. *The Reading Teacher, 55*, 10–20.

Beck, I., & McKeown, M. (1991). Conditions of vocabulary acquisition. In R. Barr, M. Kamil, P. Mosenthal, and P. D. Pearson (Eds.), *Handbook of reading research* (vol. 2, pp. 789–814). New York: Longman.

Dixon-Krauss, L. (2002). Using literature as a context for teaching vocabulary. *Journal of Adolescent & Adult Literacy, 45*(4), 310–318.

Irwin, J. (1991). *Teaching reading comprehension processes* (2nd ed.). Needham Heights, MA: Allyn and Bacon.

Lapp, D., Jacobson, J., Fisher, D., & Flood, J. (2000). Tried and true word study and vocabulary practices. *The California Reader, 33*(2), 25–30.

Nagy, W., & Anderson, R. C. (1984). How many words are there in printed school English? *Reading Research Quarterly, 19*, 304–330.

Nilsen, A., & Nilsen, D. (2003). A new spin on teaching vocabulary: A source–based approach. *The Reading Teacher, 56*, 436–439.

Rasinski, T. V. (2000). Speed does matter in reading. *The Reading Teacher, 54*, 146–150.

Rosenbaum, C. (2001). A world map for middle school: A tool for effective vocabulary instruction. *Journal of Adolescent & Adult Literacy, 45*(1), 44–48.

Simmons, D. C., & Kameénui, E. J. (1990). The effect of task alternatives on vocabulary knowledge: A comparison of students with learning disabilities and students of normal achievement. *Journal of Learning Disabilities, 23*(5), 291–297.

SECTION I

WORD- AND SENTENCE-LEVEL COMPREHENSION

Some of the most important factors in understanding what you read are the knowledge of words and the ability to process text fluently. This section provides strategies for developing strong vocabulary knowledge by giving students active experiences related to the words they will encounter in text. Because it is important for readers to have multiple exposures to words in a variety of contexts, several different vocabulary development strategies are included in this section.

Fluency in reading contributes greatly to comprehension, and chapter 8 focuses on a variety of strategies for developing fluency. Vocabulary knowledge, of course, is directly related to fluency, and so the vocabulary development chapters precede those on developing fluency. The organization of this book into sections should in no way be construed as a sequence of instruction, but rather a collection of unique strategies that should be related to the needs of individual students as identified through ongoing assessment. Although section VI focuses on assessment strategies, the teacher should be assessing continuously as the other strategies are taught and used. Students' background knowledge should be assessed and built on no matter what strategy is being employed. The crucial point to understand is that good readers employ a variety of strategies to support their understanding of text. This section provides teachers with multiple approaches for supporting student comprehension, both at the word and sentence level.

COLLECTING WORDS

Learning the Nuances of Word Meanings

Collecting words (Jordan & Herrell, 2001) is a strategy for helping students develop a better understanding of the nuances of words that have the same or similar meanings. Research clearly indicates that the development of extensive vocabulary and understanding of word meanings are essential to successful and fluid comprehension in reading (Allen, 2000). By "collecting" words, students are constantly building a repertoire of words and word meanings that will serve to increase their understanding of text and improve and strengthen their descriptive writing.

The strategy involves making charts of words discovered by the students in their reading or conversations, categorizing and briefly defining them as they are encountered. The word charts provide a record of the words students acquire as they add to the collections. In addition, they serve as a reference for the students who compile them and other students. As students locate and add words to the charts, they are responsible for helping other students understand the meanings and nuances of the new words. This may be accomplished through simple explanations or may require more elaborate picturization or acting out.

STEP BY STEP

The steps in implementing the strategy of collecting words are:

STEP 1   INTRODUCING WORD COLLECTIONS

The teacher introduces the strategy by asking students to think of all the different ways that they can "walk." She writes the word *walk* at the top of a chart. She then lists the other words for *walk* that the students suggest. As students suggest a word for *walk*, the teacher asks them to demonstrate that kind of walk. After the demonstration the teacher asks the other students to describe how the walk looked. The description/definition that the students give is added beside the word on the chart. This activity continues until a representative selection of words has been added to the chart. Students may add more words to the chart as they are discovered at later times.

FIGURE 1.1 Examples
of word collections.

**Focus on
English Learners**

Presenting new vocabulary
in multiple ways such as
pictures, acting out, seeing
the word written, and oral
practice is vital to
understanding and
comprehension.

WALK	
Tiptoe—walk on the tips of your toes	Saunter—walk casually with a confident air
Parade—walk tall with the knees raised high	March—walk with feet planted firmly
Slither—walk in a sneaky way, like a snake	Crawl—move on all fours, knees and hands
Mince—walk with tiny steps	Strut—take large steps with a prideful carriage
Flounce—walk with large steps and arms swinging	Stride—take large steps and swing arms forcefully
Cavort—walk in a playful manner, arms and legs flying	

SAID	
Whispered—said very quietly	Shouted—said in a very loud voice
Shrieked—said in a loud, shrill voice	Replied—answered
Responded—answered	Suggested—said in a helpful way
Stated—said in a clear, calm way	Snickered—said in the midst of giggling

TASTY WORDS			
Sweet	Yucky	Tangy	Delicious
Sour	Yummy	Fruity	Smooth
Bitter	Cheesy	Salty	Lumpy
Crunchy	Slimy	Hot	Fishy
Slippery	Chocolaty	Spicy	Rubbery

STEP 2   ADDING NEW CATEGORIES

New categories will be added on additional charts as the need arises during reading. Students may discover words with which they are not familiar, thus providing an opportunity to classify the words and create a new collection of words on a chart. See figure 1.1 for examples of a variety of word collections by category.

STEP 3   USING THE WORD COLLECTIONS

The word collections can be used as resources during reading and writing. Students may refer to the word collection charts when they encounter words that have previously been placed on the chart. If they encounter new words that are not on the chart, they may add these to the word collection. In writing, the words are used to increase the descriptive nature of the students' work, encouraging them to seek new and different ways of expressing more common words.

STEP 4   MANAGING THE WORD COLLECTION

As collecting words becomes an ongoing activity in the classroom, the word collection charts begin to use a lot of wall space. The charts can be put into big book form by making a cardboard cover for them, three-hole punching them, and holding them together with rings. Students will enjoy returning to them and adding new words. The big books can be spread out on the floor or placed in a big book easel for use. Teachers have found additional ways of building word collections. Strips of magnetic tape can be cut into word-sized pieces and words written on them with permanent marker. These words can be collected on the side of a filing cabinet, on an automotive drip tray, or even a cookie sheet. Sentence strip word cards can be collected in a pocket chart. Some teachers have used word rings (individual words written on small cards, single-hole punched, and held together with a medium-sized ring) for word collections and find that students use the word rings for sorting and classifying words in multiple categories. Word collections can be printed on overhead transparency sheets and filed in a notebook adjacent to the overhead projector so that students can project the collections onto a screen for access.

APPLICATIONS AND EXAMPLES

For an example of using word collections in a 9th-grade history class, see File 1 of the CD provided with this text.

Mrs. Rosales's third graders are beginning to write stories including dialogue. She notices that they are overusing the word *said*. She calls the class together to talk about other words that they might use instead to make their writing more interesting.

Using Pat's story as an example, she reads a sentence containing the word *said*, and then asks him to demonstrate how the person "sounds." Patrick responds, "He is very scared and he is just barely whispering."

Mrs. Rosales asks Pat to say the words exactly the way the character is saying them. Pat whispers the words in a very shaky voice, and she asks him what he could say in his story that would make it clear to the reader how the character sounds when he is saying these words.

Pat answers with enthusiasm, "oh, I get it, instead of saying, 'he said, I don't want to go out in the dark by myself,' I could say, 'He whispered with a shaky voice, I don't want to go out in the dark by myself.'" "Exactly," agrees Mrs. Rosales, "and now we all know just how he sounds."

Mrs. Rosales asks the rest of the children to find the word *said* in their own stories. She then asks them to replace the word *said* with more descriptive words to help the reader understand how the characters sound and feel. The class then begins using their own stories to fill in a word collection chart for more descriptive ways of expressing the word *said*. Mrs. Rosales also asks her students to look in books for other examples of how authors clarify the way in which a character is speaking. See Figure 1.1 as an example of the word chart they created.

CONCLUSION

Word collecting is an easy way to interest students in word study. In some categories the words can be rated or sequenced in some way. Little words can be sequenced, for example. A list such as *infinitesimal, tiny, small, little, petite,* and *micro* could be arranged in order of size. Although there is not always one correct answer in these cases, students give a lot of thought to their sequences and learn some valuable oral language skills defending their choices.

The main purpose of collecting words is to spark interest in nuances of word meaning and to build vocabulary for reading and writing. Interacting with the words, acting them out, and discussing their meanings and the acceptable contexts for their use are all valuable activities to increase word knowledge and reading comprehension. An added benefit is the students' improved writing skills as they begin to incorporate the new words into their writing.

The teacher's observation of the students' understanding and use of the new vocabulary provides the perfect assessment/instruction connection. If the students are not using the new vocabulary or are misunderstanding the meaning of new words, the teacher should provide additional experiences and examples to help them internalize the nuances of meaning. This is especially vital with English learners.

REFERENCES

Allen, R. (2000). *Before it's too late: Giving reading a last chance.* Alexandria, VA: Association for Supervision and Curriculum Development.

Jordan, M., & Herrell, A. (2001). Collecting and processing words: Strategies for building vocabulary in young children. *Kindergarten Education: Theory, Research and Practice, 3,* 17–25.

SUGGESTED READING

Laframboise, K. L. (2000). Said webs: Remedy for tired words. *The Reading Teacher, 53*(7), 540–542.

Rodriguez, T. A. (2001). From the known to the unknown: Using cognates to teach English to Spanish-speaking literates. *The Reading Teacher, 54*(8), 744–746.

STRUCTURAL ANALYSIS

Focusing on the Meaning of Word Parts

> **Focus on English Learners**
>
> By studying root words and affixes, English learners begin to develop a system for accessing the meanings of unfamiliar words.

Students who are familiar with the added meanings of the small parts of words they read—prefixes, root words, and suffixes—can figure out the meanings of unknown words when they encounter them in text. They do this by looking for something they know within the word (Fox, 2000).

To use the meanings of prefixes, root words, and suffixes, students must be exposed to the concept of structural analysis, breaking a word apart to discover its meaning. In addition, they must be taught the meanings of common prefixes, root words, and suffixes in a way that engages their interest and gives them multiple exposures to the definitions. Affix (prefixes and suffixes) studies may be presented as a learning game, giving students an opportunity to manipulate word parts to create complex words. Students are also encouraged to explain the meanings of prefixes, root words, and suffixes when they encounter them in text and make the connections between the gamelike approaches used to learn the meanings and the application of that knowledge within the context of a reading experience.

Several approaches are necessary for the knowledge of affixes to be mastered and applied. The meanings of individual prefixes, root words, and suffixes must be studied and practiced in multiple ways. The application of this knowledge is emphasized during both reading instruction and reading for pleasure. Teachers present the information in a variety of ways and encourage students to keep a personal affix dictionary where they record words they discover that include the affixes being studied. This journal is only a small part of active word study that is ongoing in the classroom, involving students in multiple ways of building vocabulary. This focus on vocabulary building supports students' growing repertoire of comprehension strategies. See figure 2.1 for a list of common prefixes, figure 2.2 for a list of common suffixes and their meanings, and figure 2.3 for a list of common root words.

STEP BY STEP

The steps for teaching structural analysis are:

STEP 1   INTRODUCING PREFIXES, ROOTS, AND SUFFIXES

The teacher introduces the meanings of the words *prefix, root word,* and *suffix* by explaining that many words have several parts. He shows a root word from figure 2.3 and talks about the meaning of the word. He adds a prefix and explains how the addition of

FIGURE 2.1 Common prefixes.

PREFIX	MEANING	EXAMPLE
a-	not or without	atypical
ab-	from	absent
ad-	to, toward	admit
an-	not, without	anonymous
anti-*	against	antibiotic
amphi-	both, around	amphibious
bene-	well, good	benefit
co-, con-	with, jointly	cooperate
de-*	from, away	deliver
dis-*	apart from, not	disagree
en-, em-*	in	enclose
e-, ex-	out	exit, exhale
fore-*	in front of, before	foreground
im-, in-, ir-, il-	not	impossible
in-, im-*	in or into	inward
inter-*	between, among	interact
intro-	inside	introduce
mal-	bad, badly	malicious
mid-*	middle	midweek
mis-*	wrong, bad, not	mistake
non-*	not	nonsense
over-*	too much	overcook
para-	beside, by	paraphrase
per-	throughout	pervade
pre-*	before	preview
pro-	forward	project (verb)
post-	after	postscript
re-*	back, again	retell
semi-*	half, partly	semicircle
sub-*	under, inferior	submerge
super-*	above, beyond	supervise
trans-*	across	transport
ultra-	beyond	ultramodern
un-*	not	untrue
under-*	too little	underestimate

*Denotes prefix as one of the 19 most commonly used in American English.

the prefix changes the meaning of the word. Then he demonstrates adding prefixes to several words and introduces a chart with three common prefixes and their meanings.

The next step is starting a chart of root words with three words and their meanings. The teacher and students combine the prefixes and root words and talk about their meanings. Suffixes are then introduced in the same way. A chart of suffixes is begun, and the teacher and students practice the combination of root words and suffixes. The teacher asks the students to watch for words that use the prefixes, root words, and suffixes they have learned. He also alerts the students that there are many more prefixes, root words, and suffixes to learn and they will be adding to the charts.

FIGURE 2.2 Common suffixes.

SUFFIX	MEANING	EXAMPLE
-able, -ible*	able to	curable
-ac	related to	cardiac
-acy, -acity,		
-acoius	having the quality of	democracy
-al, ial*	relating to	personal
-ant	one who	servant
-ard	one who	coward
-ary	place for	library
-cide	to kill or cut	homicide
-cle, -cule	small	particle
-crat	to rule	democrat
-ee, -eer	one who	volunteer
-en	to make	harden
-ence	state of	violence
-er, -or*	one who	teacher
-er*	more	harder
-est*	most (comparative)	biggest
-ette	small	dinette
-ful*	quality of	playful
-ic*	like, pertaining to	historic
-ice	act of, time of	novice
-ion, -ation,		
-ition, -tion*	act or state of	construction
-ism	state of, quality of	baptism
-ity, -ty*	state of, quality of	necessity
-ive, -ative, -itive*	tending to, relating to	creative
-kin	small	napkin
-less*	without	fearless
-let	small	booklet
-logy, -ology	study of	biology
-ly*	having the quality of	mannerly
-ment*	state, quality, act	excitement
-ness*	quality of	happiness
-or	one who	actor
-ory, -orium	place where	observatory
-ous, -eous, -ious*	full of or state of	joyous
-s, -es*	plural	dogs
-y*	quality, full of	muddy

*Denotes suffix as one of the 17 most commonly used in American English.

FIGURE 2.3 Examples of common root words.

ROOT WORD	MEANING	EXAMPLE
acri, acer	sharp, bitter	acrid
act	do	action
amicus	friend	amicable
ann	year	annual
aqua	water	aquarium
ast(er)	star	astronaut
aud	hear	audience
bell(i)	war	rebellion
bi	two	bicycle
bio	life	biology
cess	go, yield	process
cred	believe	credit
chron	time	chronicle
cycl	circle or wheel	bicycle
dic	speak	dictate
fac	to make, do, see	factory
flor	flower, flourish	floral
flu	to flow	fluent
fid	trust, have faith	fidelity
grad	go, step	graduate
grat	pleasing, grateful	gratitude
grav	heavy	gravity
greg	flock, herd	congregate
hol	whole	hologram
luc, lumen	light	luminous
pathos	feeling	sympathy
pug	fist	pugilist
plac	make calm	placid
spec, spic	to see, observe	spectacle
tract	pull, drag	tractor
vid	see	video

STEP 2   MODELING STRUCTURAL ANALYSIS

The teacher introduces the study of structural analysis by decoding an unfamiliar word that has a common root word and thinking aloud as he models breaking down the word. For example, he uses the word *unsuitable*. He talks the students through the use of structural analysis:

> *I see a word that has both a prefix, something added to the beginning, and a suffix, something added to the end of the word. If I take off the prefix—un—and the suffix—able—I am left with the root word,* suit. *Now, what does the word* suit *mean? Suit means something that fits or is correct, as in "it suits me just fine."*
>
> *If I know the meaning of the word* suit, *then I have to think about the meaning of the prefix* un. *It means "not," so I know the meaning of the word* unsuit *is "not fitting." Now, let's look at the suffix* able. *This suffix is used when we want to use the word to describe something. So we could say that the suffix* able *means "able to." If we use*

the word unsuitable *to describe a color, we could say, "This color is unsuitable for painting the house." What would this mean?*

The teacher moves through this think-aloud process, talking about the meanings of the word parts and the meaning of the word and how it changes as different affixes are added to it.

STEP 3   PRACTICING STRUCTURAL ANALYSIS

The teacher provides a piece of text that includes a number of words with affixes, and the students read the text silently, underlining words with affixes. After they have read the passage, the teacher leads them through a think-aloud process in which they analyze the words and talk through identifying the root word and its meaning. They then add the prefix and discuss how the word meaning changes. Finally they add the suffix and discuss how its addition changes the meaning. The students then begin to keep a word study journal. See figure 2.4 for an example of a word study journal for structural analysis.

STEP 4   ADDING TO THE PREFIX, ROOT WORD, AND SUFFIX CHARTS

The teacher takes a few minutes each day to make three new additions to the charts introduced in the first step. The students are assigned the task of finding words for their journals that use the newly added prefixes, root words, and suffixes in addition to the words and affixes already on the charts.

STEP 5   CELEBRATING STUDENT PROGRESS

The teacher finds time to recognize students who are adding regularly to their word study journals. Students are encouraged to share the words they locate. A bulletin board with newly located words can be an ongoing project that helps focus the students on the fact that they are making progress in vocabulary building.

APPLICATIONS AND EXAMPLES

Focus on English Learners

Providing multiple exposures to new words in English along with having opportunities to hear the words used and defined supports English learners in better understanding word meanings.

The notice on the bulletin board of Miss Damon's 10th-grade English class reads:

prefix for the day—anti
root word for the day—bell
suffix for the day—ous

As the students enter the classroom they sit down and quickly take out their books. They begin searching for words that contain the prefix, suffix, or root word for the day and adding them to their vocabulary notebook. The room is hushed and

FIGURE 2.4 An example of a word study journal page.

Word—meaning	Prefix—meaning	Root word—meaning	Suffix—meaning
Remarkable	re	mark	able
Something that is out of the ordinary	*to do again*	*to take note*	*capable of*

Prefix + Root Word + Suffix = Something remarkable would be something that is capable of making you note, or notice it more than once.

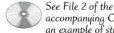
See File 2 of the accompanying CD for an example of structural analysis study with third graders.

students seem to scurry in and get right to work. The bell rings, Miss Damon gives the students 5 more minutes, and then she calls, "Time."

The students then begin to share the words they have located. As words are read orally by each student in turn, the others add the words to their lists. The students give a brief definition for each word they suggest and then use the word in a sentence. When they add the total of the words they have discovered, their "word score" for the day is 37.

"I believe that is a new record," says Miss Damon with a smile. "Now let's see if we can find ways to use these words today. Tomorrow be ready to share the uses you found for them. Who found some ways to use yesterday's words?" As Miss Damon goes on with the lesson for the day in literature, a vocabulary usage notebook is circulated. Students add a short message to the journal giving the word from the day before that they were able to use and how they used the word. Miss Damon finds ways to use the new words for the day in her literature lesson and each time one of the words is used hands shoot up all over the room. The students are listening and focused.

At the end of the class, Miss Damon looks at the class vocabulary notebook and chooses two or three entries to read aloud. The students seem excited by their word studies and eager to use their new words. Miss Damon is eager to see their vocabulary scores on the standardized test at the end of the year. She already notices a difference in their spoken vocabularies.

CONCLUSION

In order for students to acquire the word knowledge they need to be successful in school and in life, teachers must plan and implement many different approaches to make them aware of word meanings and methods they can use to build their repertoire of words and meanings. Any approach the teacher can introduce that gets the students actively engaged in word study has great potential for getting students interested in words, word parts, and their meanings. The study of prefixes, root words, and suffixes expands word knowledge greatly. Instead of studying individual words, affix and root study gives the students the power to unlock words by structural analysis. This approach, teamed with motivational strategies like vocabulary journals and class bulletin boards recognizing students who are conducting ongoing word analysis and vocabulary building, provides a rich source of word learning to students.

Giving students opportunities to build words in literacy centers, discuss the meaning of words in reading groups, and use new words in vocabulary journals gives teachers multiple views of students' understanding of word meanings. This information is vital in planning additional instruction as needed.

REFERENCES

Fox, B. (2000). *Word identification strategies* (2nd ed). Upper Saddle River, NJ: Merrill/Prentice Hall.

WORD MAPPING

Exploring Word Meanings and Applications

Word maps (Schwartz & Raphael, 1985) are graphic representations that require students to list the definition and examples of ways in which a word can be used. To build on students' prior knowledge and support their ability to make connections to words they encounter in reading, an expansion of typical word maps is suggested. Because students need to be adding constantly to their store of known vocabulary, teachers need to be conducting ongoing, direct instruction in vocabulary. Basing vocabulary study on words of relevance to the science, social studies, and literature being explored in the classroom makes sense and gives students opportunities to use their new vocabulary knowledge in context. Word mapping is one way to explore new vocabulary and help students connect the new words to multiple contexts.

Typical word maps require that students list the word, definition, and some examples of the word's use. Expanding the word map to include specific examples of the way the word is used in context and possibilities for use of the word in other contexts supports the students' understanding of multiple meanings and uses of the words. See figure 3.1 for an example of a word map expanded in this way.

To be effective in expanding students' vocabularies, building word maps should be included in the daily routine. Once constructed, word maps should be available for use by all students in the classroom. To make word maps accessible to all students, they can be stored alphabetically in a binder. Some teachers have experienced great success with students adding sentences as additions to other students' word maps as a way of sparking interest in ongoing word study.

> **Focus on English Learners**
>
> Examples of how a word might be used encourages English learners to include new words in their oral and written English production.

FIGURE 3.1 A word map for the word *map*.

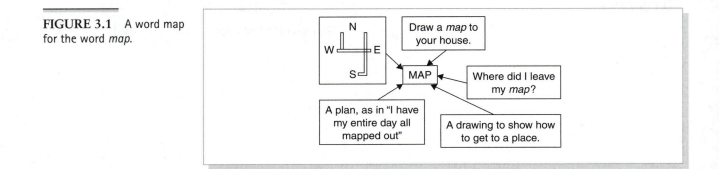

Step by Step

The steps in implementing the use of word maps are:

Step 1   Explaining and Modeling the Procedure

The teacher explains and models how to construct a word map. She explains that to develop a wide knowledge of words, we need to learn about 8 to 10 new words each day. Because we learn words best by using them in many different contexts, we will begin our study of words by mapping the word. Mapping a word involves defining it, using it in sentences, and trying to find ways to use it frequently to make it part of our daily vocabulary. The teacher draws an example of a word map and discusses each part as she adds it to the map.

Step 2   Providing Guided Practice

The teacher encourages students to find a word in their daily reading that has given them difficulty or one that interests them. They can choose a word from the reading done the previous day or any other content-area reading. The teacher then walks the class through the construction of a word map for the words the students have chosen. Students discuss meanings of the words and look them up in the dictionary, if necessary. They are encouraged to list the sentence in which they found the word on their map.

Then students encounter the challenge of word maps. They are encouraged to think of other ways in which they might use or encounter the word. In this part of the strategy, they might need to construct a second or third word map for the same word. If a second or third definition of the word is found, then additional sentences are added to the new maps, representing the ways in which the word can be used. Some students may also want to include illustrations of the words, when appropriate.

Step 3   Sharing the Information

The teacher establishes a routine for sharing the word maps and storing them so that they are available to use. The word map binder becomes a resource within the classroom and should be constantly updated as students find new and interesting words. A bulletin board near the word map binder can be used to display especially unique words and give encouragement to students' active pursuit of word study.

Step 4   Encouraging Use of the Words

The teacher sets up an expectation that students will be creating new word maps daily. She makes materials for constructing word maps readily available to the students, provides a short time each day for talking about new words and word maps, and offers incentives for word study. See chapter 5 on vocabulary processing for additional suggestions, such as word journals and bulletin boards.

Applications and Examples

Miss Benninghoven's first graders are enjoying the exploration of movement as they hear the book *The Third Story Cat* (Baker, 1987) read to them. As the cats in the story prowl and parade, Miss B. gets the students up from the rug where they usually sit to hear stories, and they prowl and parade around the room like the cats in the story. Because there are so many wonderful movement words to explore, Miss B. posts each movement word on sentence strips in the pocket chart as she and the students act them out. Soon the pocket chart is full of movement words like *parade, prowl, leap, twitch, wink, climb, chase,* and *nip.*

After Miss B. and the students finish reading the book, Miss B. sends the students back to their tables. She introduces word maps by saying, "We have talked about a lot of new movement words today. I think we should begin to make some word maps for the new words we are learning. Have you ever heard the word *map* before?"

Rosita raises her hand, "My daddy uses a map when we go on vacation. It tells him where to go."

"Yes, Rosita," responds Miss B. "That's a very important kind of map. It helps you to keep from getting lost.

"Word maps are a little different kind of map," continues Miss B. "Word maps help us to learn more about words. Let me show you how to make a word map. Let's take the word *parade* from our story. I'll start by putting the word in the middle of my paper and drawing a box around it." Miss B. demonstrates as she talks. "Now, I want to write what the word means. What did we say about the meaning of the word *parade*?"

Tina raises her hand. "Yes, Tina?" asks Miss B.

"It means to walk tall and lift your knees up high."

"Exactly," says Miss B. with a smile. She writes the definition under the word and draws a rectangle around the definition. "Now, we can draw a picture of the cats in the story parading. We can also write the sentence from the book that talked about the cats parading. We can write a sentence about how we paraded around the room, too." Miss B. demonstrates each of these steps as she talks about them. "Now, we have made a word map for the word *parade*. But, is this the only meaning of the word *parade*?"

"No, Miss B. We talked about another kind of parade this morning. You remember, the kind with bands and floats," suggests Emile.

"Yes, you are right," replies Miss B. "Let's make another word map for the word *parade*. We will start the same way. The definition will be different, though. What did you say the new definition was, Emile?"

"Bands and floats going down the street?" asks Emile tentatively.

"Good definition," says Miss B. as she writes Emile's words. "Now use this kind of *parade* in a sentence."

"We went to see the Christmas parade," responds Emile as Miss B. writes his sentence on the word map.

"Can anyone think of another sentence using this kind of parade?" asks Miss B.

"The high school band lined up to be in the big parade." suggests Tina.

Miss B. writes Tina's sentence on the word map. "I'm going to give this word map to Emile so he can draw the picture," says Miss B. "Now I want you each to make a word map for one of the words in our story." As Miss B. passes out the word map paper, she asks each student which word they want to map. If two students choose the same word, she suggests they work together and try to find different sentences for each map.

After the students have completed their word maps, Miss B. calls them together in a celebration circle to share their maps and talk about the meanings of the words. "I will leave some word map paper and markers over in the vocabulary center. Word maps will be another choice that you have as you choose literacy centers each day," explains Miss B. "I have this pretty new binder for us to use to store our word maps," she says as she shows the class a binder decorated with pictures the students have drawn in the past. "This is hard," she says as she shows them how to file the word maps in alphabetical order. "You have to remember your alphabet and put the word maps behind the right letter. Where will I put the word maps for the word *parade*?"

"Behind the *P*. That's easy, Miss B.!" responds Rosita.

"You're too smart for me!" says Miss B. with a smile. "How do you suppose you can use these word maps?"

"When we find a new word, we can make a new word map," suggests Colin.

Focus on English Learners

Physically involving students in acting out words and situations helps provide them with a context related to new vocabulary. The word map engages them in using the new word in multiple contexts.

See File 3 of the accompanying CD for ways to use word mapping to combine vocabulary and social studies instruction in sixth grade.

"Yes, you can," replies Miss B. "But when will you use the word maps?"

"We can go to the binder and find a word we don't know and look at the picture and the meaning and the sentences to help us," says Emile. "Then we'll know what the word means."

"Very good idea," says Miss Benninghoven.

CONCLUSION

As Miss Benninghoven demonstrates, a focus on vocabulary can be an exciting addition to any classroom. Students who are awakened to ways in which they can explore word meanings and origins acquire a lifelong interest in words and what they mean. It takes more than the introduction of simple activities like word maps and vocabulary journals to create this kind of interest, however. The teacher must find ways to provide discussion, celebration, and application of the words studied if the students are to "catch the fever." Vocabulary study will greatly enhance reading comprehension and writing abilities, but vocabulary acquisition requires multiple exposures to the new words in multiple contexts to be most effective.

Word maps are helpful for several reasons. They help students to draw on their background knowledge, explore different contexts in which the word may be encountered, and use different language modes. Listening and speaking are involved in the instruction related to word maps and in the sharing and practicing of the words in context. Reading and writing are involved in the construction of the word maps and in the reading to find the words to be mapped. Viewing and visually representing are involved as the students illustrate words and explore word maps by others. As with any effective strategy, word maps must be explored on a regular basis to be effective.

Observing students as they construct and use word maps provides an authentic look at their understanding of the multiple meanings of words as well as their understanding of word maps as a resource. Lessons can be planned to encourage students to use word maps as alternatives to dictionaries if a resource file of word maps is built and made available to students in the classroom.

REFERENCES

Baker, L. (1987). *The third story cat*. Boston: Little, Brown, and Company.

Schwartz, R., & Raphael, T. (1985). Concept of definition: A key to improving students' vocabulary. *Reading Teacher, 39*, 198–205.

SUGGESTED READING

Bluestein, A. (2002). Comprehension through characterization: Enabling readers to make personal connections with literature. *The Reading Teacher, 55*, 431–434.

Laframboise, K. L. (2000). Said webs: Remedy for tired words. *The Reading Teacher, 53*(7), 540–542.

Rosenbaum, C. (2001). A word map for middle school: A tool for effective vocabulary instruction. *Journal of Adolescent & Adult Literacy, 45*(1), 44–48.

4

WORD ORIGIN STUDIES

Linking Word Histories and Roots to Word Comprehension

Focus on English Learners

The study of root words and word origins may aid many English learners in recognizing cognates in their first language.

Traditionally students in American schools were taught Greek and Latin root words to help them understand the meanings of words, prefixes, and suffixes. In recent years this practice has been lost in many schools, and some educators believe that students' word knowledge and comprehension have suffered from the lack of this instruction. As a new millennium begins, school districts across the nation are moving to standards-based education, and the reappearance of the study of word origins in language arts standards is one outgrowth of this movement. The study of the meanings of common Greek and Latin root words, prefixes, suffixes, and word histories can be helpful to building more extensive reading, writing, and speaking vocabularies in students and adults alike (Tompkins, 2000).

In addition to supporting vocabulary growth and comprehension, word origin studies can be motivational. Some of the words we use daily have interesting histories. Students lukewarm about studying root words and affixes are sometimes motivated to read and discuss unique stories about how words, expressions, and idioms came into use. By sparking students' interest in word study, teachers can start a lifelong pursuit of word knowledge. This is an ongoing cycle of learning that serves students well throughout their lives.

STEP BY STEP

The steps in implementing word origin studies are:

STEP 1   SPARKING AN INTEREST

The teacher introduces interesting stories about the origins and histories of words as they are encountered. The teacher must do some research and preparation. Before introducing a unit of study or a piece of literature, he identifies key words and looks up their origins. As the lesson is presented, the teacher tells the word history story or demonstrates the root word meaning. Once this approach is begun, the teacher does daily mini-lessons concerning word histories and meanings. A bulletin board designated as a word study board is introduced so that the information the teacher is researching and sharing is accessible to students who show an interest.

STEP 2   PROVIDING MATERIALS FOR WORD STUDY

A few books such as dictionaries that include word etymologies, thesauruses, and other word reference materials (see reference list at the end of this chapter) are put into a word study center in the classroom. Students are encouraged to use the materials for locating definitions, pronunciations, and histories of words. A format for documenting word research is provided, and students are encouraged to display their work on the bulletin board or include their research in a binder at the word study center. (See chapter 3 on word maps.)

STEP 3   CELEBRATING STUDENTS' EFFORTS

A time is set aside each day for the discussion of new words the students have researched. The teacher prepares a word to be presented each day as well, ensuring the ongoing study of word origins and histories.

STEP 4   CONNECTING WORD STUDY TO ALL AREAS OF CURRICULUM

The teacher identifies key vocabulary needed for students' understanding of reading material and concepts to be studied across the curriculum. Key words in science, social studies, math, and literature are identified and researched. Depending on the ages of the students, the teacher may provide most of the research and simply share the information with the students, or researching key words in any unit of study may be an ongoing part of the assignment.

STEP 5   ENCOURAGING WIDE USE OF THE DEVELOPING VOCABULARY

Just defining and researching the origins of words will not accomplish the necessary mastery of vocabulary. Students need to use the new words in multiple ways to comprehend them fully. Using vocabulary journals and personal word study notebooks in which students keep a list of new words along with definitions, word histories, and personal notes about use both support the word study initiative in the classroom. Most important of all, though, is the provision of time to discuss the word study that is taking place and to celebrate students' research and use of the new vocabulary.

APPLICATIONS AND EXAMPLES

Focus on English Learners

Helping students to recognize common root words and their meanings supports the understanding that language has an underlying system. With Spanish speakers, many of the Latin roots are very close to the same spelling, pronunciation, and meaning in their first language. Such words are called *cognates*.

Mr. Roberts is teaching a unit on ancient Greece in his sixth-grade class. As a part of the social studies unit, he is initiating an ongoing word study project. He is challenging his students to discover the roots, origins, and meaning of new words. He is also sharing fascinating stories about the histories of words throughout the day. His goal is to get his students interested in word study and to increase their vocabularies daily.

Mr. Roberts introduces the word study by saying, "As we study about ancient Greece, I want you to be aware of how many of our English words have Greek roots. I am going to introduce some Greek root words to you today, and we will see if we can think of some common words that we know with these root words. The first Greek root word we will try is the root *scope*, which means *see*. How many words can you think of that contain the root word *scope* and have something to do with seeing?"

Mr. Roberts writes *scope* on the chalkboard and adds the words the students suggest. He then introduces the root *hydro*, which means *water*, and asks, "How many words can you think of that contain the root *hydro* and have something to do

FIGURE 4.1   Greek roots and English words.

Scope (see)	Hydro (water)
Tele<u>scope</u>—an instrument for seeing stars	<u>hydro</u>gen—one of the elements in water
Horo<u>scope</u>—looking at the stars to tell your future	<u>hydro</u>electric—using flowing water to make electricity
Kaleido<u>scope</u>—a toy that allows you to see patterns	<u>hydro</u>phobia—fear of water
Micro<u>scope</u>—an instrument for making small things visible	

For an example of word origin study in an 11th-grade ESL (English as a second language) class, see File 4 of the CD provided with this text.

with water?" See figure 4.1 to see the words Mr. Roberts' sixth graders added to the chart that day.

As the unit of ancient Greece continues, Mr. Roberts adds a new Greek root to the chart each day, and the students discover resources in their readings and research books for locating words to add to the word study charts. Mr. Roberts is excited about their interest, especially since he plans to continue the word study throughout the year. His next social studies unit is on ancient Rome.

CONCLUSION

Mr. Roberts has found ways to integrate word origin studies into his curriculum in an ongoing manner. Sparking student interest in the study of word origins, definitions, and histories is not always easy. Students become interested when they see practical applications for the studies they do. Relating word origin studies directly to science, social studies, math, and literary curriculum is helpful for two reasons. Students see the connections between studying words and understanding the total unit of study. They are also much more able to recall word meanings and histories when the study of the words is related to a meaningful context.

Assessment of students' understanding of root words and affixes is vital in planning instruction and creating connections across disciplines. These connections enable students to transfer their knowledge of words and continue to build their usable word knowledge. Teaching through this approach supports students' addition of many new words to their speaking, reading, and writing vocabularies without the discrete study of thousands of individual words.

Vocabulary knowledge is an extremely important aspect of reading comprehension. In the recent report of the National Reading Panel (NRP), vocabulary is cited as one of the most important aspects of reading instruction (Allen, 2000). Although more research is needed, the studies reviewed by the NRP reveal the power of vocabulary study in increasing word knowledge and comprehension across the grades.

REFERENCES

Allen, R. (2000). *Before it's too late: Giving reading a last chance*. Alexandria, VA: Association for Supervision and Curriculum Development.

Tompkins, G. (2000). *Reading for the 21st century*. Upper Saddle River, NJ: Merrill/Prentice Hall.

RESOURCE BOOKS FOR TEACHING WORD ORIGINS

Almond, J. (1985). *Dictionary of word origins: A history of the words, expressions, and cliches we use*. Secaucus, NJ: Citadel Press.

Asimov, I. (1969). *Words from the myths*. Boston: Houghton Mifflin.

Brook, D. (1998). *The journey of English*. New York: Clarion.

Bryson, B. (1994). *Made in America*. New York: Avon Books.

Cox, J. A. (1980). *Put your foot in your mouth and other silly sayings*. New York: Random House.

Funk, C. E. (1948). *A hog on ice and other curious expressions*. New York: HarperCollins.

Funk, C. E. (1958). *Horsefeathers and other curious words*. New York: HarperCollins.

Henrickson, R. (1997). *OPB encyclopedia of word and phrase origins*. New York: Facts on File.

Lederer, R. (1990). *The play of words*. New York: Pocket Books.

Merriam-Webster. (1991). *The Merriam-Webster new book of word histories*. Springfield, NY: Author.

Metcalf, A., & Barnhart, D. K. (1997). *America in so many words: Words that have shaped America*. Boston: Houghton Mifflin.

Nilsen, A. & Nilson, D. (2003). A new spin on teaching vocabulary: A source-based approach. *The Reading Teacher, 56*, 436–439.

Steckler, A. (1979). *101 words and how they began*. Garden City, NY: Doubleday.

Steckler, A. (1980). *101 more words and how they began*. Garden City, NY: Doubleday.

Terban, M. (1983). *In a pickle and other funny idioms*. New York: Clarion.

Terban, M. (1987). *Mad as a wet hen! And other funny idioms*. New York: Clarion.

Terban, M. (1988). *Guppies in tuxedos*. New York: Clarion.

Tompkins, G. E., & Yaden, D. B., Jr. (1986). *Answering students' questions about words*. Urbana, IL: National Council of Teachers of English and the ERIC Clearinghouse on Reading and Communication Skills.

Watkins, C. (1985). *The American heritage dictionary of Indo-European roots*. Boston: Houghton Mifflin.

5

VOCABULARY PROCESSING

Multiple Strategies Approach

Students exposed to vocabulary in a variety of settings and through multiple activities have a much higher incidence of retention and understanding of the meanings and proper uses of words (Pressley & Woloshyn, 1995). Although students can learn a cursory meaning of a word quickly, it takes multiple interactions with a word over a period of time to establish "extended mapping," or thorough comprehension (Carey, 1978). Multiple exposure activities might include word association, the introduction of realia, active learning process, vocabulary role play, meaning-based vocabulary games, and use of the word outside of class in real-life situations.

Students' ability to comprehend reading material is often limited by their understanding of the vocabulary presented to them in the context of the reading. Their prior reading experiences may have a direct influence on their perception and integration of the new vocabulary into the contextual setting in which words are being used. The use of a multiple activities approach will greatly enhance the likelihood that students will be able to incorporate their new knowledge of unfamiliar vocabulary and thereby enhance their comprehension and retention of the material being presented.

STEP BY STEP

The steps in implementing vocabulary processing are:

STEP 1 IDENTIFYING KEY VOCABULARY WORDS

Whenever a narrative story or information text is to be read to the students or by the students, the teacher prereads the selection. She/he identifies any vocabulary that may be unfamiliar to the students, or is being used in an unfamiliar context and writes these words on sentence strips or cards. Careful analysis is required to ensure that appropriate consideration is given to all words that might play a role in the students' understanding of the material. The teacher's task is to select those words or phrases that might interrupt the flow of understanding for students and to organize possible approaches for presenting this vocabulary to students. The teacher should choose words carefully without making assumptions that all students know even the simplest of words. Special attention should be given at this point to words that might be unfamiliar to English language learners and to words that have multiple meanings. The goal is not to preteach all these words but rather to have a clear plan for presenting the vocabulary to students. If in the course of reading the selected text it becomes obvious that students do not understand a particular word or phrase that was not preselected, then that word or phrase should be added to the list and incorporated into the vocabulary processing activities.

STEP 2 ASSESSING PRIOR KNOWLEDGE

Before the text is introduced, the teacher engages the students in an activity that allows for the determination of students' levels of prior information, background knowledge, and vocabulary related to the material to be read.

See figure 5.1 for examples of activities that might be used for assessment of prior knowledge.

FIGURE 5.1 Activities for assessing background knowledge.

KWL Chart (Ogle, 1986)	A large piece of paper is divided into three columns, labeled *K* for what the students "know," *W* for what the students "want" to know, and "L" for what the children "learned" from the experience. The topic of the text is discussed, and children provide input for the various sections of the chart. The assessment of background knowledge is most evident, of course, in the first two sections of the chart while the last section is reserved for review of comprehension and understanding.
Focused Discussion	Use visuals, illustrations, book covers, etc., to generate a short discussion about the text to be read. Note students' conceptual understanding, connection to past experiences, and vocabulary use during the discussion.
Quick Write	Older students may be asked to write briefly what they know about the topic addressed in the chosen text. These should be easily accomplished in a short time period, such as 5 minutes or less. The focus of these writings is on content rather than structure and might even take the form of a list or a conceptual web rather than narrative writing.
Double-Entry Journals (T Charts)	The teacher selects key concepts and vocabulary related to the text to be read and places them on the left side of a two-column chart (T chart). The students are then asked to write brief summations of their knowledge relating to the chosen concepts and vocabulary.

Examples of KWL and T Charts for Jane Yolen's (1987) *Owl Moon*

KWL CHART			T CHART	
K	**W**	**L**		
Owls are birds They can fly They are big Fly at night Heads turn all the way around Have big eyes Eat mice	Where do they live? When do they sleep? What do baby owls look like? Why do they "hoot"?	For review and checking for comprehension	A clearing Flew on silent wings Trees stood like statues Owling A meadow Hope	Student writings go here . . .

STEP 3   ## READING, RELATING, AND ACTING

During the reading of the text, the teacher may choose to stop to check for understanding and to relate words and events to past experiences. This will help students clarify the meanings of words and phrases or clear up misconceptions relative to the assigned reading. This gives the teacher the opportunity to model some of her own strategies for processing the text, especially as they might apply to decoding and making sense of new words. See figure 5.2 for examples of processing strategies appropriate at this stage. Acting out words is very helpful in providing experiences to make the vocabulary more meaningful.

STEP 4   ## MAKING CONNECTIONS

After the class finishes reading the text, it is important to spend some time discussing the reading and reviewing the new vocabulary that has been processed. Further use of these words serves to reinforce and solidify the connections made in exploring them through the various strategies suggested. See figure 5.3 for example of activities for making connections with the new vocabulary.

STEP 5   ## APPLYING WORDS TO REAL LIFE

To encourage students to internalize new vocabulary, they must be prompted to use the words in real-life settings as much as possible during the initial acquisition phase of vocabulary development. Students can be asked to keep a vocabulary log in which they relate instances in which they used the new word(s). These logs can be shared at some point during the day, so that all students have the opportunity to share vicariously in the use of new vocabulary. See figure 5.4 for an example of vocabulary log entries.

FIGURE 5.2   Examples of processing strategies.

Think Aloud	The teacher verbalizes for students the strategy that she would use to approach the unraveling of the meaning of unfamiliar words. This might include one or more of the following: ■ *Clues from context*—continue reading to determine if the word is later defined in the text or if "clues" in the text help to determine the meaning of the word. ■ *Clues from illustrations*—examine illustrations related to the immediate text to see if they might provide clues to the meaning of the word. ■ *Drawing from personal and/or background experiences*—does the word bring to mind any other similar situations you might have experienced that would provide clues to the meaning of the word? ■ *Intertextual experiences*—relate to other books that may have been read on the same topic, or written by the same author, or contain similar situations related to the new vocabulary words.
Vocabulary Role Play	Using physicalization of words, that is, acting out the words to help students internalize the new meanings and understandings. This technique may be used at appropriate points during the reading of the text to provide physical experiences related to the word and clarify nuances of meaning.
Periodic Paraphrasing	Stopping at logical points in the text to summarize and paraphrase the sequence of events, new words, or unfamiliar phrases.

FIGURE 5.3 Activities for making connections.

Generating Sentences	Have students review how a word is used in the text, either from memory (best) or by looking back in the text to find the word in a sentence. After reviewing how the word is used in the selected text, the students are asked to create a sentence of their own that incorporates the vocabulary word in the same or similar context in which it is used in the selected reading. This may provide the opportunity to explore multiple meanings of words as students may create sentences using the words in a variety of contexts other than that presented in the selected reading. Although all of the multiple meanings presented would be "celebrated," it is important that the students be able to present the word in the same context as it used in the selected text. This would indicate contextual understanding of the word's meaning.
Sentence Prompts	Using sentence starters or fragments to prompt students to use new vocabulary encourages appropriate use of new words in correct textual settings. Students are provided with a list of new vocabulary words and directed to place them in the appropriate sentence "stems" (Cudd & Roberts, 1993/94). The amount of writing required may be adjusted to the levels of the students. With younger children this might involve oral responses that are transcribed for them. prancing mane owling dependable shrugged She didn't know the answer to the question, so she simply _____ her shoulders. At the parade I saw........... The pony was loved by the children because...... When Pa told me to get his rod and reel, I knew we were going fishing. But tonight, he said we were going to look for owls in the woods; we were going _____.
Semantic Mapping Based on a Concept	The central theme or idea of the story is used as the center point of a semantic map. Other words in the vocabulary are then related to the central theme or idea. **Feeling** Cold Fear Hope **Sights** Trees Shadows Clearing Moon **Sounds** Silence Train Barking Crunching Whooooo Owling

FIGURE 5.4 Sample vocabulary log entries.

Vocabulary Word	Vocabulary Log Entry
pandemonium	At the basketball game Friday night, *the crowd went wild* when we scored the winning basket in the last two seconds. I said to Robbie, "Let's get out of this pandemonium and head for The Burger Barn."
shadow	I showed my dad my shadow and said, "Look, my shadow is swimming in the pool."

FIGURE 5.5 Double-entry journal for practical chemistry.

Combination	Definition
Muddy Water	Mixture is not consistent throughout the sample. This is a heterogeneous mixture.
Sea Water	Mixture that no matter where you sample it has the multiple substances (salt and water) in the same ratio. This is a homogeneous mixture.
Sand	Mixture is not consistent throughout the sample. This is a heterogeneous mixture.
Fresh Water	This is composed of two or more elements, chemically combined (hydrogen and oxygen). This is a compound.

APPLICATIONS AND EXAMPLES

Vocabulary processing in a third-grade integration study of science and literature is illustrated on File 5 of the accompanying CD.

Mr. Bateman, a high school chemistry teacher, is faced with trying to get his students to learn a number of new vocabulary words to assure that they will be able to comprehend the material contained in the next unit of study. He divides the class into several small groups and gives each group a set of materials and a list of the definitions that he wants them to learn. Some of the materials include sand, water, sugar, food coloring, and salt. He then instructs the students to combine the materials in a variety of ways that might conform to the definitions for the words he has given them. The words include *compound, mixture, homogeneous mixture,* and *heterogeneous mixture.* The groups busily engage in creating combinations that they believe conform to the desired combinations to fit the definitions.

After each group completes a combination, Mr. Bateman asks them to share their results with the rest of the class and to explain how the particular combination they have created serves as an exemplar for the definition they have chosen. Once definitions and appropriate exemplars are agreed upon, they are logged into their lab journals, and students are given a crossword puzzle to complete based on the definitions they have "discovered" in the process of creating the combinations of materials. Mr. Bateman then asks the students to look for everyday examples of mixtures, compounds, heterogeneous mixtures, and homogeneous mixtures. He instructs them to list these everyday scientific observations in a double-entry journal with the substance in the left column and the definition of the combination in the right column. See figure 5.5 for sample double-entry journal.

Each day as the students share their journal entries, Mr. Bateman uses this as an opportunity to relate the chemistry they are learning to their everyday experiences. In this way he is supporting the internalization of the word meanings rather than just having the students memorize the terms and definitions.

CONCLUSION

To move students from a superficial understanding of vocabulary (fast mapping) to a more in-depth conceptual knowledge (extended mapping) it is necessary to give them multiple exposures in a variety of formats or modes. This should include practical applications to bring real-life understanding to the word meanings and contextual frameworks. The classroom example included in this chapter explores the wide range of vocabulary activities that may be used with students to ensure their movement toward the extended mapping that will support their success in all areas of the curriculum.

Just being able to read and pronounce a word does not assure understanding. Teachers should provide opportunities to clarify meanings, use words in multiple contexts, and assess the students' understandings of words by asking them to explain word meanings, use words in sentences, or discuss possible ways that given words might be used.

REFERENCES

Carey, S. (1978). The child as word learner. In M. Halle, J. Bresman, & G. Miller (Eds.), *Linguistic theory and psychological reality* (pp. 265–293). Cambridge, MA: MIT Press.

Cudd, E., & Roberts, L. (1993/94). A scaffolding technique to develop sentence and vocabulary. *The Reading Teacher, 47,* 346–349.

Ogle, D. M. (1986). K-W-L: A teaching model that develops active reading of expository text. *The Reading Teacher, 39,* 564–570.

Pressley, M., & Woloshyn, V. (1995). *Cognitive strategy instruction that really improves children's academic performance.* Cambridge, MA: Brookline Books.

Yolen, J. (1987). *Owl moon.* New York: Scholastic, Inc.

SUGGESTED READING

Adams, T. L. (2003). Reading mathematics: More than words can say. *The Reading Teacher, 56,* 786–795.

Beck, I. L., & McKeown, M. G. (2001). Text talk: Capturing the benefits of read-aloud experiences for young children. *The Reading Teacher, 55,* 10–20.

Dixon-Krauss, L. (2002). Using literature as a context for teaching vocabulary. *Journal of Adolescent and Adult Literacy, 45*(4), 310–318.

Lapp, D., Jacobson, J., Fisher, D., & Flood, J. (2000). Tried and true word study and vocabulary practices. *The California Reader, 33*(2), 25–30.

6

TEXT TALK

Scaffolding Comprehension through Oral Discussion

Focus on English Learners
Hearing and participating in text talk and the accompanying vocabulary study benefits students as they acquire English.

Text talk (Beck & McKeown, 2001) is an approach to discussing text that focuses the reader (or listener) on thinking strategies that support comprehension. In discussing the text, the teacher asks open-ended questions, requiring the students to develop problem-solving and/or experience-related responses rather than simply gleaning facts and basic information from the text. This strategy also includes vocabulary study following the reading. This helps students to connect the vocabulary encountered in the reading to their understanding of the text and to a deeper knowledge of the words.

Text talk is a combination of literature discussion and vocabulary study that provides a basis for students to be able to actively participate in such classroom approaches as "grand conversations" (Serafini, 2000) with more success. It provides guided practice in all three of the experiences necessary to effectively discuss literature: exposure, exploration, and interaction (Serafini, 2000).

Text talk is typically taught and demonstrated during read-aloud, but can also be incorporated into reading instruction groups and literature discussion activities once the students are familiar with the approach. Upper-grade students also respond enthusiastically to this approach (Ivey, 2003).

STEP BY STEP

The steps in implementing text talk are:

STEP 1   SELECTING APPROPRIATE TEXT

The text selected should be intellectually challenging and provide opportunities for children to explore ideas and use language to explain their perceptions. Look for texts that have some complexity in plot and presentation of unfamiliar ideas and topics. Books that rely heavily on the story, rather than the pictures, for communicating the sequence of events are especially effective (Beck & McKeown, 2001).

STEP 2   FORMULATING INITIAL QUESTIONS

Plan questions to open the discussion that require children to describe and explain ideas rather than to just recall words or events from the text.

STEP 3   READING THE TEXT

Whether reading the text aloud or having the students read the text themselves, it is important to stop periodically and discuss what was read. Use the preplanned questions to get the discussion started.

STEP 4   SCAFFOLDING THE INITIAL RESPONSES

As the children begin to answer the questions, the teacher should ask follow-up questions to scaffold their thinking. These follow-up questions encourage the students to elaborate on and further develop their initial responses.

STEP 5   FOCUSING ON TEXT INFORMATION RATHER THAN ILLUSTRATIONS

Because children often answer questions based on information they glean from illustrations, the pictures should be presented after they have heard/read and responded to the text. When text talk is being used as a part of reading group activities, the illustrations should be covered. Children are informed ahead of time not to look at the pictures until after reading and discussion of the text. Tell them that the illustrations are being used to confirm ideas rather than to predict what will happen.

STEP 6   DIFFERENTIATING BETWEEN BACKGROUND KNOWLEDGE
            AND TEXT KNOWLEDGE

Because students tend to over-rely on background knowledge, which can actually disrupt comprehension rather than enhance it (Trabasso & Suh, 1993), teachers help them to differentiate between responses based on their prior knowledge and responses that come from knowledge gained from the text. To do this, the teacher simply confirms that the student has made a true statement, but needs to look to see what the text says about the question. The purpose of these exchanges is to help students identify when they are responding from their prior knowledge and when they are responding from information found in the text. This process helps students to avoid interference in comprehension based on their prior experiences, and also helps support them in gaining information from the text and integrating it into their overall schema.

STEP 7   EXPLORING VOCABULARY

Identify words from the text that are relatively unfamiliar to the students. Begin by reviewing the words in relation to the text, explaining the meanings, and having the children repeat the words to confirm that they are pronouncing them correctly. Plan a series of activities that will enable students to become more familiar and comfortable with using the words. Display the words in pocket charts and refer to them consistently over a period of time. For suggestions on ways to actively involve students in vocabulary study, see collecting words, word mapping, vocabulary role play, and vocabulary processing strategies found in this text.

APPLICATIONS AND EXAMPLES

See File 6 of the accompanying CD for a third-grade example of text talk used to encourage higher-level reading.

Mrs. Arthur's 10th-grade social studies class is studying Christopher Columbus and his voyages to the "new world." In this study, Mrs. Arthur hopes to help her students look at varying viewpoints and compare the published accounts of history to look for commonalities and differences. Mrs. Arthur has located a text entitled *Westward with Columbus: Set Sail on the Voyage That Changed the World* (Dyson, 1991). This text gives a very descriptive and detailed account of Columbus's first voyage along with the story of a scientist who re-created the voyage in 1988 in order to look into some conflicts in Columbus's logs.

Mrs. Arthur has designed some questions to pose to her class after each segment of the text is read. The purpose of each set of questions is to move her students beyond fact finding and help them to do some in-depth thinking and problem solving related to the reading and their understanding of history.

The class is completing the reading of the first section of the text in which Dr. Coin, a present-day scientist, is meeting the author of the book to talk about the proposed reenactment of the journey and the questions posed by Columbus's log.

Mrs. Arthur wants the students to delve into the knowledge Dr. Coin possesses that enables him to recognize the inconsistencies in Columbus's log. Because the students are 10th graders, Mrs. Arthur wants to support their problem-solving skills and alert them to ways in which authors slant their writing in order to influence the reader's thinking.

Mrs. Arthur prepares a list of questions to get the discussion started:

1. What type of research would Dr. Coin have to do to recognize the inconsistencies in Columbus's log?
2. What were some of the problems he would encounter in mounting a reenactment voyage?
3. What do you think his motivation might be?
4. What type of records will he have to keep in order to compare and contrast his voyage with that of Columbus?

After a thorough discussion of the first section of the text, Mrs. Arthur will prepare the students to read the second section. In this section the traditional story of Columbus, his early life, and his attempts to obtain funding for his voyage to the far east is told. Mrs. Arthur has the students complete a personal KWL chart before reading the second section. They complete the K and W ("know" and "want to know") sections of the chart before reading the text and then fill in the L ("learned") section after reading. To prepare for the discussion, the students are to think about differences in the version in this book and versions they have read in the past. They are also to make a list of vocabulary words they have difficulty understanding.

Mrs. Arthur plans to lead a discussion in which the students will be asked to talk about the inconsistencies in this version of Columbus's early life and those they've read in the past. The focus of this discussion will be the reasons for the inconsistencies, the type of information that is available related to events of the distant past, and ways that writers might tell the story in order to influence the reader's opinions.

The vocabulary study that Mrs. Arthur plans to conduct after the reading of each section of the text will help the students to relate the new words to their past experiences, look at root words, and create a vocabulary journal. In the vocabulary journal they will chronicle their use of the words in speech or writing and their personal experiences with the words.

CONCLUSION

Mrs. Arthur is using strategies of text talk to support her students in understanding text. Through discussions focusing on inference and problem solving followed by in-depth vocabulary study, she is building her students' repertoire of self-help strategies to use when encountering tough text. She is also helping her students understand the importance of recognizing the author's intent in writing descriptions in certain ways. Mrs. Arthur recognizes the importance of planning in conducting higher-level discussions.

REFERENCES

Beck, I. L., & McKeown, M. G. (2001). Text talk: Capturing the benefits of read-aloud experiences for young children. *The Reading Teacher, 55,* 10–20.

Dyson, J. (1991). *Westward with Columbus: Set sail on the voyage that changed the world.* New York: Scholastic Inc.

Ivey, G. (2003). "The teacher makes it more explainable" and other reasons to read aloud in the intermediate grades. *The Reading Teacher, 56,* 812–814.

Serafini, F. (2000). Before the conversations become "Grand." *The California Reader, 33,* 19–24.

Trabasso, T., & Suh, S. (1993). Understanding text: achieving explanatory coherence through online inferences and mental operations in working memory. *Discourse Processes, 16,* 3–34.

SUGGESTED READING

Sipe, L. R. (2002). Talking back and talking over: Young children's expressive engagement during storybook read-alouds. *The Reading Teacher, 55,* 476–483.

Suits, B. (2001). A second look at literature circles. *The Reading Teacher, 35,* 21–29.

Wood, K., Roser, N., & Martinez, M. (2001). Collaborative literacy: Lessons learned from literature. *The Reading Teacher, 55,* 102–111.

MICROSELECTION

Introducing the Concepts of Key Words and Main Ideas

Finding the main idea in individual sentences, also called *microselection*, is a prerequisite for teaching students to find the main idea in longer reading passages (Baumann, 1982). By beginning with individual sentences, students find success and gradually transfer this ability to longer text. The ability to locate the main idea in sentences and passages is a critical skill for several reasons. Students are better able to retain the meaning of the reading when they can locate and recall main ideas rather than trying to remember each detail because they haven't been able to prioritize the information read. Once they can identify the main idea, they are more likely to be able to paraphrase the meaning of the sentence rather than having to memorize it as written.

Microselection is done at the sentence level and practiced in several ways before it is expanded into finding the main idea in paragraphs and whole passages. Students are taught first to identify important key words and then to paraphrase the meaning of the sentence. Although microprocessing (Irwin, 1991) involves the understanding of individual words, phrases, and sentences, the skills of identifying key words and paraphrasing are important skills in comprehension at the paragraph and whole-selection level as well.

STEP BY STEP

The steps in teaching microselection are:

STEP 1   INTRODUCING THE CONCEPT OF MICROSELECTION

The teacher explains that understanding the meanings of important words in a sentence aids in understanding the meaning of the whole sentence. No one can be expected to remember every word read or heard. By identifying the important words in a sentence, it is easier to be able to understand and talk about the meaning of the sentence rather than having to memorize the whole sentence.

STEP 2   MODELING THE IDENTIFICATION OF KEY WORDS

The teacher reads a sentence from a reading selection required of the students. For example, using the social studies text, she may read, "The role of women in industry changed dramatically due to their widespread employment in traditional male jobs during WWII." She models the selection of important words in the sentence by writing the words *women, industry*, and *WWII* on the board. She then demonstrates how, by remembering the key words, she can restate the sentence, keeping the meaning, without saying it exactly as it was written. She says, "I can restate the main idea in my own words by saying, 'During World War II, women proved they could work in any job in industry by performing tasks usually done by men.'"

> **Focus on English Learners**
>
> Modeling new processes helps support understanding.

STEP 3   GUIDING STUDENTS IN PRACTICING MICROSELECTION

The teacher begins guided practice by asking the students to read a sentence and identify the most important words to remember. She then asks the students to tell what the sentence was about without repeating the original sentence. This exercise is repeated several times until the teacher is sure that the students understand.

STEP 4   PAIRING STUDENTS FOR FURTHER PRACTICE

The teacher puts the students into practice pairs, making sure that she doesn't pair two weak readers. The students are given a reading assignment and instructed to read the passage one sentence at a time. After each sentence is read silently, one student identifies the important words and the partner states the sentence in his or her own words. Once the important words are identified, they can be written on a list or highlighted in the text using removable highlighting tape. The partners take turns identifying important words and restating the sentence.

STEP 5   DISCUSSING THE PROCEDURE

The teacher brings the class back together for a debriefing activity. Each pair is asked to share the important words identified for each sentence and discuss the word meanings. Any controversy about the most important words in the sentence is discussed, and students are encouraged to defend their choices.

APPLICATIONS AND EXAMPLES

Mrs. Dowling's second graders are having difficulty with word problems in math. She decides that a lesson on microselection might serve to help them identify the important words in the word problems that give the students information about the appropriate math operation to use. Mrs. Dowling writes the following word problem on the overhead projector:

> *John and Susan each have three cookies. Their friend Sara comes to play with them. They want to share the cookies with their friend but don't know how to make it fair. How many cookies will each child get to eat?*

Mrs. Dowling asks the students to read the first sentence. "What are the important words in this sentence?" she asks the class.

"I think the word *each* is important. It tells you that John has cookies and so does Susan," replies Juan.

"Very good. The word *each* is important. You know there are more than three cookies," responds Mrs. Dowling.

"The word *three* is important, too," adds Don. "You have to know how many cookies each of them has."

"*Each* and *three* tell you that you have to add three and three to find out how many cookies they have, since there are two children," says Cindy.

"Are the names of the children important?" asks Mrs. Dowling.

"Well, no. You just need to know that there are two children who each have three cookies," replies Martha.

"Knowing their names helps you to keep it straight when Sara comes to play, though," adds Consuela.

"That's true," says Mrs. Dowling. "Now, who can tell me what this sentence says?" she asks as she covers up the words on the overhead.

"There are two children who each have three cookies," says Cindy quickly.

"Exactly! You don't have to memorize the sentence once you know the important words to remember," says Mrs. Dowling with a smile. "Now, do you have to do any math yet?"

"Well, you have to add three and three so you know how many cookies they have altogether," notes Juan. "You'll need to know that."

"OK, we're getting ahead of ourselves," says Mrs. Dowling. "Let's read the next sentence and find the important words."

"Well, *Sara* or *friend* would be important. If she's a friend, they're going to want to share their cookies," says Martha.

"Yes, you are right. What do you think you're going to have to do?" asks Mrs. Dowling.

"We have to figure out how to share six cookies between three children," suggests Consuela.

"I think you're right, but let's read the next sentence and find out," urges Mrs. Dowling.

"Oh, we were right!" says Consuela. "The important words in the next sentence are *share* and *fair*, Mrs. Dowling. They want to know how to make it fair."

"You are really good at this, Consuela. Now, read the last sentence to see if you're right."

"Let me do this one," says Juan. "The important words are *how, many, each,* and *eat.*"

"I think you're right," says Mrs. Dowling. "How many do each of them get to eat?"

"This is so easy," says Cindy. "They each get two cookies. John gives Sara one cookie and Susan gives her one cookie. Everybody gets two cookies and it's fair."

"OK, that's one way to do it," says Mrs. Dowling. "Is there another way that will work?"

"They can put all six cookies down and each one of them can take one cookie and then go back and take another one. That way everyone gets the same amount," suggests Juan.

"That will work, too," says Mrs. Dowling with a smile.

"Now, I'm going to give you some more word problems to do. I want you to work in partners and we'll do the same thing. Read one sentence at a time, choose the important words in each sentence, and talk with your partner about the words and what math you have to do to solve the problem. Remember, they are called *word problems* for a reason. You have to pay attention to the words you're reading and what they mean."

As the students are working, Mrs. Dowling moves around the room. She observes the students as they choose the important words and talk about them. Every now and then she asks students to restate the sentence to make sure they are understanding. She is very pleased with the knowledge the students show.

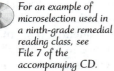

For an example of microselection used in a ninth-grade remedial reading class, see File 7 of the accompanying CD.

Focus on English Learners

Working in pairs provides opportunities for discussion and problem solving. Pairing with one strong English speaker in each team supports content understanding and English development.

CONCLUSION

Instruction in microselection is an important step to take with students who are having difficulty summarizing or paraphrasing. If students cannot identify the main idea in a passage they have read, it is often helpful to teach them microselection. Being able to identify important words in a sentence is much less overwhelming than facing a paragraph or more of text. Once students can microselect, they often move into paraphrasing and summarizing with much more success. As Mrs. Dowling demonstrates, the ability to identify important words in math problems and science experiments is a strategy that supports comprehension across the curriculum. By identifying important words in the individual sentence, it becomes easier to identify the causes of vocabulary and comprehension difficulties as well.

Modeling the use of microselection and then monitoring student use of the strategy is vital in determining when students need more instruction or guided practice. Using pairs or small groups of students in the initial practice phases provides important scaffolding for students struggling with the process.

REFERENCES

Baumann, J. (1982, December). *Teaching children to comprehend main ideas*. Paper presented at the annual meeting of the National Reading Conference, Clearwater, FL.

Irwin, J. (1991). *Teaching the comprehension processes* (2nd ed.). Needham Heights, MD: Allyn and Bacon.

SUGGESTED READING

Williams, J. A. (2001). Classroom conversations: Opportunities to learn for ESL students in mainstream classrooms. *The Reading Teacher, 54*(8) 750–757.

FLUENCY STRATEGIES

Multiple Approaches

Reading a sentence with proper phrasing and fluency has a great impact on the student's ability to understand what is being read (Irwin, 1991; Kuhn & Stahl, 2003). When a reader struggles with word recognition, stops to decode words in a sentence, or reads word by word, comprehension suffers.

A number of factors enter into the student's ability to read fluently. The knowledge of high-frequency words, which appear throughout any text to connect words carrying the unique meaning of the sentence, are always important to understanding. They should be a major focus in reading instruction, of course. Another important factor in understanding meaning in individual sentences is the reader's phrasing. Instruction in *chunking* at the sentence level, the ability to connect important phrases into cohesive "chunks," is enhanced through the use of a series of techniques.

Initial modeling by the teacher is essential. The teacher should read the sentence fluently, using appropriate phrasing and expression. Students then are encouraged to engage in a series of practice strategies that progressively put more of the responsibility on them for reading with appropriate phrasing and expression. The series of techniques that supports this gradual use of proper phrasing includes:

1. Modeling by the teacher (Kuhn & Stahl, 2003)
2. Echo reading, in which the teacher models and students echo the teacher's phrasing and expression (Rasinski, Pakak, Linnek, & Sturtevant, 1994)
3. Choral reading, in which a student reads along with the teacher and sometimes other students
4. Chunking practice exercises to mark the reading material in some way to indicate proper phrasing
5. Opportunities to reread familiar text practicing fluency and expressive reading

For many students, the use of this whole series of strategies is not necessary. With only a few demonstrations, they can see the difference in their fluency and understanding, and they begin practicing phrasing almost naturally. For those students who read most hesitantly, the series of exercises provides the support necessary to move them toward more fluent reading. By hearing proper phrasing and expression, their auditory sense is activated. This helps them hear the grouping of ideas and aids in their comprehension of the sentence. While practicing appropriate phrasing and expression, the students also are rereading the sentences a number of times, which also supports comprehension.

STEP BY STEP

The steps in implementing sentence-level "chunking" instruction are:

STEP 1   ## MODELING FLUENT AND EXPRESSIVE READING

The teacher reads the sentence with proper phrasing and expression. It is important to talk about the value of phrasing and expression in assisting in the comprehension of what we are reading. The oral reading of a sentence brings the auditory sense into play. By grouping words in a way that helps us to hear them in a conversational connection, our auditory sense helps us to process the meaning of the phrases and the sentence.

STEP 2   ## ENGAGING THE STUDENT IN ECHO READING

The teacher repeats the modeling of reading with proper phrasing and expression and asks the student to "echo" the expressive reading. If the student has difficulty doing this while looking at the words, it may be necessary to ask the student to echo without following the print for a couple of times until the echo pattern is established. Once the student is echoing fluently without attending to the print, the print is used once again.

STEP 3   ## PRACTICING CHORAL READING

The teacher introduces a simple paragraph and reads it with appropriate phrasing and expression while the student reads aloud along with the teacher. At first, the student may lag behind. The teacher may have to slow the pace of reading slightly, but it is important to keep the pace steady so that the reading remains fluent and expressive. The choral reading of the sentence or passage is repeated several times until the student is reading with fluency and expression. The final component of this step is to have the student read the passage alone, demonstrating fluent expressive reading. Short poems are also very effective for practice in choral reading.

STEP 4   ## PRACTICING FLUENT, EXPRESSIVE READING WITH MATERIAL MARKED WITH PROPER PHRASING

The student should be provided with reading material that is marked in some way to indicate proper phrasing. The marking of the reading material can be done in several ways. The student can be involved in marking the material, helping him or her to recognize the meaning factors that aid in determining which words are grouped together when reading. Some methods of marking reading materials to be used for this phase of practice are shown in figure 8.1.

STEP 5   ## PRACTICING SENTENCE-LEVEL CHUNKING IN ORAL READING

Once the student is comfortable reading with phrasing and expression using marked materials, the use of unmarked materials is introduced. Whenever the student experiences difficulty in decoding or reverts to word-by-word reading, the teacher should establish a signal to use that reminds the student to reread for fluency. When the student remembers to do this spontaneously, the teacher can recognize the fact by providing some kind of simple signal to congratulate the student on the new-found independence.

FIGURE 8.1 Marking the text for chunking practice.

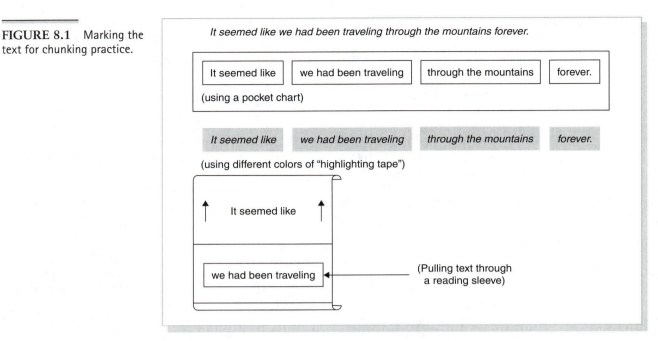

APPLICATIONS AND EXAMPLES

An example of fluency instruction in first grade is provided on File 8 of the accompanying CD.

Mr. Estrella tells his 10th graders, "Shakespeare uses a number of symbolic references in his writing. In this scene Marcellus is explaining the symbolic importance of the ghost disappearing once the rooster crows. Listen as I read this text aloud."

Printed text	*Text repunctuated for phrasing*
It faded on the crowing of the cock.	*It faded, on the crowing of the cock.*
Some say that ever 'gainst that season comes	*Some say that, "Ever 'gainst that season comes*
Wherein our Savior's birth is celebrated	*wherein our Savior's birth is celebrated,*
This bird of dawning singeth all night long,	*this bird of dawning, singeth all night long."*
And then they say no spirit dare stir abroad;	*And then they say, "no spirit dare stir abroad."*
The nights are wholesome, then no planets strike,	*The nights are wholesome. Then no planets strike,*
no fairy takes, nor witch hath power to charm,	*no fairy takes, nor witch hath power to charm;*
So hallowed and so gracious is that time	*so hallowed and so gracious is that time.*

Mr. Estrella reads the text aloud, with expression, phrasing so that the text can be clearly understood. He asks, "What does the cock's crowing symbolize?"

Mario responds, "Well, the rooster usually crows at dawn so I think the quote is saying that the ghost disappeared at dawn, but don't all spirits usually do that? I mean, in all the scary stories, ghosts roam the houses at night."

"Exactly," replies Mr. Estrella. "The ghost is a spirit and disappears at dawn, but Shakespeare is also saying that the motion of the planets and witches and fairies lose their power at dawn. I know this is tough text but when you read it paying attention to the phrasing, it really begins to make sense. Let's practice it together. Read it along with me."

Mr. Estrella displays the passage on the overhead projector and leads the students in the choral reading of the quote, demonstrating by underlining the phrases with different colors of transparency pens as they read. He then hands out a photocopied handout with the passages that follow the quote they are practicing (Swope, 1994). "I want you to work in pairs to underline the phrases in these passages and then practice the oral reading of the passages with your partner. After you each read a passage aloud, talk about the meaning of the passage. We will get back together as a group to read each passage aloud with proper phrasing and expression. Then we will talk about the meanings of each of the sections of text."

The students work in pairs as Mr. Estrella circulates around the room. He stops to do some modeling whenever the students are having difficulty with phrasing. He listens to the students discussing meaning and supports their exploration of the text.

At the end of the period, the students demonstrate their fluent reading of Shakespeare and find that their understanding of the text is greatly improved as a result of their practice. They leave Mr. Estrella's literature class feeling successful.

> **Focus on English Learners**
>
> Paired practice with focus on fluency and expression encourages repeated readings of text, a major tool in increasing fluency.

CONCLUSION

No matter what grade level is involved, students' comprehension of text is improved when they are taught to read in meaningful chunks, phrasing well and using expression. Although this is easier for some students than others, almost all students can benefit from this instruction. Instruction in sentence-level chunking is especially valuable for struggling readers and readers for whom English is not their native language. Hearing teachers or peers model good phrasing and expression often helps students to better understand that good reading is not necessarily rapid but should be paced and phrased to focus on meaning. In addition, the rereading that takes place in the sequence of hearing, echo reading, and choral reading supports the learning of new vocabulary. The techniques used to mark materials into meaningful phrases support the students in understanding which words must be grouped together to encourage understanding.

Providing opportunities for repeated readings of familiar text is a vital addition to any instruction in reading fluency. The reading of poetry, reader's theater scripts, and text of varying genres is important in building the reader's confidence. Observation and planned interventions by the teacher in the form of brief echo reading and modeling places value on fluency and encourages students to focus more on this important aspect of the comprehension process (Kuhn & Stahl, 2003).

REFERENCES

Irwin, J. (1991). *Teaching comprehension processes* (2nd ed.). Needham Heights, MA: Allyn and Bacon.

Kuhn, M. R., & Stahl, S. A. (2003). Fluency: A review of developmental and remedial practices. *Journal of Educational Psychology, 95*, 3–21.

Rasinski, P. V., Pakak, N., Linnek, W. I., & Sturtevant, E. (1994). Affect of fluency development on urban second-grade readers. *The Journal of Educational Research, 87*, 158–165.

Swope, J. W. (1994). *Ready-to-use activities for teaching Hamlet.* West Nyack, NY: The Center for Applied Research in Education.

SUGGESTED READING

Briggs, C., & Forbes, S. (2002). Phrasing in fluent reading: Process *and* product. *Journal of Reading Recovery, 1,* 1–9.

Denman, G. A. (2000). Poetry in the classroom: Reading a poem well. *The California Reader, 33*(2), 12–14.

Rasinski, T. (2000). Speed does matter in reading. *The Reading Teacher, 54,* 146–151.

Richards, M. (2000). Be a good detective: Solve the case of oral reading fluency. *The Reading Teacher, 53*(7), 534–539.

Worthy, J., & Broaddus, K. (2002). Fluency beyond the primary grades: From group performance to silent, independent practice. *The Reading Teacher, 55,* 334–343.

SECTION II

PARAGRAPH-LEVEL COMPREHENSION

The strategies explained in this section relate to the connections among sentences within a paragraph. The section begins with two approaches that support readers in understanding the ways in which adjacent sentences combine information to make sense. The chapter on anaphoric relationships is especially vital knowledge for helping students understand the ways in which pronouns and other words are substituted for one another in reading passages and how to interpret these relationships to make sense of text.

Subsequent chapters in section II allow the teacher to support students in comprehending paragraphs as coherent entities within a larger text. They encourage students to become active processors of text and to learn to paraphrase, ask themselves questions, and become actively engaged in making meaning as they read. As in section I, it is important that the teacher activate prior knowledge before these strategies are presented to students. The teacher must observe and question throughout the process so that the students' levels of understanding, both of the meaning of the text and of the use of the comprehension strategies, are being constantly monitored. Whenever the teacher recognizes that students are not fully understanding, reteaching and/or additional guided practice should be scheduled.

Because no strategy is appropriate for all students within a classroom situation, we encourage teachers to use a variety of approaches to support readers in making connections within paragraphs in text. Some students will respond best to strategies that they can employ independently, while others will find more support in collaborative strategies. Each student should be given instruction in several approaches so that she or he has a number of strategies available for use whenever a group of sentences or a paragraph proves challenging.

ANAPHORIC RELATIONS

Word Substitutions

Anaphoric relations are associations between words when one word or phrase is being used to take the place of another. The most common anaphoric relations are between nouns and the pronouns that replace them. The word that is being replaced in the sentence is called the *antecedent*. Often, a group of several words may be used to replace a single word. For example, in the following sentences a substitution is made for the noun *computer*.

> John bought a computer. The **box of fascinating components** gave him quite an intellectual challenge.

Identifying anaphoric relationships in sentences is a difficult task for some students. When readers cannot easily identify the antecedent of the pronoun (substitution), they often misunderstand the meaning of the passage. The antecedent is more easily identified when it is found in an adjacent sentence (Barnitz, 1980), so students must often be taught to look before or beyond the sentence being read to find the antecedent and make the meaning connection. In addition to the location of the antecedent, other factors that influence the difficulty of understanding the relationships are the difficulty of the reading material, the prior knowledge of the readers, and the clarity of the writing (Irwin, 1991). Examples of different types of anaphoric relations are shown in figure 9.1.

Teachers can check the students' understanding of the relations between and among pronouns, substitutions, and their referents by asking questions. If it appears that students are confused by these word substitutions, then explanations of the word connections may be woven into the fabric of the lesson. However, the difficulty of making the connection may justify the explicit teaching of these relationships. In this context, teaching anaphoric relations can be done in both incidental and explicit ways.

STEP BY STEP

The steps in implementing the explicit teaching of anaphoric relations are:

STEP 1   SELECTING MATERIAL RICH WITH ANAPHORIC RELATIONS

The teacher selects several passages containing anaphoric relations. The individual sentences in the first passage are copied onto sentence strips and displayed in a pocket chart.

FIGURE 9.1   Examples of anaphoric relationships.

Pronoun	Word Substitutions
John bought a computer.	John bought a computer.
He got a really good deal.	The box of fascinating components gave him quite an intellectual challenge.
He bought it at the computer store.	The salesman was able to answer all his questions.
He bought the printer there too.	He was able to get all his questions answered by the customer service representative.

FIGURE 9.2   Using a pocket chart to identify antecedents, one type of a anaphoric relationship.

Most of all Clifford thought about his mom

He decided to spend Thanksgiving with her

She lives in the city

Most of all Clifford thought about his mom

He decided to spend Thanksgiving with His mom

His mom lives in the city

STEP 2   SUBSTITUTING THE ANTECEDENTS FOR THE PRONOUNS OR SUBSTITUTIONS (REFERENTS)

The teacher and students read the sentences aloud. The teacher asks students to identify the relationships between the pronouns, substitutions, and antecedents. She writes the antecedent words on sentence strips and places them over the pronouns and substitutions so that the sentences can be reread to determine whether or not they make sense with the antecedents in place. See figure 9.2 for an example of how this is done.

STEP 3   DIAGRAMMING THE ANAPHORIC RELATIONS

The teacher writes another passage on an overhead transparency, chart paper, or the chalkboard. Instead of substituting the antecedents for the referents as was done with the sentence strips, this time arrows are drawn from the referents to the antecedents. Each time this is done, the sentence can be reread substituting the antecedent for the referent to determine whether the meaning of the sentence remains the same.

STEP 4   DISCUSSING THE PURPOSE OF THE ACTIVITIES

The teacher ends the lessons with some discussion that relates the activities to problem solving during reading. The students are encouraged to find additional anaphoric relations within the reading material they are studying. The teacher and students discuss the strategies that proficient readers use. Students discuss ways to make sense of the text when pronouns and other word substitutions cause confusion. They can use the strategies practiced during this lesson whenever they become confused about the meaning of a sentence containing pronouns or other word substitutions.

APPLICATIONS AND EXAMPLES

See File 9 of the accompanying CD for an example of a lesson in a 10th-grade social studies class that focuses on anaphoric relations in text.

Ms. Decker's second graders love stories about Clifford the big red dog. Just before Thanksgiving, Ms. Decker brings in a new Clifford book entitled *Clifford's Thanksgiving Visit* (Bridwell, 1993). As Ms. Decker is reading the story aloud, one of the students comments, "Why are the words *she* and *her* on this page? Clifford is a he."

Ms. Decker decides that this is a unique teachable moment, and she writes the three sentences on sentence strips. She displays the sentence strips on the pocket chart like this:

Most of all Clifford thought about his mom.

He decided to spend Thanksgiving with her.

She lives in the city.

Ms. Decker asks, "Who is the author talking about when he says *she* and *her*?" Janine answers, "Clifford's mom."

"Yes," agrees Ms. Decker. "It says Clifford thought about his mom. Let me show you how you can tell if you're right."

Ms. Decker writes *his mom* on a piece of sentence strip and places the words over the word *her*. "Now, let's read the sentences and see if they make sense."

Ms. Decker and the students read, "Most of all Clifford thought about his mom. He decided to spend Thanksgiving with his mom."

"Well? What do you think?" asks Ms. Decker. "Does that make sense?"

Geoffrey responds slowly, "It makes sense but it sounds funny."

"Yes, you are right, Geoffrey. It does sound funny because we don't talk that way, but is Clifford going to spend Thanksgiving with his mom? Is that who he means when he says *she*?"

"Yes," agrees Geoffrey.

"Now," says Ms. Decker, "what about the next sentence? Who is the author talking about when he says, 'She lives in the city?'"

The students agree again, "His mom!"

"Let's try it," says Ms. Decker as she places the words *his mom* over the word *She*.

As the students read the sentence along with Ms. Decker, they agree that it makes sense. "I know the author means Clifford's mom when he says *her* and *she*," says Janine. "But it sure sounds better when you don't keep saying *his mom* over and over."

"That's exactly why we use the pronouns. They make the story sound better," says Ms. Decker.

CONCLUSION

Students often confuse the meanings of sentences and phrases due to a misunderstanding of the anaphoric relationships contained in the text. They need to explore strategies for identifying and relating these words to each other in order to have a clear meaning of the material being read. Finding ways for them to physically or visually make these connections serves as an important aid to their comprehension of the text and understanding of the anaphoric relationships. As Ms. Decker has demonstrated in her classroom, there are several ways to make these connections visible to the students. Because this can be a difficult strategy for the students, it is best for the teacher to demonstrate and then have the students practice using the strategies during the assigned reading.

Using techniques to point out students' use of their knowledge of anaphoric relationships aids teachers in observing whether or not the instruction is effective. Students can highlight places in the text where they find these relationships. Using highlighting tape makes their use of the strategies evident, but is still removable. This allows teachers to observe the usage more readily and to plan additional instruction if students are not making connections.

REFERENCES

Barnitz, J. (1980). Syntactic effects on the reading comprehension of pronoun-referent structures by children in grades two, four, and six. *Reading Research Quarterly, 15,* 268–289.

Bridwell, N. (1993). *Clifford's Thanksgiving visit.* New York: Scholastic, Inc.

Irwin, J. (1991). *Teaching the comprehension processes* (2nd ed.) Needham Heights, MD: Allyn and Bacon.

CONNECTIVES

Focusing on Words That Support Cohesion and Inference

Connectives are words in sentences that help the reader to understand relationships between and among people, time sequences, and events in paragraphs. Students' comprehension and ability to infer meaning is greatly enhanced when they are taught to recognize the clues provided by connectives (Irwin, 1991).

Connectives can be used to relate two events, as in this sentence:

I feel good today because *I finished all my work.*

They can also provide a link in terms of sequence, as in this sentence:

I went for a walk after *I completed my homework.*

Some connectives are implied, as in the sentences:

I feel sick to my stomach. (because) *That ride is very rough.*

The sentences do not contain a word that makes the connection, but the connection is obvious because of the proximity of the sentences. For examples of other types of connectives, see figure 10.1.

To support students in making the connections represented or implied by connectives, teachers need to address the words, their literal meanings, and the ways in which they are used in sentences within the text being read.

STEP BY STEP

The steps in teaching connectives are:

STEP 1   IDENTIFYING TEXT RICH IN CONNECTIVES

The teacher reads content-area text to be read by the students and notes sentences containing connectives. He prepares questions to ask the students after they read so that he can determine their understanding of the meaning the connectives add to the sentences. For example: "The people needed homes, *but* there were no trees in the area, *so* they built their homes of rock." The teacher might prepare the questions,

FIGURE 10.1 Examples of connective relationships.

Type	Key Words	Example
Causality	because, so, consequently	John went to school *because* he had a test.
Concession	but, although, however, yet	John went to school *but* he didn't want to!
Condition	if . . . then, unless, except	*If* John passes the test *then* he will be promoted.
Contrast	in contrast, similarly (comparative adjectives)	John sings well; *in contrast,* his dancing is awful.
Conjunction	and, in addition to, also, along with	John went to school *along with* Mary.
Disjunction	or, either . . . or	*Either* John went to school *or* he went to the game.
Location	there, where	John went to school, *where* he took a test.
Manner	in a similar manner, like, as	John was elated to pass the test *as* he had been worried about his knowledge of the topic.
Purpose	in order to	John went to school *in order* to take a test.
Time	before, always, after, while, when, from now on	*Before* John takes the test, he will review the materials.

Focus on English Learners

Understanding the meaning of connectives helps make compound and complex sentences more comprehensible.

"What does the word *but* in this sentence tell you?" and "What does the word *so* lead you to believe?"

STEP 2   ASKING QUESTIONS TO DETERMINE THE STUDENTS' LEVEL OF UNDERSTANDING

The teacher asks the questions he prepared as he read the text. If the students can relate the fact that the people couldn't build wooden homes because there were no trees, they are making the connections in the sentences. They also should be able to relate that the word *so* conveys that the people chose to build homes of rock because it was available. It also implies that they might have preferred to use wood. If some students do not understand the implications of the connectives, the teacher should make note of this so that direct teaching of connectives can be done with those students.

STEP 3   PLANNING AND IMPLEMENTING DIRECT TEACHING OF CONNECTIVES

After the teacher identifies the students who need instruction in connectives, the lessons can be planned and taught using a number of formats.

Connective cloze (Pulver, 1986)—Sentences with connectives are prepared by leaving out the connectives and substituting a blank. Students are asked to supply the appropriate connective. For example: Paul didn't go to the movies with his friends, _____ he didn't have any money.

Sentence combining —In this approach students are given sentence strips with short sentences written on them and a variety of connective words. The students choose two sentences and combine them using a connective that connects the sentences in a meaningful way. For example: Jane went swimming. It was raining. These two sentences would be combined as: Jane went swimming *although* it was raining.

Identifying and labeling connectives —In this activity students are given a paragraph containing connectives and asked to label them. The teacher presents the chart of the types of connectives (see figure 10.1). The chart is reviewed and discussed and then the students read the paragraph given to them, labeling each connective they find using the label from figure 10.1.

STEP 4   REVIEWING CONNECTIVES IN READING

After the focus on and direct instruction of connectives, the teacher reviews the types of relationships shown through the use of connectives any time these associations seem to confuse students. The chart of connectives (figure 10.1) is left on display in the classroom and used to remind students about inferring connections, identifying relationships between sentences, and supplying implicit (unstated) connectives in text.

APPLICATIONS AND EXAMPLES

Mr. Garcia's 10th-grade social science students began looking at a series of events surrounding the time period inclusive of World War I. They discovered that the women's suffrage movement was gaining a lot of headway during this period and began a discussion as to the reasons behind the growth of the movement during this period in history. He decides to see if the students can make a connection between events related to the war and the progress of the suffrage movement. He distributes an article about the suffrage movement and asks them to read the text and to use the connectives chart on the board to identify any connectives they find in the reading. The text is as follows:

See File 10 of the accompanying CD for a second-grade connectives example used to teach cause-and-effect relationships.

> It is 1917 and the President of the United States has a number of problems on his mind. In addition to WWI, which is raging in Europe, there are women marching in front of the White House! In order to gain the attention of the President and the press, they carry a huge banner stating "TWENTY MILLION AMERICAN WOMEN ARE NOT SELF-GOVERNED!" While in Europe American soldiers are fighting for Democracy with aggressive warfare, in contrast these women are fighting for Democracy peacefully. Day after day, the women march in front of the President's house so that women across the nation can gain the right to vote.
>
> Many people dislike the suffragists' picketing because of the war effort in Europe. Consequently, the police feel justified in arresting the pickets. In order to maintain attention for their cause, the jailed women go on hunger strikes. However, the prison matrons in an effort to keep the women alive resort to force-feeding them. Although the women feel that they are fighting an uphill battle, they speak out in court,
>
> > "As long as the government and the representatives of the government prefer to send women to jail on petty and technical charges, we will go to jail. Persecution has always advanced the cause of justice, therefore, the right of American women to work for Democracy must be maintained." (Hakim, 1995)

The students read the article and identify the connectives by underlining them in the text. Mr. Garcia then leads a discussion on how the phrases and ideas joined by the connectives relate to each other and what implications that might have as to why the suffrage movement was so strong during this particular time in history. To see the questions Mr. Garcia uses to lead this discussion, see figure 10.2.

FIGURE 10.2 Connectives and discussion points.

It is 1917 *and* the President of the United States has a number of ⟶	CONJUNCTION Why was the date used as an introduction in this sentence? How is the date important to the rest of the sentence?
problems on his mind. *In addition to* WWI, which is raging in Europe, ⟶	CONJUNCTION What does this word tell us about the war and the women marching?
there are women marching in front of the White House! *In order to* gain ⟶	PURPOSE These words help us to examine the reasons that the women were marching. What were they trying to do?
the attention of the President *and* the press, they carry a huge banner ⟶ stating "TWENTY MILLION AMERICAN WOMEN ARE NOT SELF-GOVERNED!"	CONJUNCTION What was the connection between the president and the press in this sentence?
While in Europe American soldiers are fighting ⟶	TIME What is the purpose of pointing out what was going on in Europe?
for Democracy with aggressive warfare; *in contrast* these women are ⟶ fighting for Democracy peacefully. Day after day, the women march in front	CONTRAST How was the approach the women were using different from the approach the soldiers had to use?
of the President's house *so that* women across the nation can gain ⟶ the right to vote.	PURPOSE Why were they marching?
Many people dislike the suffragists' picketing *because* of the war ⟶	CAUSALITY What caused some people to find the women's marching inappropriate?
effort in Europe. *Consequently,* the police feel justified in arresting the ⟶	CAUSALITY What is the connection between this sentence and the previous one?
pickets. *In order* to maintain attention for their cause, the jailed women ⟶	PURPOSE What does this phrase tell us about the hunger strike?
go on hunger strikes. *However,* the prison matrons ⟶	CONCESSION What does this word tell us about what is coming in the rest of the sentence?
in an effort to keep the women alive resort to force-feeding them. ⟶	PURPOSE Who is making an effort? What are they trying to do?
Although the women feel that they are fighting an uphill battle, they ⟶ speak out in court,	CONCESSION This word also gives us a preview of something to come in this sentence. Can you predict what might be coming?
"*As long as* the government and the representatives ⟶ of the government prefer to send women to jail on petty and technical charges, we will go to jail. Persecution has always advanced the cause of justice,	CONDITION What are the circumstances that will probably remain to be true?
therefore, the right of American women to work for ⟶ Democracy must be maintained."	CAUSALITY What is the connection implied in this word?

CONCLUSION

As Mr. Garcia demonstrates in this brief classroom vignette, students of all ages can be supported in their understanding of connectives in reading. By providing active discussion and rewriting of text to clarify connective concepts, teachers provide scaffolding to improve the comprehension of sentences containing connectives. Most of the connectives used as examples in this chapter are explicitly stated. Even more difficult are implicit connectives. Once students have experience identifying and defining explicit connectives, it becomes easier to identify implicit connectives. By teaching students to insert a familiar connective word or phrase that clarifies the implicit connective, students can improve their ability to understand adjacent sentences whose meanings are intertwined in some way. Strategies for teaching connective concepts are particularly important when working with English language learners. They often require direct instruction in identifying words and phrases whose meanings are not easily identified on a literal level. With all students who find the identification of these connectives difficult, the use of the chart of connective types and examples makes the connections more visible and eventually easier to understand.

REFERENCES

Irwin, J. (1991). *Teaching the comprehension processes* (2nd ed.) Needham Height, MD: Allyn and Bacon.

Hakim, J. (1995). Mom, did you vote? In *A history of US: War, peace, and all that jazz.* New York: Oxford University Press.

Pulver, C. (1986). Teaching students to understand explicit and implicit connectives. In J. W. Irwin (Ed.), *Understanding and teaching cohesion comprehension.* Newark, DE: International Reading Association.

TEXT CHARTING

Exploring the Connections among Sentences

In order for students to recognize the importance of reading beyond one sentence to gather all the information contained in a paragraph, it is necessary to call their attention to the elements of information contained in each of the sentences within a paragraph. An activity that supports this understanding of the interdependence of sentences within a paragraph is called *text charting*. In this exercise, students read each sentence in a paragraph and determine what information is added to the "big picture."

The charting of the sentences also supports the reader in understanding the use of connectives in sentences and how they can alert the reader to the relationship of the phrases, clauses, and subsequent sentences in the passage.

Text charting is a powerful tool in supporting students in their understanding of integrative processes, the connection between adjacent sentences in text. While reading, students are then better able to recognize what questions might be posed in one sentence and answered in another. For instance, one sentence may tell us that someone is going home, while the next sentence may give us the reason they need to go home. The students' understanding of this interrelatedness of the two sentences is essential in increasing their comprehension skills. See figure 11.1 for an example of a simple story demonstrating the interrelatedness of several independent sentences through text charting.

STEP BY STEP

The steps in implementing text charting are:

STEP 1   SELECTING THE TEXT

The text selected should be one that does not provide all the information needed in the initial sentence of a paragraph. The students should have to glean needed information from several sentences to make a comprehensible whole of the text.

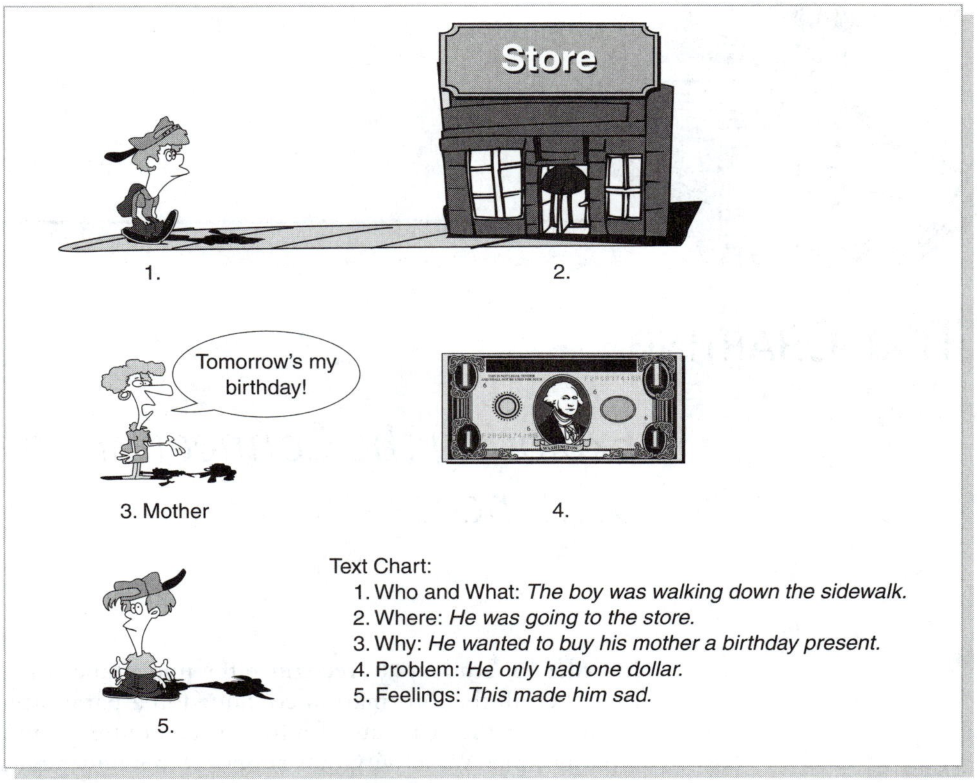

FIGURE 11.1 Text charting.

Text Chart:
1. Who and What: *The boy was walking down the sidewalk.*
2. Where: *He was going to the store.*
3. Why: *He wanted to buy his mother a birthday present.*
4. Problem: *He only had one dollar.*
5. Feelings: *This made him sad.*

FIGURE 11.2 Using a pocket chart to organize a text chart.

STEP 2   MODELING THE PROCESS

The teacher introduces text-charting "question words" to the students. They include such words as *who, what, why, when, where,* and *how.* The actual words chosen depend on the text used. The text used for initial exposure to the process should be relatively simple so that students can become comfortable with the skill of asking themselves those questions. As the text becomes more involved and intricate, other words and phrases may be needed to connect the thoughts in the text. In addition, concepts such as *problem, conflict, resolution,* and *cause and effect* can be charted. Using a pocket chart or similar organizational device, the teacher places sentences on the chart and asks students to identify which sentences answer the question words they have chosen to analyze the text. See figure 11.2 for an example of using a pocket

FIGURE 11.3 Marking prepared text.

A Slip in Time

Who
Joey walked slowly past the store. It was cold and windy that afternoon, and he had forgotten to   *Problem*

what
wear his jacket. He stopped and looked in the window of the sporting goods store, staring at the

new leather NFL jackets that were on display. Suddenly he had an idea!

what
He walked into the store and asked the owner if he could try on one of the jackets he saw in

who
the window. The owner agreed and Joey quickly chose the bright green and yellow one he had

when   *what*
been admiring. While Joey was admiring himself in the mirror, the owner moved to another

where
part of the store to assist another customer. "This is my chance," thought Joey.

what
He bolted for the door, setting off a noisy anti-theft alarm as he passed through it. He ran

when
quickly out the door and turned sharply to his right. Then it happened. Joey slipped on a patch of

cause and effect
ice on the sidewalk and fell suddenly to the ground.

As he gathered himself to get up, he saw a pair of shiny black shoes standing near his head. As

how
he looked at the shoes, somewhat dazed, and began moving his eyes up the blue trousers rising

problem
above them, he knew his luck had run out. He had slipped and fallen directly in the path of Officer

feelings
Mulcahey, the biggest, meanest cop on the beat. His heart sank.

chart to organize text charting based on the use of question words. An optional approach is to chart the additional information added by reading each sentence as the paragraph or story develops.

STEP 3   GUIDING PRACTICE

The teacher distributes a prepared text handout to the students. She instructs them to read the text and write the appropriate question words in the text to identify where information is supplied. See figure 11.3 for an example of appropriately marked prepared text. She walks around the classroom, monitoring students' progress and encouraging and guiding the questioning process.

STEP 4   PRACTICING INDEPENDENTLY

Students are given another prepared text or a selection from a current reading assignment, whether from literature or a content area, with a list of focus-question words. They are instructed to place the words in the appropriate places in the text and bring the assignment back the next day for discussion.

FIGURE 11.4 Text-review questions.

A Slip in Time

Joey walked slowly past the store. It was cold and windy that afternoon, and he had forgotten to wear his jacket. He stopped and looked in the window of the sporting goods store, staring at the new leather NFL jackets that were on display. Suddenly he had an idea!

He walked into the store and asked the owner if he could try on one of the jackets he saw in the window. The owner agreed and Joey quickly chose the bright green and yellow one he had been admiring. While Joey was admiring himself in the mirror, the owner moved to another part of the store to assist another customer. "This is my chance," thought Joey.

He bolted for the door, setting off a noisy anti-theft alarm as he passed through it. He ran quickly out the door and turned sharply to his right. Then it happened. Joey slipped on a patch of ice on the sidewalk and fell suddenly to the ground.

As he gathered himself to get up, he saw a pair of shiny black shoes standing near his head. As he looked at the shoes, somewhat dazed, and began moving his eyes up the blue trousers rising above them, he knew his luck had run out. He had slipped and fallen directly in the path of Officer Mulcahey, the biggest, meanest cop on the beat. His heart sank.

Focus Word	Text-Review Questions
Who?	Who is this story about?
	Who is the main character in this story?
What?	What did Joey do wrong in the story?
	What was Joey looking at in the window of the sporting goods store?
	What caused Joey to fall?
Where?	Where did Joey stop to look in the window?
	Where did Joey fall?
	Where was Joey's own jacket?
How?	How was Joey able to get out of the store?
	How did Joey feel at the end of the story?
	How did Joey get caught?
When?	When did the anti-theft alarm go off?
	When did Joey decide to steal the jacket?
	When did Joey get caught?
Why?	Why did Joey go into the sporting goods store?
	Why did Joey steal the jacket?
	Why did Joey's heart sink?

STEP 5   REVIEWING AND DISCUSSING

Students are placed in small groups the following day to compare and discuss their placement of the focus question words. After the groups report their findings, a larger discussion ensues during which the teacher points out the use of the skill in formulating answers to similar but broader questions that often appear in standardized testing. See figure 11.4 for an example of text-review questions.

APPLICATIONS AND EXAMPLES

Miss Lillie's second-grade class has begun to study the relationship between words and phrases. She is working with them on identifying what questions might be answered related to key words or phrases that she gives them. Today they are talking about the weather, and she has placed some key words and phrases in a pocket chart for the children to see and read along with her. The first word that she shares with

FIGURE 11.5   A wall full
of answers.

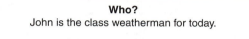

Who?
John is the class weatherman for today.

Where?
John went outside.

Why?
John went to check the weather.

What?
John saw that the sun was shining.

An example of text charting in a seventh-grade language arts class is provided on File 11 of the accompanying CD.

the children is *outside*. She tells them that they need to send a weatherman *outside* to see what the weather is like today. Then she places individual cards containing question words across the top of the pocket chart. She uses *who, what, when,* and *where*.

She asks the children, "When we told our weatherman to go *outside*, have we told him *who* to go, *what* to go, *when* to go, or *where* to go?" The children respond almost in unison, "*Where* to go."

Miss Lillie places the word *outside* under the question word *where* in the pocket chart. "That's right, boys and girls, we told him *where* to go, so we will put the word *outside* under our question word *where*."

She repeats the process with a series of words and phrases and then places them in the chart under the appropriate question word. She guides the students in writing short sentences related to the weather activity that they will then place under appropriate headings on a wall chart she has prepared for the lesson. Students write sentences on sentence strips. Some of the sentences include: "John is the class weatherman for today." "John went outside." "John went to check the weather." "John looked up at the sky." "John saw that the sun was shining."

Miss Lillie asks the students to read their sentences and then to place them under the question word that shows which question is answered by the sentence they have written. See figure 11.5 for a "wall full of answers" that the second graders created.

Use of the who, what, when, and why question words provides a structure for students to use in understanding all aspects of a text. These same questions provide the teacher an opportunity to check for understanding and to plan additional instruction or guided practice.

Focus on English Learners

Group problem solving and discussion accompanied by charting provides exposure to oral English supported by written examples.

CONCLUSION

As demonstrated in this classroom scenario, it is important for teachers to help students recognize predictable patterns in text. Understanding the interdependence of sentences within and among paragraphs is essential to gather all the information the text contains. It is necessary to call students' attention to the elements of information contained in each of the sentences within a paragraph and to find ways to visually and actively represent these relationships.

SUGGESTED READING

Staal, L. (2000). The story face: An adaption of story mapping that incorporates visualization and discovery learning to enhance reading and writing. *The Reading Teacher, 54,* 26–31.

INFERENCES

Filling in the Missing Pieces

Inferences are thought processes that readers go through to uncover information based on their own knowledge that is not explicitly stated in the text. Students often need direct instruction in how to determine the pieces that are missing in the text. Oftentimes, making inferences requires reading several sentences and combining the concepts they convey to reach an implied conclusion. The information readers need to supply comes from a combination of their background knowledge and life experiences. A good example of these is Trabasso's (1981) *slot-filling inferences*, which require the reader to supply vital information mentally, such as:

Who was performing the action? (Agent)

To whom was it done? (Object)

What was used to do it? (Instrument)

Who experienced the feeling or thought? (Experiencer)

Where does it come from? (Source)

What was the result and/or goal? (Goal) (Irwin, 1991)

Instruction in making inferences is best done in the context of reading real text. The teacher introduces the students to the idea that not all the information they need to understand from the reading material is contained within the words on the page. The teacher should be knowledgeable enough about different types of inferences and the information that readers must infer so that he can ask the appropriate questions at the point of need.

STEP BY STEP

The steps in teaching inferences are:

STEP 1 CHOOSING APPROPRIATE READING MATERIAL

Before beginning a lesson on inferences, the teacher selects reading material that will require the students to make a variety of inferences. The teacher then prepares the questions he will ask to help the students understand the concept of supplying missing information to fully comprehend the material being read.

STEP 2   ## INTRODUCING AND MODELING INFERENCE

The teacher introduces the concept of inference by explaining that some information you need to understand what is happening in a story is not stated in the words of the story but must be supplied in your mind. He uses simple examples:

"She added sugar to her cereal." (The reader might infer that she's eating breakfast or that she uses a spoon for the sugar.)

"Joanna rode away quickly on her bike. Larry looked sadly at his flat tire." (The reader infers that Larry also has a bike.)

The teacher also makes the point that we do this thinking almost automatically unless we do not understand what is happening or we infer mistakenly. When confusion occurs, we must know the kinds of inferences that we make in reading to help ourselves figure out the meaning.

At this point the teacher introduces the six different types of inferred information listed in the questions at the beginning of this chapter to help students see different kinds of information that can be inferred. This list is not exhaustive, however. Sometimes the reader must infer much more complicated points such as the character's motivation or the guilt or innocence of a character in a mystery story. These kinds of inference require readers to gather clues from the text or infer from a combination of the author's description along with their own background experiences.

STEP 3   ## PROVIDING GUIDED PRACTICE IN INFERRING

Having chosen a passage rich in inferences, the teacher assigns the passage for reading. He may choose to read the selection aloud or have the students read it silently. The teacher stops the students at the points in the reading where inference is required. He asks the questions he has prepared to help them recognize that they are using inference. He also helps them identify the type of information they are supplying mentally. Depending on the success of this practice, the teacher decides whether or not to continue guided practice with the whole group or selected students within the group. Students who are successful in identifying and supplying inferences move on to the next step, independent practice. For those students struggling with the identification and supplying of inferences, the teacher schedules extended guided practice so that he can support their mastery of this vital skill. Sometimes these students require easier reading material.

STEP 4   ## DOCUMENTING AND CELEBRATING INDEPENDENT PRACTICE

The teacher suggests a way in which the students can document their understanding of the concept of inference as they read independently. The students can use highlighting tape to mark places in their reading materials where they used inference. They can mark the spots with Post-it Notes® or they can keep a journal of inferences. After the students have completed their independent reading, the teacher brings them together to talk about and celebrate their uses of inference and compare the places in the text where they found it necessary to infer.

APPLICATIONS AND EXAMPLES

Inference instruction in a third-grade social studies lesson is illustrated on File 12 of the accompanying CD.

"I notice a lot of you are reading Harry Potter books during your free reading time," says Mrs. Littleton to her seventh graders. "What do you like about these books?"

"They are exciting," says Martha. "They are full of action and you are always being surprised."

"You can almost see the action," says Martin. "It's like a video in your head. It's never boring."

"Find a passage like that and read it to me," suggests Mrs. Littleton. "I haven't read any of the books and wonder why they are so popular."

"These are the first two sentences in the third book," starts Eliana. "'Harry Potter was a highly unusual boy in many ways. For one thing, he hated the summer holidays more than any other time of the year.'"

"You have to be thinking all the time as you read the books," Eliana continues. "The author could have said, 'Harry Potter is a 13-year-old boy, who is also a wizard. He doesn't do anything like regular 13-year-olds.' But instead she gives you one example of why he is unusual and you have to figure it out. It makes it much more interesting to read."

"Let's do something with this book today," suggests Mrs. Littleton. "We're going to be studying making inferences. It sounds like your Harry Potter books require a lot of that. We'll use some of the passages in the books you are reading to talk about the kinds of inferences you are having to make."

Mrs. Littleton picks up the third book in the series, *Harry Potter and the Prisoner of Azkaban* (Rowling, 1999), and turns to a page at random and reads,

> *She didn't often stay at Privet Drive, because she couldn't bear to leave her precious dogs, but each of her visits stood out horribly vividly in Harry's mind.*

"Now that's an interesting sentence," Mrs. Littleton says. "What might I infer, just from that sentence alone, that helps me understand Harry's relationship with his Aunt Marge?"

"Well," Kyreesha begins, "it doesn't sound like Aunt Marge comes to visit very often, and that when she does come, it's not a lot of fun for Harry."

"What makes you say that, Kyreesha?" Mrs. Littleton asks.

"'Cause it says she doesn't stay there very often and that when she does, he has some very bad memories of her visits."

"That's a good observation, Kyreesha," Mrs. Littleton notes. "It does say that he had very bad memories of her visits. When you have very bad memories of something, that would indicate it wasn't a very pleasant experience. It doesn't look like Harry and his aunt hit it off too well when she came to visit. Now everyone open your books and let's see if we can find some other instances where just what we read might not tell the whole story."

CONCLUSION

Good readers often supply missing information by inferring what is not explicitly stated in the text. Those readers who are unable to do this automatically, or who do not realize the need for supplying this missing information, often miss the point of the reading or become confused by a lack of explicit information. This sometimes slows down their reading and makes the text more difficult for them to understand. As Mrs. Littleton has discovered, some students require direct instruction in the process of constructing or inferring material that is not explicitly stated in the text. Even good readers need to recognize that they are supplying additional information toward their comprehension of the text by using their background knowledge and experiences. Being aware of the assumptions they are making, and the basis for them, allows them to monitor their understanding and to go back and correct any misconceptions they may have gained from inaccurate inferences.

REFERENCES

Irwin, J. (1991). *Teaching reading comprehension processes* (2nd ed.). Needham Heights, MA: Allyn & Bacon.

Rowling, J. (1999). *Harry Potter and the prisoner of Azkaban*. New York: Scholastic, Inc.

Trabasso, T. (1981). The making of inferences during reading and their assessment. In J. T. Guthrie (Ed.), *Comprehension and reading*. Newark, DE: International Reading Association.

READ, PAIR, SHARE

Working with a Partner to Answer Questions

Read, pair, share is an adaptation of a partner activity called think, pair, share (McTighe & Lyman, 1988) in which partners read together and stop after reading each paragraph or appropriate section of text to answer the traditional who, what, when, where, and how questions related to the text they just read. Whenever the partners cannot answer a question, they return to the selected text to find the answer. See figure 13.1 for the questioning format used with this strategy.

The teacher introduces the strategy by teaching a lesson on the who, what, when, where, and how questions. The students learn to read with a partner, stopping periodically to see how many of the question words are appropriate for the section just read and to answer the appropriate questions. The teacher encourages the students to reword the questions whenever necessary to make them fit the section they have read. She concludes the activity by conducting a class discussion and review of the strategy and the main ideas contained in the reading material.

STEP BY STEP

The steps in implementing read, pair, and share are:

STEP 1 INTRODUCING THE QUESTION WORDS

The teacher begins the activity by introducing the question words. Who? What? When? Where? Why? and How? are explained. The teacher talks about newspaper reporters and the fact that they must include the answers to all five of these questions in a newspaper article to make sure they tell the entire story. The teacher also explains that some paragraphs don't include information about all five question words but sometimes the questions can be reworded so they are more appropriate for a certain paragraph. The teacher uses a sample paragraph to introduce answering the questions and adapting questions to make them more appropriate. In some instances, a longer section of text might be more useful in this activity.

FIGURE 13.1
Questioning format for read, pair, share.

Narrative Form

Title _____

Paragraph Number _____

Answer each question with a word, sentence, or phrase from the paragraph.

Who is the paragraph about?

What is the character doing?

When does this action take place?

Where does the action take place?

How does the character perform the action?

Informational Form

Title _____

Paragraph Number _____

Answer each question with a word, sentence, or phrase from the paragraph.

Who? Are there any people mentioned in the paragraph?

What? What is the paragraph about?

When? Is the time important in the paragraph?

Where? Is the location important in the paragraph?

How? How do the other elements relate to the main idea of this paragraph?

Note: Any time a question does not fit the context of the paragraph, readers are encouraged to rephrase the question, retaining the question word in some way, to make the question more appropriate.

STEP 2   MODELING THE STRATEGY

The teacher asks one student to act as her partner and gives the class a paragraph and a questioning format page for use in practicing the strategy. She introduces the title of the strategy and says, "This tells exactly what we will do. First we all read the paragraph silently. Let's do that now."

She stops and models silent reading while the whole class does the same. "Next, we pair. That means we work together to try to answer the questions. The share step means that we go back to the paragraph to share the location of the answers to the questions or share the responsibility of rewording the questions to fit the paragraph. Now, let's demonstrate how to do this."

The teacher and her partner then model answering the questions together and writing words, phrases, or sentences on the questioning format page. They also model looking in the paragraph to find the answers and rewording any questions to make them appropriate for the paragraph. The teacher reminds the students that the whole class will share their answers later, after the entire reading assignment has been completed in read, pair, share format.

STEP 3   MODIFYING THE QUESTIONS

Students often have difficulty in modifying the questions so the teacher takes time to show how the various questions can be reworded to make them more appropriate. Using some sample paragraphs on overhead transparencies, the teacher demonstrates how the questions often need to be reworded. She provides some examples and involves the students in guided practice in modifying questions.

STEP 4   *USING THE STRATEGY TO COMPLETE A READING ASSIGNMENT*

The teacher pairs students, being careful not to pair two weak readers. She gives the students a reading assignment and questioning format pages with formats for each paragraph. Four to six questioning formats copy onto one page easily. She then gives the students time to use the strategy in reading the assignment and moves around the room as they practice the strategy. The teacher provides assistance as necessary during this initial practice session.

STEP 5   *DISCUSSING THE ACTIVITY*

Once the students have completed the reading assignment using the read, pair, share strategy, the teacher brings them together to discuss their answers. They also discuss how they modified questions and what they learned from the reading assignment. They are encouraged to share their experiences in using read, pair, share and how well it worked for them.

APPLICATIONS AND EXAMPLES

The use of read, pair, share in a third-grade literature discussion is explained on File 13 of the accompanying CD.

Mr. McMillan wants his 11th-grade U.S. history class to understand some of the prominent figures of the war years of the 1940s and to see some of their more personal characteristics. He wants to make some of these icons of history come alive for his students. He wants to introduce them to reading biographies, which is a new experience for many of his students. He decides to use the read, pair, share processing strategy during his introduction to the genre.

He explains the procedure to his students and models it by bringing one of the students to the front and actually going through the procedure as a demonstration for the class. In the process he introduces the set of questions that students will be using during the process. For informational text, in particular, he feels that this is an extremely important part of the read, pair, share process.

Mr. McMillan reveals a chart he has prepared for the lesson that contains the questions the students will use with each other during the process:

> Who? Are there any people mentioned in the paragraph?
>
> What? What is the paragraph about?
>
> When? Is the time important in the paragraph?
>
> Where? Is the location important in the paragraph?
>
> How? How do the other elements relate to the main idea of this paragraph?

He then requests that his students read chapter 20, "A Lonely Little Girl," in Joy Hakim's *History of US: War, Peace, and All That Jazz* (1995). This chapter discusses some of the personal characteristics of Eleanor Roosevelt's early life and gives the students some insights into her early struggles and what made her the person she ultimately became.

After they complete the reading, Mr. McMillan pairs the students and gives them the read, pair, share questioning form. He instructs them to go through the questioning process with their partner that he demonstrated for them. They are to fill in the form and then the class will share their responses.

As the students read the text and share the question-answering process, they are surprised to find out about the struggles that this grand lady went through in the early years of her life. By sharing the information through questioning, they are also gaining the point of view of the other students and becoming more aware of the personal side of an individual that can be discovered through reading and interacting with biographies.

CONCLUSION

The interaction of students during reading and comprehension processing provides an excellent scaffold for developing these skills. They begin to see through the eyes of another and to more readily understand the processes that might be necessary to obtain a deeper understanding of reading material. They begin to see that even informational text can include elements of personal interest and involvement. Encouraging students to think and share thoughts together can help them develop stronger tools for relating to and understanding text.

REFERENCES

Hakim, J. (1995). *A history of US: war, peace, and all that jazz.* New York: Oxford University Press.

McTighe, J., & Lyman, F. (1988). Cueing thinking in the classroom: The promise of theory-embedded tools. *Educational Leadership, 45,* 18–24.

14

COOPERATIVE SCRIPTS

Working in Pairs to Improve Comprehension and Recall

<table>
<tr>
<td>

Focus on English Learners

This strategy provides English learners an opportunity to summarize orally with a partner listening, correcting misconceptions, and elaborating for more complete understanding.

</td>
<td>

Cooperative scripts (Dansereau, 1985) is a term for the practice of two students working together to summarize material and support one another's understanding and recall of the important facts and concepts contained in the material read. The students take turns summarizing the material. One student summarizes while the partner listens actively, correcting any errors and prompting when omissions are made. This strategy has been widely researched and shown to be highly effective in facilitating information recall. While both partners have been found to benefit from the activity, larger gains were found for the sections for which the readers served as summarizers rather than the sections for which the students served as listeners (Spurlin, Dansereau, Larson, & Brooks, 1984). An important aspect of the use of this strategy is the length of the sections to be summarized. The teacher must be clear in the instructions to students so they know when to stop reading and engage in cooperative scripts.

</td>
</tr>
</table>

STEP BY STEP

The steps in implementing cooperative scripts are:

STEP 1   MODELING THE PROCEDURE

The teacher chooses a partner and models the silent reading of a paragraph, asking all students to read the same paragraph silently. Once the paragraph has been read silently, the teacher briefly summarizes it, asking his partner to listen for misstatements and omissions. The teacher deliberately makes some misstatements and omissions so that the importance of active listening by the partner is evident. The second paragraph is read silently and the partner summarizes while the teacher serves as listener.

STEP 2   EXPLAINING THE PURPOSE OF THE STRATEGY

The teacher explains that this strategy is used to help students to recall and summarize reading material. He stresses the importance of both partners being actively involved as they create cooperative scripts, summarizing the paragraphs and supporting one another to identify the most important ideas in each paragraph.

STEP 3   ## PRACTICING THE STRATEGY

The teacher divides the class into pairs, being careful not to pair two weak readers. He gives students the reading assignment with specific instructions as to when to stop and summarize. The summarizer is instructed to summarize the paragraph as completely as possible without looking at the reading material. The listener is instructed to follow along in the book, serving to correct any misstatements and supply any important facts or concepts that the summarizer omits. In the beginning it is wise to ask the students to summarize after each paragraph, but the reading sections can be lengthened when the teacher recognizes that students are ready to handle longer reading passages. The teacher moves around the room for the first few sessions of cooperative scripts observing, monitoring, and giving suggestions.

STEP 4   ## DISCUSSING THE PROCEDURES AND OUTCOMES

The teacher brings the students back together as a whole group to discuss the procedures used and the students' perceptions of how the strategy works. If students have experienced problems, this discussion serves to provide suggestions for solving the problems. This discussion also serves as a celebration where the teacher can give recognition to the partners who worked well together.

APPLICATIONS AND EXAMPLES

See File 14 of the accompanying CD for an example of cooperative scripting in an eighth-grade geography class.

Miss Athena and her second graders have been studying insects. She has discovered an interesting book entitled *World's Weirdest Bugs and Other Creepy Creatures* (Roberts, 1995) that she feels will be a good text to use to introduce cooperative scripting. She begins by introducing the book and having the students look at the pictures of the interesting insects. She then tells the students that they are going to practice a new way to study. "We are going to learn to do something called *cooperative scripts* today. Who can tell me what a script is?" she asks.

"It's like a play," answers Martha. "The words you are to say for your part are written down. That's called a script."

"Exactly," replies Miss Athena. "But these cooperative scripts we are going to create are not going to be written down. You will work with a partner to create a script called a summary. You will read the book one paragraph at a time and take turns telling what the paragraphs say. When you are the summarizer, you talk about the paragraph you read, trying to remember all the important parts without looking at the book. Your partner, the listener, has the book open in front of him or her and helps you to create the script by reminding you when you forget something or make a mistake. Then you will read the next paragraph and the person who was the listener the first time will become the summarizer for the second paragraph. Let me show you how it works. Open your book to page 2 and let's all read the first paragraph silently." Miss Athena waits until everyone has read the first paragraph and then she closes her book and asks her partner Hank to watch the book as she summarizes the first paragraph. "If I make a mistake or leave something out, your job is to help me, Hank. We are cooperating to create a script of the first paragraph."

"OK," nods Hank. "Go ahead."

Miss Athena says, "This first paragraph tells about the Hercules beetle. It says that the beetle walks around with big pincers on its head."

"It says that the pincers are like a big pair of pliers that open and close every time the beetle moves its head," adds Hank.

"Very good! Now let's all read the second paragraph, and I'll be the listener and Hank will be the summarizer," says Miss Athena. Everyone reads the second paragraph silently.

Hank closes his book and begins his summary while Miss Athena watches the text. "The Hercules beetle is one of the biggest beetles in the world. The male beetle can be 7 inches long from the horns to the tip of the body. The female is smaller because she doesn't have horns."

"Very good, Hank," says Miss Athena. "The only thing you left out was the fact that there are 300,000 different kinds of beetles in the world."

"Now, boys and girls, you see how important it is that both of the partners work together," reminds Miss Athena. "I'm going to put you into pairs and you are to work together to read and create cooperative scripts as you read."

Miss Athena pairs the students and walks around the room monitoring their use of cooperative scripts. When they have finished reading the book and taking turns summarizing and listening, she calls them back together. "How did you like this strategy?" she asks.

"It was fun," replies Yvonne. "I think I'll remember more because I really had to think about what I was reading."

"We really read everything twice when we were the listeners," states Monroe solemnly.

"Exactly," replies Miss Athena. "That's one of the reasons why this strategy will help you to recall the information you read."

CONCLUSION

As Miss Athena demonstrates, cooperative scripting can be used for several purposes. It is most effective in supporting students as they read informational text. Because they must read carefully in order to be able to summarize, they obtain more information. The recalling of the text and the active listening and correcting done by the partner also serves to focus the pair. Because the roles of the partners switch regularly, students tend to stay on task without becoming bored. Their cooperation is necessary for success, and the strategy exemplifies cooperative learning because of the need for both summarizing and listening skills. This is also a good strategy to be used for studying factual information in preparation for testing.

REFERENCES

Dansereau, D. F. (1985). Learning strategy research. In J. Segal, S. Chipman, & K. Glaser (Eds.), *Thinking and learning skills: Relating instruction to basic research.* Hillsdale, NJ: Erlbaum.

Roberts, M. L. (1995). *World's weirdest bugs and other creepy creatures.* New York: Troll Associates.

Spurlin, J., Dansereau, D., Larson, C., & Brooks, L. (1984). Cooperative learning strategies in processing descriptive text: Effects of role and activity level of the learner. *Cognition and Instruction, 1,* 451–463.

15

GIST (Generating Interaction between Schemata and Text)
Making Comprehension Connections

GIST, or generating interaction between schemata and text (Cunningham, 1982), is a strategy used for supporting comprehension of informational text. GIST is especially helpful when students are required to read long texts containing a significant amount of new information. Students work in cooperative groups and read sections of the text silently. If the need arises, stronger readers may read aloud to the group. After each short section is read silently, members of the group work collaboratively to generate one sentence that summarizes the "gist" of the passage. In some lengthy and difficult text, this generation of a summary sentence is done paragraph by paragraph. Once a sentence is generated, members of the group write it on their own papers so that each group member ends up with a concise summary of the text. The teacher circulates among the groups to facilitate and provide support. Because group members have a chance to discuss and clarify meaning as they decide on the best summary sentence for the section or paragraph, this is a particularly effective strategy for use with students having difficulty with comprehension.

Step by Step

The steps in implementing GIST are:

Step 1   Identifying and Preparing the Text

The teacher identifies text that may cause some difficulty for students. She decides whether the text must be read and summarized paragraph by paragraph or section by section and determines logical places for the students to stop and summarize information they have read.

Step 2   Grouping

The teacher divides the class into heterogeneous cooperative groups and identifies a facilitator and recorder for each group. Each group should contain a strong reader.

When possible, English language learners should be placed in a group with another student who can provide primary language support to increase the interaction and full participation of all students.

STEP 3   MODELING THE STRATEGY

The teacher briefly discusses background knowledge to set the stage for the activity related to the selection to be read. She chooses a relatively short, simple passage and reads it aloud to the class. She then asks the students to work together in their groups to create a one-sentence summary of what was read. After the students have completed their summary sentence, the teacher asks the reporter in each group to share the summary sentence with the class. The class discusses and compares the statements and adds details that the class feels will enhance the statements. Then students write the summary sentence on their own papers.

These summaries may then be used later for review of the main ideas of the selection read. The teacher serves as facilitator and quality controller, making sure that the summary sentences capture the gist of the paragraphs. It is important that the quality control be done in a supportive manner through questioning and supporting the students' understanding of the text.

STEP 4   GUIDING PRACTICE

The teacher explains to students that they will be reading the entire selection using the GIST strategy. The selection is divided into logical segments for the purpose of stopping and summarizing. Students read the first selection silently. As they wait for the rest of their group to finish reading, they should be thinking of the main points in the section and formulating a summary sentence in their minds or writing it on a piece of paper. The group should then discuss the section read and negotiate the best summary sentence they can write. At this point, the teacher should have the student groups share their sentences, discuss the main points of the section, and the various ways those could appropriately be expressed in the summary sentences. The teacher serves as facilitator and questions the students to lead them to capture the meaning and nuances of the text.

STEP 5   PRACTICING INDEPENDENTLY

Having practiced the GIST process, the groups work collaboratively to complete the reading and summarizing of each subsequent section. The groups share their final reports. This provides an effective review of the passage read and gives an opportunity to correct any misconceptions. In addition, summaries may be posted on wall charts to serve as a review for fellow classmates.

APPLICATIONS AND EXAMPLES

 File 15 of the accompanying CD provides on example of a GIST lesson in a fourth grade social studies class.

GIST can also be used effectively in introducing students to literary passages and works that might otherwise seem too complex and convoluted for them to understand and appreciate. In early explorations of Shakespeare, for example, GIST can be useful in teaching the students how to process the original Shakespearean text in a way that will provide a clearer understanding of the author's intent and message.

Mr. Jefferson has decided to introduce his seventh graders to the works of William Shakespeare. He decides to begin the exploration by taking one of Shakespeare's better-known passages and introducing the students to it through the use of GIST to make the text more clear and understandable.

FIGURE 15.1 The GIST of "the seven ages of man" as retold by Mr. Jefferson's seventh graders.

Original Text	Summary (GIST) Statements
Jaques: All the world's a stage,	
And all the men and women merely players:	Everybody plays a role in life
They have their exits and their entrances;	They're born and they die
And one man in his time plays many parts,	People do lots of different things
His acts being seven ages. At first the infant,	
Mewling and puking in the nurse's arms.	First we're babies
And then the whining school-boy, with his satchel	Then we go to school
And shining morning face, creeping like snail	
Unwillingly to school. And then the lover,	Then we fall in love
Sighing like furnace, with a woeful ballad	
Made to his mistress' eyebrow, Then a soldier,	We go off to war
Full of strange oaths and bearded like the pard,	and become a "man"
Jealous in honour, sudden and quick in quarrel,	
Seeking the bubble reputation	We know everything
Even in the cannon's mouth. And then the justice,	
In fair round belly with good capon lined,	We grow older and fatter
With eyes severe and beard of formal cut,	We mature, grow more serious
Full of wise saws and modern instances;	
And so he plays his part. The sixth age shifts	
Into the lean and slipper'd pantaloon,	We are getting "old"
With spectacles on nose and pouch on side,	
His youthful hose, well saved, a world too wide	
For his shrunk shank; and his big manly voice,	
Turning again toward childish treble, pipes	We are getting "senile"
And whistles in his sound. Last scene of all,	
That ends this strange eventful history,	
Is second childishness and mere oblivion,	We go out like we came in
Sans teeth, sans eyes, sans taste, sans everything.	We die

Mr. Jefferson looks through several well-known soliloquies and decides to use the "seven ages of man" speech from *As You Like It*. He transfers the text to an overhead transparency and prepares individual copies of the speech for each of the students.

On the day he chooses to begin the exploration, he reviews with the students what they know about the use of GIST to clarify text. He asks, "Can someone review for us the steps we use in analyzing text using the GIST method?" Bakar raises his hand and says, "GIST is a way of working with each other to decide what the important points are about what we're reading. And then we have to come up with some ideas about what the stuff means."

"That's right," says Mr. Jefferson. "So now we need to move into our cooperative learning groups and take a look at some of this 'stuff' that Bakar is talking about." The students have been previously assigned to cooperative learning groups and quickly move to their respective places in the room.

Mr. Jefferson begins an introductory discussion with students on what they know about William Shakespeare. He uses a KWL chart (see chapter 25) to assess prior knowledge and to plan along with the students for the further exploration of Shakespeare and in particular of the text they are going to be reading in their groups.

Following the short discussion, he sets up the lesson by showing a video clip from *As You Like It* in which Jaques delivers the famous speech.

He then distributes the printed version of the speech and asks the students to follow along with the text as he replays the video of the speech. After the video plays for the second time, Mr. Jefferson says, "Now, to me, the first two lines of the speech mean that everybody has a role to play in life. So, I'm going to write what I think it means right here beside the lines in the speech." Mr. Jefferson writes his interpretation of the first two lines to the right of them on the transparency.

"Now, I want you to work in your groups and see if you can come up with some ideas about what the rest of the lines mean to you. And I want you to write your interpretations out beside the lines just the way I have done here." He points to the transparency projection.

While the students are beginning to discuss the next part of the speech, Mr. Jefferson walks around the room, checking to see that the procedure he suggested is being followed. He facilitates with some groups to assist in clarifying their processes.

The students complete their interpretations of the speech by discussing and sharing ideas, interchanging thoughts, and coming to consensus related to the meanings of the lines of the speech. Then they are asked to share their ideas as to the meanings found in the speech, giving the class an opportunity to review the passage and to correct any misconceptions about the text. See figure 15.1 for examples of how Mr. Jefferson's students interpreted various lines of the text.

CONCLUSION

Using the GIST strategy allows students to discuss meaning, reread text, hear a variety of interpretations, and reach consensus about the meaning of the text. This strategy also serves as a beginning point for their own skill building in self-analysis of text and writing summary statements. The final discussion as a full class serves as another review of the text and demonstrates the variety of ways in which a summary of a particular text might be stated.

REFERENCES

Cunningham, J. (1982). Generating interactions between schemata and text. In J. A. Niles & L. A. Harris (Eds.), *New inquiries in reading research and instruction* (pp. 42–47). Washington, DC: National Reading Conference.

SECTION III

INTEGRATING BACKGROUND KNOWLEDGE

Students come to school with a variety of background experiences. Some students have enjoyed a wealth of book-related activities, while others may have limited exposure to reading and literature. In addition to their acquaintance with literacy, students have a wide range of other life experiences such as travel or exposure to different peoples and cultures. As they begin to read, all students rely on past experiences to make sense of the texts they are reading. Teachers have traditionally relied heavily on activating prior knowledge before students begin to read a passage. Many teachers use prediction and discussion prior to reading to bring students' experiences to mind so that the readers can integrate their prior knowledge as they process the reading materials. Rarely do teachers explain the importance of activating prior knowledge in order to make sense of reading material. Even more rarely do teachers support students in understanding how their past experiences, both in life and in reading books, affect their perception of the book they are currently reading.

Section III contains a collection of strategies designed to teach students to use their background knowledge effectively. It also provides approaches to support readers in understanding the importance of the relationship between the text currently being read and past experiences with books and in life.

In today's society, there are times when students are asked to read material for which they have little background knowledge. Section III provides some examples of how teachers can build background knowledge when students are lacking in experiences to draw from as they read.

As we have noted previously, teachers should assess students' background knowledge prior to the reading of text. In addition, students should be monitored in an ongoing manner to determine their use of integration strategies and their need for further instruction. Strategies for using background experiences before, during, and after reading are included in this section. Most importantly, strategies provided in this section encourage teachers to engage students in active processing of text while they integrate their past experiences, real and literary, into the formulation of meaning as they read.

16

PREDICTING

Using Past Experiences to Support Comprehension

Focus on English Learners

Predicting is an important strategy for English learners for two reasons: They will need to think of experiences that relate to their reading, and they will practice their oral English to explain the connection.

Predicting, "hypothesizing about what will happen" (Collins & Smith, 1980, p. 4), is a well-researched strategy for increasing reading comprehension. Good readers have been found to create certain expectations when they read. Their expectations may be based on their life experiences or on past reading experiences, but they support comprehension in several ways. Expectations alert readers to possible character motivations, situational concerns, and even character traits that may influence the character's future actions. Knowledge of different literary genres alerts readers to expect certain types of plots. A mystery story provides different expectations than an adventure story or a biography.

Although predicting is well established as a strategy that supports understanding, it is often used with students without formal teaching or even much discussion. In order to use prediction most effectively, students should be taught the power of prediction and the different aspects of story and information that can be predicted. The use of prediction in the reading of expository (informational) text is especially supportive of comprehension.

STEP BY STEP

The steps in the teaching of prediction are:

STEP 1 EXPLAINING AND MODELING PREDICTION

The teacher introduces prediction as a reading strategy by asking the students why they think the teacher often asks, "What do you think is going to happen next?" If the students seem to have a good understanding of the power of prediction, the teacher can go on to model effective predicting behaviors. If the students have no understanding or only a vague understanding of why predictions are made, she explains that predicting is used for several reasons:

1. Predicting helps you bring your own experiences to mind. You make predictions based on your own experiences or other books that you have

read. Bringing those experiences to mind helps you to understand the book you are currently reading.

2. Predicting gives you a purpose for reading. You read to find out if your predictions are correct or if the author is going to add information that will change your predictions.
3. Predicting helps you to think of all the possibilities of things that might occur. It gets your mind working and actively engages your interest.

Once the purpose of predicting is established, the teacher models how it works by introducing a book and engaging the students in a discussion about all the different experiences that might influence their predictions. The teacher starts with the title and the cover and helps the students to identify possibilities and ways in which different personal experiences might influence their predictions about the story to be read. The teacher and class then predict what they think the story is about and they list their predictions on the chalkboard, chart, or overhead transparency.

STEP 2   STOPPING PERIODICALLY TO CHECK, CHANGE, AND ADD PREDICTIONS

The teacher explains that depending on only one initial prediction, it is not enough to harness the power of prediction. As new information is gained through reading, predictions can be changed. As new situations develop in the story, additional predictions may be necessary. The reader is always confirming or changing predictions according to the text being read and new information that is being gained. After you learn how and when to predict, it becomes something that you do almost unconsciously, and good readers do it constantly.

STEP 3   GUIDING PREDICTION PRACTICE

As the teacher reads a book aloud, she guides the students in making predictions, confirming or changing predictions, and adding predictions as warrnated. In the initial stages it is important to ask questions as predictions are made so that the sources of the predictions become obvious. Relating predictions to past experiences, other books read, traits and motivation of the characters, or even signals from the illustrations helps the students to recognize that they are accessing their prior knowledge and knowledge about how books and illustrations work. Students can provide evidence from the text as to the veracity of their predictions. This helps them to identify inferential statements that support their prediction although the facts are not stated directly.

STEP 4   PROVIDING INDEPENDENT PRACTICE

Students can practice predicting independently as they read with focus on predicting by adding a simple step whenever they predict. The teacher can distribute small Post-it® tabs so that the students can mark the places in the text where they predicted with one color, prediction check stops with another color, and prediction changes with a third color. This procedure helps the students to recognize their use of prediction and provides a way to bring the students together to discuss their use of predictions, the reasons for their predictions, and any changes they make in their predictions.

STEP 5   USING PREDICTIONS BEFORE, DURING, AND AFTER READING

Once the students have practiced both predicting and marking their predicting places, the differences in the ways in which prediction are used prior to reading and during reading should be made clear. The teacher encourages the students to discuss the kinds of predictions that can be made prior to reading and how those predictions are based on past experiences. During reading, prediction are made as new information is being processed. Predictions are dynamic, changing as more information is read. After reading, reviewing the predictions that were made and their accuracy or the changes made through processing new information helps readers recognize ways in which their comprehension is affected. Were they led astray by an incorrect definition of a word? Were they making errors in understanding because they read too rapidly? Did their past experiences cause them to expect things to develop in a way that was different from what the author intended?

APPLICATIONS AND EXAMPLES

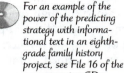

For an example of the power of the predicting strategy with informational text in an eighth-grade family history project, see File 16 of the accompanying CD.

Some of Miss Fionna's second graders are having difficulty with reading comprehension. Because she is focusing on comprehension in her daily guided reading groups, Miss Fionna decides to use her read-aloud time to teach some additional comprehension strategies. As she gathers her class on the rug for read-aloud time, she opens the discussion by asking, "Why do I always ask you what you think this book will be about?"

"To see if we're paying attention," replies Gregory.

"Well, that could be one reason," responds Miss Fionna. "What other reason might I have?"

"To get us to look at the picture on the cover," states Margaret.

"Yes, it's important to look at the picture on the cover. But, why do I want you to look at the picture?" asks Miss Fionna.

"So we'll know what the story is about," says Gail emphatically.

"How does the picture help you to know what the story will be about?" asks Miss Fionna.

"Well, if there's a cow on the cover, the story's going to be about a cow. If there's a boy in the picture, the story's about a boy," says Melissa in a tone that implies Miss Fionna has lost her mind.

"Exactly, Melissa," answers Miss Fionna. "Because you've read a lot of books, you know that the picture on the cover tells you a lot about what the book will be about. But other things you've done also help you to predict. Predicting means you think about what will be in the story and you have some ideas even before you read the story. Good readers predict all the time when they read. Now, let's look at the cover of this book. The title is *Hey, Al!* (Yorinks, 1986). I see a man, a dog, and a lot of birds. What do you think the story is going to be about?"

"Well," begins Carl, "the man is mopping and he isn't smiling. Maybe the birds made a mess and he has to clean it up."

"But I don't see a mess," says Jennifer. "I think the man's a janitor named Al, because the title of the book is *Hey, Al!* and he works at a zoo."

Miss Fionna writes, "Birds made a mess" and "Man's a janitor at the zoo" on the chalkboard. Then she asks, "Does anyone else have a prediction?" When no one else responds, she continues, "Carl and Jennifer both made predictions and they both used information from their past experiences to make them. Carl saw that the man wasn't smiling and he thought it was because he was upset with the birds for making a mess that he had to clean up. Does your mom get upset with you when you make a mess, Carl?"

Carl smiles and answers sheepishly, "Yeah."

"Jennifer connected the birds to a zoo and noticed the man's clothes and hat and thought he was a janitor. Jennifer also read the title and decided that the man was the Al in the title. Both Carl and Jennifer used their observation skills and their experiences to make predictions about the story. Now we have to read to check their predictions." Miss Fionna turns the page and reads. On the first page of the story Jennifer's prediction that the man is a janitor is confirmed. The text poses the question, "What could be bad?"

Miss Fionna asks, "Well, what could be bad? It says that Al is a nice, quiet janitor, and he and Eddie, the dog, do everything together. What could be bad?"

Melissa answers, "Just look at the picture, Miss Fionna. They're living in this tiny little room with cracks in the ceiling. They don't even have a chair, just a bed. They must be very poor."

"Good observations, Melissa. Do you think being poor is bad?"

"I think they'd be sad not to even have a chair," replies Melissa.

"Al has groceries in his hand, and they are carrying boxes that look like Chinese food," offers Carl. "I don't think they're hungry."

"Now, that's an interesting observation, Carl," replies Miss Fionna. "You are right, they have food. But what made you think the containers they are carrying hold Chinese food?"

"Because that's the kind of box Chinese food comes in," states Carl decidedly.

"Exactly," says Miss Fionna. "And how do you know that?"

"Because my mom gets Chinese food for dinner sometimes," replies Carl.

"That's what I mean when I say you know from experience," explains Miss Fionna. "Your mom brings home Chinese food in these little white boxes with handles on them and so when you see them carrying those kinds of boxes you think, 'Oh, that's Chinese food like my mom brings home.' You think that because you've had an experience that you're reminded of when you see the picture. Now, could the boxes hold something else, instead of Chinese food?"

"Yes, I guess," says Carl. "But that's the only thing I've ever seen in those boxes."

"OK, we'll have to read and see what's in the boxes. I just want you to realize that sometimes we are surprised when we read, because the things we predict don't happen. The author tells the story in an unexpected way. Our prediction can come true, but sometimes we have to read to get more information before we really understand the story. When we predict, it makes us think about what might happen and then we have to keep reading to see if we get more information. Sometimes we change our predictions from page to page. Let's read some more and see if our predictions about what is bad are true."

As Miss Fionna reads the next page aloud they find that Melissa's prediction was exactly right, but they didn't find out what was in the food boxes. After she reads this page aloud, Miss Fionna asks, "What do you think will happen next?"

Leslie answers, "Well, they're unhappy about where they have to live, so usually in these kinds of stories, they do something about where they live. Maybe Al will get a better job or they'll meet someone and move in with their new friend."

"Great predictions, Leslie," says Miss Fionna. "Does anyone else have any thoughts about this?"

"Well, they were talking about the moon. Maybe they'll move to the moon. Maybe Al will be an astronaut."

"That's an interesting thought," replies Miss Fionna. "Sometimes the author does give us hints like that."

Miss Fionna and the students read through the book stopping at almost every page to predict and discuss where their ideas originate. At the end of the book, which has a wonderful surprise ending, Miss Fionna asks, "Well, what do you think? Did our predictions come true?"

"Not many of them," laughs Melissa. "This book has lots of surprises."

"But we were thinking all the way through the book," says Miss Fionna. "We were thinking about things that had happened to us and things that we have seen in other books. Did any of those things help you to understand the story?"

"Thinking about what might happen makes it interesting. I want to read to see if our predictions are true. This book is hard to figure out, though. It's very different," says Jennifer. "I think I want to write a story like this. I'll think about what people will think is happening and then make something else happen."

"Good idea, Jennifer. Sometimes those unexpected things make the book more interesting to read."

"I never thought about how we know what's going to happen," says Carl. "I still wonder if that was Chinese food in the box."

Miss Fionna laughs, "Well, maybe you should write a letter to the author and ask him."

"I think I will," responds Carl.

Miss Fionna brings the lesson to a close by reviewing what they have learned about predicting. She passes out small Post-it® notes to the students. "As you are doing sustained silent reading today, I want you to stop every now and then and jot down some predictions on these Post-it® notes. Check to see how many of your predictions are correct, but also think about where the ideas for your predictions come from. Sometimes we predict because of something we have done or read. Sometimes we get hints from the author or from the illustrations. After SSR we'll talk about how well you predicted and what types of predictions you made."

CONCLUSION

Predicting in narrative text serves to engage the students and help them to use their past experiences, hints from the author and illustrator, and information they have gained from other books they have read to support their understanding of the book they are reading. Predicting in expository text serves a different purpose because the students are also using their knowledge of informational text structure to support their predictions. While some students use prediction automatically without thinking about what they are doing, many students need direct instruction in how to use the resources they have, including their own past experiences and their knowledge of how books are organized. Prediction is powerful in supporting students' reading comprehension. The use of prediction helps students to focus on the sequence of events and how they build on one another. It helps students to notice the hints that are given through text and pictures and to relate them to their own past experiences in supporting their understanding of the plot. In informational text, prediction based on expository text structure is especially valuable in demystifying the wide range of information found in nonfiction texts.

REFERENCES

Collins, A., & Smith, E. E. (1980). *Teaching the process of reading comprehension* (Technical report No. 182). Urbana-Champaign: Center for the Study of Reading, University of Illinois.

Yorinks, A. (1986). *Hey, Al!* Toronto: HarperCollins.

17

PERSPECTIVE TAKING

Getting into the Minds of the Characters

Understanding the perspectives of the various characters in a story is a necessary skill for comprehending the story as a whole (Emery, 1996). Perspective taking is also a vital skill in reading and comprehending biography, poetry, and history. Some research in recent years has demonstrated that younger readers may experience difficulty in taking the perspective of story characters. Emery (1996) found that preadolescent readers often found it difficult to separate their personal experiences from the events in the story. Though this can aid in story understanding if the character is about the same age and from the same cultural background, it often interferes with understanding in multicultural stories and in stories where characters have conflicting viewpoints. For this reason, explicit instruction in perspective taking is needed to support readers in developing sensitivity to the varying viewpoints of characters.

Perspective taking as a comprehension strategy can be taught using a series of activities that support the reader in using personal experiences, past readings, discussion, and drama to gradually build the complexity of understanding necessary to understand more than one perspective on an event or problem.

Discussion and graphic representation of the characters' perspectives are used to make students aware of the concept that people (characters) can feel differently about an event. Using visuals, such as comic strips with speech balloons showing what each character is thinking and then reenacting the scenes, helps to reinforce the concept of multiple perspectives.

STEP BY STEP

The steps in implementing strategies for perspective taking are:

STEP 1   CHOOSING A BOOK WITH MULTIPLE PERSPECTIVES

Though most narrative stories involve characters with different perspectives, in the beginning it is important to choose books in which the perspectives are fairly obvious. With very young children, traditional tales such as The Three Little Pigs help make this comparison on perspectives clear. With older readers, characters whose values differ are good choices.

STEP 2   PLANNING A DISCUSSION OF PERSPECTIVES

Using a classroom conflict can open a discussion of multiple perspectives. If John wants to use the computer to complete the printing of a story he has written and Penny needs the computer to do some research for her oral report, you can use this conflict to discuss the meaning of *perspectives*. From John's perspective he should be allowed to use the computer because he is almost through with his story and he wants to print it out so he can share it from the Author's Chair. How is John feeling about having to wait to use the computer? Ask John to tell about his feelings. Penny feels that her need to use the computer is more urgent because she *must* give her oral report tomorrow and she still needs some information. Ask Penny to talk about her feelings.

As a follow-up to this discussion of actual conflict in the classroom and how the different people feel about it, you read a story aloud and then move into the discussion of characters in a book. At this point you want to plan the types of questions you will ask to support the students in identifying the feelings and thoughts of the various characters in the story.

STEP 3   CREATING A VISUAL AID

To help students see that characters may have different reactions to or be thinking different things about the same event or problem, create a chart to represent the feelings of characters in relation to events and problems in the story. See figure 17.1 for an example of this type of visual aid for The Three Little Pigs.

STEP 4   REPEATING THIS APPROACH WITH SEVERAL DIFFERENT BOOKS

Choose a variety of books and characters and conduct discussions about the characters' feelings, thoughts, and reactions. Encourage the students to create visuals showing characters' perspectives after they've had enough exposure and practice in this technique.

STEP 5   PLANNING AND IMPLEMENTING A VARIETY OF ACTIVITIES THAT ENCOURAGE EXPLORATION OF CHARACTERS AND THEIR PERSPECTIVES

Once students understand the basic concept of perspective taking, you can provide them with several different ways of exploring stories from different perspectives. See figure 17.2 for a chart of ways to use visual aids and drama to study perspective taking in depth.

FIGURE 17.1   Perspective visual for The Three Little Pigs story.

Event	Wolf	Pig 1	Pig 2	Pig 3
Pigs build houses	Not involved	I'll build mine quickly. I want to play.	I'll use these sticks. They'll be good enough.	I want my house to be very strong. I'll use bricks.
Wolf comes to first pig's house.	I can blow this house down and eat the pig.	He's blowing my house down, I better run to my brother's.	He's blowing this house down too. We better get over to our brother's.	He can't blow this house down. We're all safe here.

FIGURE 17.2 Perspective-taking activities.

Activity	Procedure
Comic Strips	Have students draw scenes from a book they're reading in which the characters are not engaged in dialogue. Have them create "speech balloons" for each character in the scene and write what the character might be thinking in the speech balloons.
Reenactment	Using an illustration from the story being read or comic strips the students have drawn (see above), have the students dramatize the scene using expressive speech, gestures, and voices.
Subtext	Have the students write a reader's theatre script based on a story read (see chapters 29 and 30). As the students read the script, teach them to create and insert "asides," as in Shakespeare's plays. This encourages them to think about what the characters are thinking and feeling and see how these aspects of the character's perspective may differ from what the character is saying. At first, the teacher will need to stop the action and question students about the character's thoughts and feelings. The students will need to be taught how to "take the audience into the play" by speaking the asides directly to the audience.
Journals	While reading chapter books, students can be taught to stop after each chapter and write in a simulated personal journal as if they were one of the characters. Students can represent more than one character's perspective by using different colors of pen or different fonts on the computer.

APPLICATIONS AND EXAMPLES

 See File 17 of the accompanying CD for an example of perspective taking used in a third-grade classroom.

Mr. Jacob's tenth graders have been reading historical biographies and discussing the people they're reading about and the impact they had upon history. He wants his students to understand the different perspectives held by people at different times in history and decides to use a biography to help his students to put events into the commonly held perspectives of a different time.

Mr. Jacob chooses the book, *Rosa Parks: My Story,* (Parks & Haskins, 1992) to use as an example of how common perspectives have changed over time. He begins by asking his students to describe a typical ride on a city bus. The students are reluctant to participate, not knowing the purpose of the activity, so Mr. Jacob adds, "Tell me what you would see if you walked out in front of the school this afternoon and got on a city bus."

Jennifer says, "I ride the bus to my piano lessons after school on Tuesdays. I climb up the stairs, put my token into the change box and walk back down the aisle until I find a seat. There are usually many seats toward the back of the bus so I have to walk quickly so I can sit down before the driver starts the bus moving."

"Tell me about the people you see on the bus, Jennifer," encourages Mr. Jacob.

"The people on the bus tend to be older. It's not cool to ride the bus, but it's better than walking all the way downtown, for me. A lot of the bus people carry bags full of groceries or knitting. They speak a lot of different languages but there's not too much conversation. They mostly just ask each other if a seat is empty."

"What about the driver? Does he say anything?" asks Mr. Jacob.

"It depends," replies Jennifer. "One driver says hello to everyone. Another one mostly snarls at people when they take too long getting on."

"Does he tell you where to sit?" asks Mr. Jacob.

"No," replies Jennifer with a little laugh. "No assigned seats."

Mr. Jacob then displays a transparency of the first page of the Rosa Parks book on the overhead projector.

"Does this sound like the bus ride that Jennifer just described?" he asks.

"Well, that was a long time ago, Mr. Jacob. Things were different then," states Manuel firmly.

"How were they different?" asks Mr. Jocob.

"Black people didn't have as many rights then," replies Hector.

"I'm going to read the first few pages of this book aloud now," says Mr. Jacob. "I want you to think about the scene and pretend that you're sitting on that bus. When I finish reading, I want you to write down what you would be thinking as all this is happening on the bus. You're on your way home from work at the end of a long day. What would be going through your mind as this scene unfolds on the bus?"

Once he has finished reading the first few pages of the book aloud, Mr. Jacob asks the students to write their thoughts. Before they start to write, he distributes a drawing of the people on the bus with speech bubbles over their heads. The students write "thoughts" into several of the speech bubbles, often taking their cues from the facial expressions of the people in the drawing. Many of them express anger at the way Rosa Parks is being treated. Others just express frustration that their ride home is being delayed.

Once the students have written and discussed their writing, Mr. Jacob asks them to think about what would be different if the same event happened today. "Suppose the bus driver who snarls all the time asked Rosa to move. What do you think the people on the bus would think, say, or do today?"

Mr. Jacob then asks the students to talk about what Rosa was thinking.

"This book says she was tired from work, and tired of being pushed around by white people. Another book I read said that she was just tired and didn't mean to make a fuss that day," says Manuel.

"Who wrote that book?" asks Jennifer. "This book is actually written by Rosa Parks. I think I believe this one."

CONCLUSION

Mr. Jacob is supporting his students in understanding perspectives related to the reading they are doing. Although beginning readers often encounter stories whose characters are fairly easy to understand, as readers encounter more complex text the perspectives, motivations, and interactions of the character become increasingly more difficult to understand. Explicit instruction in identifying perspectives of characters is vital to the developing reader. Providing support in the form of visual aids, discussion, and story reenactment enables readers to deepen their understanding of characterization and uncover the more complex concepts being represented.

REFERENCES

Emery, D. (1996). Helping readers comprehend stories from the characters' perspectives. *The Reading Teacher, 49*, 534–541.

Parks, R., & Haskins, J. (1992). *Rosa Parks: My story*. New York: Dial Books.

SUGGESTED READING

Barton, J., & Sawyer, D. M. (2003). Our students are ready for this: Comprehension instruction in the primary grades. *The Reading Teacher, 57*, 334–347.

Clyde, J. A. (2003). Stepping inside the story world: The subtext strategy—A tool for connecting and comprehending. *The Reading Teacher, 57*, 150–160.

Marr, M. B., & Wood, K. D. (2000). The value of perspective-taking for improving comprehension. *The California Reader, 34*, 7–13.

Oczkus, L. (2003). *Reciprocal teaching at work: Strategies for improving reading comprehension*. Newark, DE: International Reading Association.

Sipe, L. R. (2000). The construction of literacy understanding by first and second graders in oral response to picture storybook read-alouds. *Reading Research Quarterly, 35*(2), 252–275.

Suits, B. (2001). A second look at literature circles. *The Reading Teacher, 35*, 21–29.

DOUBLE-ENTRY JOURNALS

Connecting Experiences to Text

Double-entry journals (Barone, 1990) are a specific type of reading log in which students respond to text on a journal page divided into two columns. Double-entry journals can be used in several ways within the reading and language arts curriculum. They are particularly effective in helping students to recognize and write about the personal experiences they have had that relate to assigned reading. The student or teacher can select a quote from the reading material and write the quote on the left side of the journal page. The student then writes a response to the quote on the right side of the page. These responses can relate to a number of elements in text, but for the purpose of relating prior knowledge and experiences to the text, students are asked to remember personal experiences that pertain to the quote. These experiences may be taken from their own backgrounds or reading they have done. See figure 18.1 for an example of a double-entry journal connecting text to prior experiences.

STEP BY STEP

The steps in implementing double-entry journals to relate experiences to text are:

STEP 1   MODELING THE STRATEGY

The teacher selects a quote from familiar reading material and reads it aloud to the class. The teacher then draws a double-entry journal format on the overhead or chalkboard and demonstrates writing the quote on the left side of the journal. He says, "This is called a *double-entry journal*. It is called double-entry because there are two columns on the journal page. On the left side I write an interesting quote, selected from the material I am reading. On the right side I write about a time when I

FIGURE 18.1 Double-entry journal based on passages from *Heroes.*

In fact, he always insisted on sitting in the back of the plane "because it's safer back there."	My grandmother always wants to sit in the back seat of the car because she says it's safer back there.
A person can survive only a few minutes in such cold water.	I remember one time I fell through the ice trying to cross a small stream and my clothes got all wet, and I thought I was going to freeze to death.

Source: From H. Billings, and M. Billings, 1999, *Heroes* (2nd ed.), Lincolnwood, IL: Jamestown Publishers.

had an experience similar to the one described in the quote. I can also write about a time when I felt the way the character in this quote felt. When I complete the double-entry journal, it helps me to understand what is happening in the story because I can relate the story to my own experiences."

STEP 2   PRACTICING THE STRATEGY

The teacher distributes reading materials and blank double-entry journal pages to students. He instructs the students to read silently until they find a quote that stimulates a memory or emotion related to a personal experience. The students write the quote on the left side of the journal and write about their personal experience on the right side. The teacher circulates among the students during this process to give them support and suggestions.

STEP 3   SHARING PERSONAL EXPERIENCES

Once the students have completed their reading and responding, the teacher asks them to share the quotes they have chosen. By sharing their personal experiences and hearing other students relate personal experiences that may mirror or differ from their own, students can see how personal experiences support the comprehension of text. Students can also relate to the events and emotions that are a part of the reading because they begin to find common threads between their own lives and those of characters.

APPLICATIONS AND EXAMPLES

See File 18 of the accompanying CD for an example of double-entry journals used in a second-grade text with environmental themes.

Ms. Moua stands in front of her 10th-grade social studies class reading a quote from *Catherine Called Birdy* (Cushman, 1994). "When I was reading this, it really brought back memories of my teenage years," she says as she quotes, "My father, the toad, conspires to sell me like cheese to some lack-wit seeking a wife."

"In my culture women traditionally get married very young, between 13 and 15. Because I wanted to go to college and become a teacher, my father tried to introduce me to as many possible husbands as he could find. I really found the medieval times very similar to the traditions in the Hmong culture."

Because Ms. Moua and the class are studying medieval history, she wants to find as many ways as possible to relate this time in history to their lives. She wants the students to compare and contrast medieval life to the present day. She also wants the students to relate the study of history to their own lives.

"It is very important for readers to be able to relate the reading they do to their own lives," says Ms. Moua. "I want to show you one way to do this. We will be reading some historical fiction in literature class at the same time we are studying medieval history. This way, you will be able to take a peek into the daily lives of people who lived during this time in history. *Catherine Called Birdy* is one book I think you will enjoy reading. It gives the reader some wonderful insights into the way of life during that time. Because it is about a young lady about your age, I think you will find some ways to relate her life to your own.

"We will be working in a double-entry journal while we read this novel. You will choose quotes from the book that remind you of events in your own life. For example, I will start my double-entry journal with the quote I just read to you."

Ms. Moua draws a large T-shaped chart on the chalkboard and writes the quote, "My father, the toad, conspires to sell me like cheese to some lack-wit seeking a wife" on the left side of the T chart. On the right side she writes, "In my culture women traditionally get married very young, between 13 and 15. Because I wanted to go to college and become a teacher, my father tried to introduce me to as many possible husbands as he could find."

After Ms. Moua demonstrates the format for the double-entry journal, she passes out blank double-entry journal pages to her students. "As you read the first few chapters of the book today, choose quotes that remind you of experiences you have had. You can also relate quotes to similar emotions you have experienced or even other books you have read. If anything in the book reminds you of discussions we have had about medieval history, you can note those connections, too. I'll be walking around the classroom while you're working. I would love to hear about the connections you are making. I will, of course, answer any questions you have."

After the students read and respond in their double-entry journals, Ms. Moua brings them back together as a group and asks them to share some of their quotes and responses. A number of the students have chosen the quote, "I am frequently told not to spend so much time with the goat boy, so of course I seek him out whenever I can." As students discuss this quote and why they selected it, it is clear that a number of the students have parents who try to choose their friends. Ms. Moua asks, "Why would Catherine deliberately seek the goat boy out when her parents object to their friendship?"

"We want to choose our own friends. We are practically adults. We need to let our parents know that we will make our own decisions about things like this," replies Joanie.

"I don't feel that way," says Nathan. "I really like a couple of my friends. They are neat people and my parents just don't know them. I sneak around to meet them just because it's not worth getting into a big argument about things like that."

"Do you think many things have changed in the ways teenagers and their parents get along or solve problems?" asks Ms. Moua.

"I thought so before I read this book," answers Nathan. "But the dialogues between Catherine and her parents sound a lot like conversations between me and my parents."

"As you are choosing quotes for your journal, you may want to point out some ways in which things have changed," reminds Ms. Moua.

"This is really a good book," comments Jose. "It really helps me to understand the ways of the medieval times."

CONCLUSION

As you can see from this classroom example of using double-entry journals to elaborate on personal experiences and the reading of texts, students can be supported in understanding text through relating it to their own lives. Choosing quotes to which personal responses are written helps students establish the habit of relating text to experiences. Often the connections between texts can be emphasized in this way as well. As students become more proficient in responding to text, they can be taught to connect other books they have read to the text currently being read. They can also learn to relate current events to reading materials in this same way. In the process they practice writing skills. The discussions that follow the journaling are equally important because they support the students in understanding the impact of life experiences in the way text is interpreted and valued.

REFERENCES

Barone, D. (1990). The written responses of young children: Beyond comprehension to story understanding. *The New Advocate, 3*, 49–56.

Cushman, K. (1994). *Catherine called Birdy*. New York: Harper Trophy.

READ/THINK ALOUD

Emphasizing Connections and Thought Processes

Read/think aloud is a simple strategy that can be used to support students' understanding of the reading process in many areas. It is especially effective in demonstrating how good readers bring their background knowledge into play as they process text. In read/think aloud the teacher uses the reading of a book to model the connections she is making as she reads the book. The teacher reads aloud, stopping periodically to think aloud about the way she is processing words, phrases, or sentences. She also verbalizes the connections she is making in her mind between the book being read and other books and past experiences.

Although this is a simple strategy, it requires some basic preparation. Reading the book in advance of using it in the classroom is important. Some teachers have found placing Post-it® notes in think-aloud spots ahead of time helps them to remember to stop and verbalize thought processes. Another adaptation of this strategy is the read/think/write activity in which the teacher reads and thinks aloud and then asks students to jot down notes at various places in the story where they have made connections to their past experiences. The teacher then gives the students time after the reading to choose one or more of their notes and expand on it or them. It is also valuable to allow time for students to share the connections they have made because the sharing often jogs the memory of other students and serves as another demonstration of the importance of making personal connections to text and the role it plays in supporting comprehension.

> **Focus on English Learners**
>
> This strategy helps English learners to hear the teacher's thought processes as she reads. It also gives them practice in verbalizing and/or writing in English after having observed the teacher's modeling.

STEP BY STEP

The steps in implementing read/think aloud are:

STEP 1 CHOOSING AND PREREADING THE BOOK

The teacher chooses a book that will provide an opportunity to make connections to other books that have been read in the classroom in the past and to personal experiences the teacher can relate to students. As she prereads the book, the teacher places Post-it® notes in places where she will stop and think aloud. The Post-it® notes can be left blank if the connection is obvious or the teacher may choose to write a word or phrase to remind her of the connection to be made.

STEP 2   READING AND THINKING ALOUD

The teacher reads the book aloud, stopping at appropriate places to think aloud, verbalizing the thought processes she is using to make a connection between past experiences, literary and actual, and the text being read.

STEP 3   DISCUSSING THE PROCESSES

After the read/think aloud is completed, the teacher goes back through the book, discussing the processes she uses to make sense of text by connecting what she reads to past experiences. At this point the teacher also encourages students to think of intertextual (literary) and actual experiences they have had that relate to the story. The teacher makes clear the importance of past experiences to comprehension. She should discuss and model the value of having experienced similar feelings, actions, activities, or events in the process of truly understanding the emotions and motivations of characters or in predicting future events.

STEP 4   ADDING WRITING TO THE PROCESS

An optional approach to this strategy is to have the students jot down words or phrases as they think of intertextual or actual experiences that relate to the text as it is being read aloud. The teacher then gives the students time after the oral reading to choose one or more of the notes they made during the reading and expand on it or them. Taking the time to encourage students to talk about their experiences and their relationship to the text serves to give other students ideas about how helpful this strategy is to understanding the text being read.

APPLICATIONS AND EXAMPLES

 For an example of read/think aloud used with sensitive topics in high school, see File 19 of the accompanying CD.

Mr. Fredric wants to provide a demonstration of read/think aloud to his fourth graders, some of whom are experiencing comprehension difficulties. As he plans a short lesson for December 7, Pearl Harbor Day, related to World War II, he decides to use Eve Bunting's beautiful story about the Japanese internment camps *So Far from the Sea* (1998). Mr. Fredric wants to teach about Pearl Harbor Day and the importance of using background to understand reading text in a combined lesson.

"I want to read a book to you today that has a very important connection to today's date. As I read the book, I will be stopping every now and then to model how I think as I read, even to myself. After we finish reading the book, we will talk about two things, so I want you to be very thoughtful listeners," begins Mr. Fredric.

"First, let's look at the picture on the cover. What do you see?" asks Mr. Fredric.

"It looks like an Eskimo family," suggests Dion.

"What makes you think that?" asks Mr. Fredric.

"Well, there's snow on the mountains and they have heavy coats on. They also look like Eskimos," replies Dion.

"OK, this is important. Dion is making a prediction based on her past experiences. She has seen pictures of Eskimos and Alaska, and this picture reminds her of those things. She thinks this story is going to be about Eskimos. She also mentioned that it looks like an Eskimo family," says Mr. Fredric.

"What made you think it is a family?" he asks Dion.

"Well, it looks like a mother, a father, and two children. It's just like my family," answers Dion.

"Oh, sounds like Dion is using her own experiences to predict again. That's a great strategy. It really helps you to begin to listen and read carefully in order to check your own impressions," says Mr. Fredric.

"Mr. Fredric," says Gaye as she raises her hand. "Could they be Japanese or Chinese? Look at the writing on the white monument. It looks Japanese or Chinese."

"Great observation, Gaye," answers Mr. Fredric. "We don't know yet, of course. We'll have to read the story but that's a good thing for us to check as we read."

Mr. Fredric reads the story aloud. He stops to ask the students if they've ever felt "spooky" the way the girl in the story feels. He talks about a trip he made with his family once when he kept "feeling spooky" and just knew that something was wrong. He found out as the trip progressed that his father had been transferred and the family was going to have to move to a new city. His mom and dad hadn't told him this ahead of time because they were investigating the new town before they made their final decision. Somehow, he had suspected that the trip was more than a pleasure trip.

When he gets to the first black-and-white drawing in the book, he asks the students why they think the picture is in black and white. The students predict that the black-and-white pictures are taking place in the past. "That's exactly right," says Mr. Fredric. "This story has something called 'flashbacks.' The father is telling about something that happened to him when he was a little boy. The black-and-white drawings tell us that this part of the story took place when he was little, many years ago. These drawings remind me of the photographs in my grandmother's album. Whenever I see black-and-white photos, they remind me of the way things were a long time ago."

As he continues reading and thinking aloud about his own experiences, Mr. Fredric uses the book to teach the importance of relating your own experiences to the book to share the feelings of the characters in the book. He talks about the sadness he felt when his grandfather died, and the fear he felt growing up as a German-American right after World War II when German and Japanese immigrants were not trusted by neighbors and school friends.

After he finishes reading the book, he asks the students to think about any other books they've read that helped them to understand this book. The students remembered books about families being separated, others about grandfathers, but most of all they talked about their own feelings as they read these books. They remembered feeling sad. Some of them talked about crying today when Mr. Fredric read about the Japanese being taken to the internment camps.

"It is important to relate your own experiences and other books you've read to the books you are reading now," says Mr. Fredric. "When you are able to do this, you begin to understand a lot more about what you are reading. You know how the characters feel. You understand why they do the things they do. It's also fun to predict based on your own experiences, because then you're testing your predictions as you read and it makes you read more carefully. Dion predicted the story was about a family, and she was right. She thought, based on her experiences, that it was an Eskimo family but she found out it was a Japanese-American family as we read the book. Gaye noticed the Japanese writing and that gave her a clue."

"Now, does anyone know why I chose to read this book today?" Mr. Fredric asks.

"I heard on *Good Morning America* that today's Pearl Harbor Day," says Jacob. "My mom says that's the day the Japanese bombed Pearl Harbor and caused our country to get into the second World War."

"You are exactly right, Jacob," answers Mr. Fredric. "That was a long time ago but I think this book helps us to learn some lessons from history. How did the father in the story feel about being forced into the internment camp just because he was Japanese, living in America?"

"He didn't seem angry. He seemed to understand why they did it," replies Fern.

"I think he was sad, though," says Teresa. "His story about dressing up in his cub scout uniform so the soldiers wouldn't take him made me cry."

The discussion about the story and the students' feelings and perceptions continues for awhile. The students seem to fully understand the story and even as they talk about the meaning of Pearl Harbor Day, they keep referring to the personal experiences of their families during this time in history. Mr. Fredric closes the lesson by asking the students to go home and talk to their grandparents or older neighbors about Pearl Harbor Day and what they remember about the day. He plans to use the read/think aloud strategy the next day, adding some writing about personal reflection as he reads another Eve Bunting book *Fly Away Home* (1991).

CONCLUSION

The explicit teaching of reading strategies, even to upper-grade students, plays an important role in developing students' abilities to interpret and comprehend text. Read/think aloud is a modeling strategy presented by the teacher so that students begin to understand the thinking processes involved in the interpretation of text. By sharing their own strategies, teachers can give students models for using their experiences and background knowledge to deepen their understanding and appreciation of what they are reading.

REFERENCES

Bunting, E. (1998). *So far from the sea*. New York: Clarion Books.
Bunting, E. (1991). *Fly away home*. New York: Clarion Books.

SUGGESTED READING

Oster, L. (2001). Using the think-aloud for reading instruction. *The Reading Teacher*, *55*, 64–69.

SERIES BOOK STUDIES

Building Background Knowledge through Familiar Story Elements

Focus on English Learners

Because series books help English learners become familiar with characters, settings, and situations, the reader tends to process more text and experience more interaction with English vocabulary and structures.

Reading books published in a series provides students the chance to accumulate background knowledge as they read each book (Krashen, 1993). Series books have become so popular with young readers that some of the series now contain a hundred or more books. Research has demonstrated that wide reading improves reading fluency and vocabulary, but the main benefit from encouraging the reading of series books is the gradual building of background knowledge from book to book. Encouraging the reading of series books depends upon two factors, however: access to many books and providing time for reading books.

The success of books like the Harry Potter series attests to the comfort young readers acquire once they become familiar with the characters, settings, and special circumstances in a series of books. The use of series books in the classroom has been questioned in the past because many teachers do not think the quality of the books meets high literary standards. Though this may be true for some series, students are motivated to read the series books and they are available in almost every reading level and interest area. See figure 20.1 for suggestions of reading series for all ages.

Using a series of books in the classroom for free voluntary reading is given more value when the students have an opportunity to discuss what they are learning about characters and plot as they read. Because the purpose of using book series is to get students reading widely, the discussion of building background knowledge should be kept at a nonstressful, creative level. Depending on the type of series being read, an appropriate reading journal could be implemented. *Sweet Valley High* readers might keep a dialogue journal in which they write back and forth to each other commenting on characters in the books. *X-Files* series readers might keep a password-guarded file on the computer in which they warn one another about events about to happen in the next book. Harry Potter series readers might keep a secret file of magic potions or Quidditch plays.

FIGURE 20.1 Book series suggestions by grade level.

Grade Level	Series Books
Primary	*Aliens for Breakfast and Aliens for Lunch,* Stepping Stone Series, Random House.
	Clue, Jr. series by P. Hinter, Scholastic.
	Commander Toad series by Jane Yolen, Coward-McCann, Inc.
	Hank the Cowdog series by J. Erikson, Puffin Books.
	Horrible Harry series by Suzy Kleing, Puffin Books.
	Magic Tree House series by Mary Pope Osborne, Random House.
	Sweet Valley Kids series by F. Pasca, Bantam Books.
	The Zack Files series by D. Greenburg, Grosset & Dunlap.
	Ziggy and the Block Dinosaurs series by S. Draper, Just Us Books.
Upper elementary	*Bailey School Kids* by Debbie Dadey & Macia Thomton Jones, Scholastic, Little Apple.
	Dragonling series, Minstral Books.
	Dragon Slayers' Academy series by K. H. McMullan, Grosset & Dunlap.
	Full House series published by Minstral books.
	Goliath series by Terrance Dicks, Barrons.
	Nate the Great series by Marjorie Weinman Sharmat, Dell Publishing.
	The Adventures of Wishbone series by A. Steele, Lyrick Pub.
	The Boxcar Children series by G. C. Warner, Albert Whitman & Co.
	The Saddle Club series by B. Bryant, Skylark Books.
	The Three Investigators series by R. Arthur, Random House.
	The Young Merlin Triology by Jane Yolen, Scholastic.
	The Harry Potter series by J.K. Rowling, Scholastic.
	Time Warp Trio series by Jon Scieszka, Viking Penguin.
Middle school	*Animorphs* series by K.A. Applegate, Scholastic.
	Babysitter's Club series by Ann Martin, Scholastic.
	Broadway Ballplayer's series by M. Holohen, Broadway Ballplayer's Publishing Co.
	Eerie Indiana series by J. Peel, Avon.
	Goose Bumps series by R. L. Stein, Scholastic.
	Replica series by M. Kaye, Bantam Books.
	Sweet Valley Jr. High series by F. Pascal, Bantam Books.
	The Harry Potter series by J.K. Rowling, Scholastic.
Senior high school	*California Diaries* series by A. Martin, Scholastic.
	danger.com series by J. Cray, Aladdin.
	Star Wars series by J. Whitman, Bantam.
	The Chronicles of Chrestomanci series by D. Jones, Greenwillow Books.
	X Files series published by HarperCollins.
	Sweet Valley High series by F. Pascal, Bantam Books.

Source: Adapted from A. Herrell and M. Jordan, 2000, *Fifty Strategies for Teaching English Language Learners,* (2nd ed.). Used with permission from Merrill/Prentice Hall.

STEP BY STEP

The steps in implementing free voluntary reading with series books are:

STEP 1   IDENTIFYING AND GATHERING MATERIALS

The teacher identifies a variety of book series appropriate for the reading levels and interests of students in the class. A system such as cards or sign-out lists is devised so that they can be circulated. It is best to include a number of books in each series rather than a greater number of different series since the object is twofold: to get the students reading and to teach them to use background knowledge gained from one book to increase comprehension in subsequent books read.

STEP 2   INTRODUCING THE BOOK SERIES

The teacher unveils the new books added to the class library. He introduces the books as being "fun reading" books for the purpose of enjoying reading. The fact that the books are written in a series should be explained. The teacher should focus on the fact that the books are best read in sequence since some information is added in each book that builds on information from earlier books in the series. Some teachers have found that providing a checklist of the titles in a series so students can keep track of the books they read is motivational for some students. As part of the introduction of the books, the teacher provides some time within the school day for free reading. If students are reading other books during this time, it's best not to require the reading of the book series as long as the free reading time is being used for reading.

STEP 3   IMPLEMENTING BOOK-DISCUSSION GROUPS

The teacher gathers a small group of students to discuss the books they are reading. The teacher should read several of the books in the series in advance so that the characters are familiar. The teacher starts the discussion with an open-ended question about the plot or a character, such as, "What do you think about Brenda?" The purpose of the discussion group is to allow the students to talk about the books as if the characters were friends of theirs and as if they had been a part of the action. The teacher should serve as facilitator and observer, not as inquisition master. Once the discussion groups are started, students should be free to meet together to discuss the books at their discretion. Dialogue journals in which students who are reading the same book series can write messages back and forth to each other can be introduced during the discussion groups. Dialogue journals posted on a book series web site have been successful in some classes.

STEP 4   FOLLOWING UP THE READING

Once students are actively engaged in reading book series, the teacher can build on their growing background knowledge as book discussions are conducted about other books being read in the classroom. As the teacher refers to background knowledge related to other literature, he can refer to the background knowledge the students have gained through reading a series of books set in a familiar place and involving familiar characters. The books in the series become shared knowledge that can be used to high-light the power of intertextual experiences (see chapter 21 on intertextual studies.)

APPLICATIONS AND EXAMPLES

Mr. Durang has included a number of book series in his ninth-grade humanities classroom, even though he recognizes that the books will never be considered great literature. Many of his ninth graders have difficulty with reading comprehension, and Mr. Durang feels that he must find ways to help them raise their reading levels

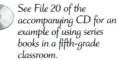

See File 20 of the accompanying CD for an example of using series books in a fifth-grade classroom.

and increase their comprehension. Mr. Durang recently read a report from the National Reading Panel (Allen, 2000) in which the need for reading instruction focusing on vocabulary development and reading strategies is mentioned as vital. As he thinks about strategies for his ninth graders, Mr. Durang is convinced that building a shared understanding of books will help his students. If he can get them interested in books, he feels they will have more knowledge to bring to the required readings for ninth grade.

Mr. Durang is not unduly concerned about the students in his classes who are avid readers. They seem to have a wealth of knowledge to bring to the humanities classroom. He has a number of reluctant readers, though, who do concern him. The series of books he has in his classroom have interested a number of the reluctant readers. It isn't until he adds the Harry Potter books (Rowling, 1997, 1999a, 1999b, 2000) to the collection that he begins to see a surge in free reading. He is surprised by the students' interest in the Harry Potter books since they are much longer than the books the students usually choose to read. He talks about this fact in the Harry Potter discussion group.

"What is it about these books that is so fascinating?" Mr. Durang asks. "I notice some of you reading them anytime you have free reading time, now."

"They are just more interesting than a lot of books. They're about very different things than normal books. Harry has magic powers he didn't even know about and he's famous with the wizards. He was living with this muggle family and they were awful to him but he got the last laugh," says Jason who seems to have a lot to say about the books.

"It's not just that," adds Becky. "The author writes in a really neat way. The books are just more fun to read. You never know what's going to happen. They're very unpredictable."

"I'm really glad you're enjoying them," says Mr. Durang. "What experiences have you had in your lives that make you able to relate to the books?"

"Well," starts Fred, "I think we've all had fights with bullies. Harry's cousin is a bully and I think that's why I was so glad to see Harry get the best of him."

"The stories kind of remind me of the Superman stories. Harry has super powers, just like Superman. Only he doesn't really know he has powers 'cause his aunt and uncle didn't want him to know."

"I can see that this group is going to have a lot to discuss," laughs Mr. Durang. "This series only has four books in it so far. It's a good thing these are long books. They'll keep you reading for a while. Once you finish the first one, you'll have a better idea of what to expect for the next three. Is this group going to keep journals?"

"We've decided to send letters back and forth to each other like they do in the books. We've designed Owl Paper to use. In the books, Harry sends letters by his owl, Hedwig. Is it OK if we have some of our owl paper copied in the office?" asks Becky. "Then we can keep scrapbooks of our owl note."

"That sounds like a good idea," responds Mr. Durang. "I can hardly wait to hear more about Harry Potter." Mr. Durang is pleased to hear the students making connections with the Harry Potter books. Their connections to their own experiences and the Superman series show him that the students are learning to draw on their prior knowledge to support their own comprehension of the stories they are reading. They are really reading a lot of text now, too. Mr. Durang is pleased.

CONCLUSION

Teachers all over the country are discovering, as did Mr. Durang, that students enjoy reading book series. They become familiar with the characters and circumstances and comfortable with reading about old literary friends. Even though many of the book series are easy reading for students, they provide a building of knowledge about books and the way sequels build on the original volumes. The reading of longer texts provides the development of plot and character not possible with short stories, and students reading the series books process a lot of text in their free reading. Reading more widely serves to improve the students' vocabularies, fluency, and interest in reading further. The biggest barrier to implementing this strategy is the accumulation of enough books to provide reading material for a class when every student is reading a great number of books each week. This is a problem, but in many ways, it's a pleasant one.

REFERENCES

Allen, R. (2000). *Before it's too late: Giving reading a last chance*. Alexandria, VA: Association for Supervision and Curriculum Development.

Krashen, S. (1993). *The power of reading*. Englewood, CO: Libraries Unlimited.

Rowling, J. K. (1997). *Harry Potter and the sorcerer's stone*. New York: Scholastic.

Rowling, J. K. (1999a). *Harry Potter and the chamber of secrets*. New York: Scholastic.

Rowling, J. K. (1999b). *Harry Potter and the prisoner of Azkaban*. New York: Scholastic.

Rowling, J. K. (2000). *Harry Potter and the goblet of fire*. New York: Scholastic.

Rowling, J. K. (2003). *Harry Potter and the order of the Phoenix*. New York: Scholastic.

21

INTERTEXTUAL STUDIES

Comparing Story Elements to Build Comprehension

Focus on English Learners

English learners often benefit greatly from reading or hearing an informational book read aloud before reading a narrative text related to the same topic. The intertextual information gained from the expository book helps build background knowledge necessary to understand the narrative text.

It is important for students to recognize that their experiences with books build a store of knowledge from which they can make assumptions and predictions when they read new stories. Students' abilities to use their personal experiences can be greatly enhanced by making them aware of intertextual knowledge, information they have gained from reading and exploring literature. Earlier use of intertextual knowledge focused primarily on simple transference of information from text to text, but the real power of intertextual knowledge lies in the reader's ability to understand textual elements, their differences and similarities, and to be able to use this knowledge in making sense of new text. Teaching the elements of a story and how these elements of character, setting, plot, conflict, and conflict resolution work together to create interest and understanding greatly enhances students' comprehension of anything they read.

Though intertextual study traditionally has been used almost exclusively with narrative text, intertexual knowledge can also support students' understanding of expository text in a slightly different and powerful way. Studying the structure of informational text supports students' knowledge of the way in which this type of text is organized. Intertextual information is useful in reading expository text because the students know that reading the headings, subheadings, illustrations, and chart captions is helpful in gaining the knowledge contained in the informational book. Understanding the purpose and use of the table of contents, index, and glossary is also important in reading future informational texts and is transferred from text to text.

Students sometimes need to be reminded of experiences they have had with other pieces of literature and informational text. Bringing their experiences to light is an important step in helping them to use the full power of elaborative processing (Irwin, 1991). Elaborative processing strategies involve the use of past experiences, including intertextual knowledge, to support the comprehension of materials currently being read.

STEP BY STEP

The steps in teaching intertextual comparisons are:

Step 1   Teaching Story Elements and Text Structure

To be able to compare books using the elements of story and text structures, these elements must be taught. The teacher should introduce students to the terms for story elements and refer to them frequently when discussing books. She introduces the characters in a story and then refers to those characters as their actions and attributes are discussed. The important elements to teach and compare vary from story to story but eventually students should recognize the elements of character, setting, plot, theme, conflict or problem, and conflict or problem resolution. It takes time and exposure to many books to teach and discuss all the elements. References to story elements should be an expected part of literature discussion to support students' thorough understanding. This understanding, in turn, supports their comprehension of the stories they are reading.

Step 2   Practicing Intertextual References

The teacher demonstrates intertextual comparisons with simple modeling anytime a book is read aloud or anytime students are engaged in reading. Questions such as "Does this plot remind you of another book we have read?" get students thinking about intertextual comparisons. Thinking about the way books are similar activates students' prior knowledge and encourages them to think more deeply about the meanings of the texts they are reading. If the teacher remains aware of the value of intertextual comparisons, she can be prepared to ask questions such as:

- Does this character remind you of another character we have encountered recently?
- What was the other book we read that was set on a desert island?
- This problem is similar to another one we read about not too long ago. Does anyone remember that book?

Once students recognize these intertextual connections, then comparisons can be explored.

Step 3   Charting the Comparisons

The teacher supports the understanding of intertextual comparisons when she makes charts or Venn diagrams (see Chapter 22) or simply lists similarities and differences with students' help. Though charting is an important step in activating students' inclination to make intertextual comparisons, this step is often dropped after a short time. The object is to get the students referring to past literary experiences as they focus on the stories they are currently reading. Activating prior knowledge and experiences with books is important in supporting comprehension; however, the use of charting should only be an introductory device to support their understanding of the ways in which books are different or similar. Eventually, the students should be able to mentally process their prior experiences without the need for visual references.

Applications and Examples

For an example of intertextual studies to stimulate higher-level thinking in a 10th-grade literature class, see File 21 of the accompanying CD.

Because Mrs. Becker's first graders have a number of different first languages, she likes to expose them to multiple readings and multiple versions of books. She is currently reading different versions of the traditional folktale, "Stone Soup," in which hungry travelers get people to feed them by making soup out of stone. Mrs. Becker talks about the characters in each version of the book and makes a chart on the

FIGURE 21.1 Comparing two versions of "Stone Soup."

Ann McGovern version:	Marcia Brown version:
Characters—young boy & old woman	Characters—3 soldiers & the villagers
Setting—old woman's house	Setting—the village square
The Problem—the visiting character(s) is(are) hungry and the locals don't want to share	
The Solution—the visitor(s) trick the locals into making a pot of soup	

chalkboard where she lists the main elements of the two versions of the story and notes their similarities and differences.

"Yesterday, we read *Stone Soup* by Ann McGovern," says Mrs. Becker as she holds the book up for the students to see. "Who are the characters in this book?"

Moua raises her hand shyly. "An old lady and a boy," she says.

"Yes, there were only two characters in this story," affirms Mrs. Becker. "But today we are going to read another story about stone soup. The story today is written by Marcia Brown." Mrs. Becker holds up the new version of the book (Brown, 1947). "What do you think will be different about this book?" she asks.

"There are two men and a lady in the picture," says Tony. "There were no men in the other story."

Mrs. Becker starts a chart on the chalkboard to help the students compare the different versions of the story. See her comparison chart in figure 21.1.

As Mrs. Becker reads Marcia Brown's version aloud, she stops periodically for the students to make comparisons. Because they are already familiar with the plot of the story, they recognize similarities and differences easily, and the students are actively engaged in suggesting items to be added to the chart.

Once the reading is complete, Mrs. Becker shows the students real ingredients for making stone soup. The students help her to prepare the ingredients and make stone soup in the crockpot she has brought for this purpose.

"Before we go home this afternoon we will have a little cup of stone soup for an afternoon snack," Mrs. Becker tells the class with a smile. Between the multiple readings of the book and the hands-on experience, Mrs. Becker knows her students understand the story and have acquired many new words and concepts in English.

CONCLUSION

To enhance students' use of elaborative processes and their abilities to use knowledge they have gained by reading literature, teachers should focus on story elements as they explore books with their students. Awareness of the importance of building shared knowledge about literature in order to expand students' background knowledge is the first step in supporting students' use of these important processes. Students may comprehend stories more completely if they can relate their personal experiences to the books. Real experiences cannot always be provided, but good literature always provides usable knowledge. The other powerful side effect of building shared knowledge related to literature is that the process of establishing these shared experiences with stories creates a strong community of learners who support one another in making sense of text. Often these types of studies also provide meaningful encouragement to expand the time spent on reading independently.

REFERENCES

Brown, M. (1947). *Stone soup*. New York: Aladdin Books/Macmillan Publishers.

Irwin, J. (1991). *Teaching the reading comprehension processes* (2nd ed.). Needham Heights, MA: Allyn and Bacon.

McGovern, A. (1986). *Stone soup*. New York: Scholastic.

SUGGESTED READING

Sipe, L. R. (2000), The construction of literacy understanding by first and second grades in oral response to picture storybook read-alouds. *Reading Research Quarterly, 35*(2), 252–275.

22

GRAPHIC ORGANIZERS

Visually Representing Ideas, Text, and Connections.

Focus on English Learners

The power of graphically organizing comparison for English learners cannot be overemphasized.

Graphic organizers are visuals or pictures created to represent ideas, text, or connections between texts. There are a number of graphic organizers that can be used to support students in reading and comprehending text (Bromley, Irwin-De Vitis, & Modlo, 1995). Venn diagrams are used to compare different texts or the reader's experiences with text in the form of overlapping circles. Flow charts are used to visually represent the sequence of events in text. The number of different ways in which graphic organizers can be used to support understanding in readers is endless. There are also several outstanding web sites that can be used to download graphic organizers for use in lessons.

Graphic organizers serve to aid comprehension by enabling the reader to label aspects of the text using language from the book and visually illustrating the connections among the events and characters.

Matching the graphic organizer to be used to the purpose of the lesson is vital. See figure 22.1 for a list of graphic organizers and their suggested uses.

As students create the graphic representation of the text, they are required to reread, discuss, and explore relationships within the text. Conceptual organizers are also effective ways to brainstorm, plan, and organize writing. In addition, teachers can use conceptual organizers to make ideas within informational text more accessible to students. Students must think more analytically to place individual characteristics and ideas in their proper position within the diagram (Tompkins, 2003).

These diagrams may also be used as a means of assessing student learning. See figure 22.2 for suggested ways of comparing and contrasting text, one use of graphic organizers.

STEP BY STEP

The steps in implementing the use of graphic organizers are:

STEP 1 IDENTIFYING TEACHING PURPOSES

Identify text to be used that can be supported with a graphic organizer. See figure 22.1 to find a graphic organizer that can be used to support student understanding of the text and your teaching point.

FIGURE 22.1
Suggestions and sources for using graphic organizers.

Graphic Organizer	Teaching Use	Source
Main Idea Mountain	Main idea/supporting details	*www.edhelper.com*
		www.edhelper.com
E Chart	Ideas/details	*www.eduplace.com*
Know/What/Found Out/Learned		*www.edhelper.com*
KWL	Basic research	*www.eduplace.com*
KWS (KWL+Sources)		*www.eduplace.com*
ISP (Information, Source, Page)		*www.eduplace.com*
Prediction/Outcome	Comprehension strategies	*www.edhelper.com*
Text Connection		*www.edhelper.com*
Timeline	Sequence of events	*www.edhelper.com*
Chain of Events		*www.edhelper.com*
Flow Chart		*www.eduplace.com*
Venn Diagrams	Compare/contrast	*www.edhelper.com*
Characters, Problem, Solution	Story structure	*www.edhelper.com*
Beginning, Middle, End		*www.edhelper.com*
Cause-Effect Charts	Cause/effect	*www.edhelper.com*
Who, What, When, Why, How		*www.edhelper.com*
Fact & Opinion Chart	Fact/opinion	*www.eduplace.com*
Describing Wheel	Descriptive writing	*www.eduplace.com*
Word Definition	Vocabulary development	*www.edhelper.com*
Word Clusters		*www.eduplace.com*
Persuasion Map	Persuasive writing	*www.eduplace.com*

FIGURE 22.2   Suggested topics for comparing and contrasting.

Comparing/Contrasting	To what?
Personal experiences	Narrative text
	Informational text
	Biography
	Poetry

Story elements:
  Characters
  Setting
  Conflict resolution
	Within the same text
	Between different texts

One character	At different points within the same text In a series of books
Concepts and/or ideas	Within the same text Between different texts
Text structure	In informational text In narrative text

STEP 2   EXPLAINING THE PURPOSE

Explain the graphic organizer and its purpose to your students and model how the organizer works. Construct an example, talking through the construction as it is built.

FIGURE 22.3   Examples of alternate shapes for Venn diagrams.

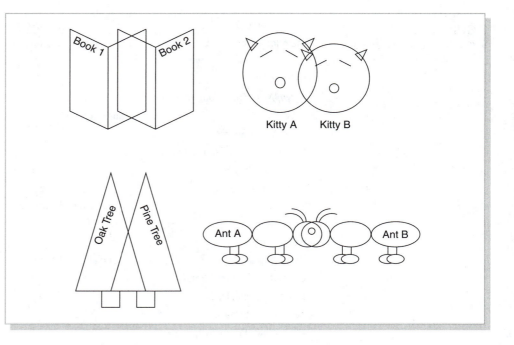

STEP 3   INVOLVING THE STUDENTS IN CONSTRUCTING A GRAPHIC REPRESENTATION

Walk the students through the building of a graphic representation, asking questions to lead them to place components into the proper places on the graphic organizer.

STEP 4   DISCUSSING THE CONNECTIONS

Support the students in discussing the connections shown on the graphic representation and using the vocabulary included in the text in the discussion.

STEP 5   PROVIDING ADDITIONAL PRACTICE IN USING GRAPHIC ORGANIZERS

As students become familiar with a variety of graphic organizers, encourage them to use the organizers to represent their understanding in a variety of contexts. See figure 22.3 for examples of various Venn diagram shapes that relate the diagrams to the content of the texts or concepts being compared.

APPLICATIONS AND EXAMPLES

See how Mr. Flores uses a Venn diagram to teach the difference between narrative and informational text in a second-grade classroom on File 22 of the accompanying CD.

Ms. Vang's tenth-grade class is beginning the production of a school newspaper. Before they begin to write news stories, Ms. Vang explains the necessity of including basic facts in their articles. She presents the students with a graphic organizer to remind them to proofread for the basic facts before they submit stories for the paper. Using a news story from that morning's paper, she walks the students through the graphic organizer, looking for the basic facts in the news story to answer the questions, who, what, when, why, and how. See figure 22.5 for the graphic Ms. Vang uses with her journalism class.

FIGURE 22.5   News release.

Softball Team Wins County Tournament

The Bears varsity softball team moves forward to the state tournament after a 4–1 win over Concord's Cougars on Friday night. Susan Harris led the team to the victory with a triple in the fourth inning. Pitcher Jenny Snow held the Cougars to one hit that was scored as a double. The hitter, Karen Harvey, scored on an error. The Bears are scheduled to play the Pittsburgh Pandas Thursday night for the first round of the state tournament. This will be the eighth straight year that the Bears have made the state playoffs.

Graphic Organizer for the News Story

Who?

What?

When?

Where?

Why?

How?

CONCLUSION

The use of graphic organizers in reading analysis enables and encourages students to examine text from a variety of perspectives. The wide variety of graphic organizers available allows students to compare and contrast ideas found in the text and analyze the relationships between concepts juxtaposed in or across readings. In the process of using graphic organizers students are required to reread text and analyze it in relation to the graphics to be displayed on the organizer. Encouraging students to work in cooperative groups to complete a graphic organizer provides them with practice in rereading, negotiation, discussion, and the exchange of ideas and viewpoints. Creating graphic organizers also encourages students to think more deeply on the meaning and contextual clues found in text.

REFERENCES

Bromley, K., Irwin-De Vitis, L., & Modlo, M. (1995). *Graphic organizers*. New York: Scholastic Books.

Tompkins, G. (2003). *50 literacy strategies*. Upper Saddle River, NJ: Merrill/Prentice-Hall.

Venn, J. (1880). On the diagrammatic and mechancial representation of propositions and reasonings. *The London, Edinburgh, and Dublin Philosophical Magazine and Journal of Science, 9*, 1–18.

SUGGESTED READING

Fisher, A. (2001). Implementing graphic organizer notebooks: The art and science of teaching content. *The Reading Teacher, 55*, 116–120.

Harmon, J., & Hedrick, W. (2000). Zooming in and zooming out: Enhancing vocabulary and conceptual learning in social studies. *The Reading Teacher, 54*, 155–159.

Oczkus, L. (2003). *Reciprocal teaching at work: Strategies for improving reading comprehension*. Newark, DE: International Reading Association.

23

CRITICAL READING

Analyzing Text through Higher-Level Thinking Activities

Focus on English Learners

Based on the level of their language and literacy development, English learners may need very specific questions to guide their analysis of text.

Students' prior knowledge of a topic has a strong impact on their comprehension of reading material, but it also influences their emotional response to reading material and their ability to "suspend disbelief" in the reading of fictional material. Critical reading (Burmeister, 1978) is traditionally defined as analyzing the validity of the author's statements. Students who read critically analyze more than just validity, though. In the reading of fictional text, critical readers are reacting to situations described in relation to their own experiences, and they are thinking and responding to dialogue almost as if they were a part of the conversation. This can support comprehension but it can also interfere with the author's intention, so it is valuable to encourage students to analyze not only the text but their own response to the text.

Critical response journals are a valuable tool in encouraging students to read analytically. A series of questions to use in analyzing text and personal responses is helpful in the initial stages of critical response journals. These questions help students to focus their thoughts and to analyze critically the material they are reading. See figure 23.1 for suggestions of questions to focus critical response.

Critical reading must be taught. Many students take any printed word as gospel and must be introduced to the concept of analyzing both what is being read and how they respond to reading material. Students who are being taught writing skills in conjunction with reading are especially able to relate the types of research and documentation done by authors whose work they read to the requirements they must meet as they prepare research reports or write fiction.

STEP BY STEP

The steps in teaching critical reading are:

STEP 1   CHOOSING READING MATERIALS AND IDENTIFYING CRITICAL ISSUES

The teacher chooses reading materials that will lend themselves to the teaching of analysis. Using the questions in figure 23.1 as a guide, the teacher chooses reading

FIGURE 23.1 Questions
to focus critical response.

For Informational Text
What are the author's qualifications for writing this material?
Is the author's logic reasonable?
Is the language used in the material biased in any way?
Were stated facts supported with evidence?
Were opinions, when stated, clearly indicated as opinion?
Was the information presented in an organized sequence?
Did the author convince me that the information was valid?

For Narrative Text
What personal experiences did the text bring to mind?
What emotions did the text evoke?
Did I discover anything new from reading this material?
Was the dialogue believable?
Did the author bring the characters to life?
Was the plot unique in any way?
Was the conclusion logical?

materials, either fiction or nonfiction, and finds examples within the reading materials to illustrate the issues to be addressed.

STEP 2   MODELING THE USE OF READING ANALYSIS

Again, using the questions in figure 23.1, the teacher models the reading of the material she has selected and models the finding of information that enables her to respond to the questions. If information about the author is not available, the publisher's web site may provide more information. If information is not available online, letters can be written to the author and sent through the publisher. Although this takes time, it serves to illustrate the importance of knowing the credentials of the author. Attention to biased language is another point that can be modeled. Typical propaganda techniques, such as name calling and the use of half-truths and over-generalizations (Pearson & Johnson, 1978), should be pointed out and discussed. If critical response journals are to be used with the students, they should be demonstrated as the analysis of the reading material is performed.

STEP 3   GUIDING THE PRACTICE OF CRITICAL READING

The teacher assigns a short reading and the students read silently. When they finish reading, they jot down brief answers to the appropriate set of questions from figure 23.1. The teacher leads a discussion of the reading, focusing on the responses the students have made to the questions. As students share their responses they should be asked why they responded as they did. Students should be encouraged to read segments from the reading assignment to document their responses.

STEP 4   PRACTICING AND JOURNALING CRITICAL READING

The students should be given opportunities to read and journal their responses to the critical reading questions. Three-hole punched copies of the questions for informational and narrative reading can be duplicated so that students can answer the critical reading questions and then write more about their responses, if appropriate.

Some teachers have even asked students to document their responses with brief quotes from the materials or page numbers referring to the sections in the reading being discussed in the critical journal.

STEP 5   ## DISCUSSING THE ANALYSIS

The teacher brings the group together to discuss the analysis. Students are encouraged to share their analysis and talk about how they made their decisions. It is especially important to discuss personal and intertextual references during these discussions to support the students' understanding of the role of these experiences in their analysis of reading materials.

APPLICATIONS AND EXAMPLES

Mr. Castillo explores critical reading in his eighth-grade drug awareness unit on File 23 of the accompanying CD.

Mrs. Frolli's first graders are studying ocean life. Because they have become interested in whales, Mrs. Frolli introduces them to the book *Baby Whale Rescue* (Arnold & Hewett, 1999). Even though her students are only 6, Mrs. Frolli wants them to know about the importance of reading critically. She tells the students that the book they are reading is a true story. "This story really happened. We know that the people who wrote the book know all about whales because here, in the front of the book, it tells about all the people who helped with writing the book. There are people from Sea World and people from Hubbs-Sea World Research Institute who helped the authors make sure that all the information is correct."

Mrs. Frolli reads the book aloud, stopping at times for the students to discuss what they are hearing. Since the book is illustrated with actual photographs of J.J., the whale and her rescuers, the students have no trouble understanding the story. Mrs. Frolli focuses on their emotional response to the story by asking questions such as, "Have you ever gotten separated from your mom or dad when you were out shopping? How did you feel?" She allows the students to talk about their experiences and then relates their experiences to the story. She talks about the whale and how close to death she was when she was found and asks, "How would you eat if your mom and dad weren't there to cook for you for a whole week?" She also relates the feelings of the people who worked to rescue the baby whale. She asks, "Have you ever tried to help a pet who was sick?"

Some of the students talk about how sad they felt when their pets were sick. Others talk about how hard it is to help a pet who is sick and how the pet may snap at you. After the discussion, Mrs. Frolli gives the students some simple journals, paper stapled together with construction-paper covers. "I want you to draw a picture of the whale when they first found her on the beach and next to that picture draw yourself. Show how you felt when you heard that part of the story. On the next page draw a picture of the people returning J.J. to the ocean, after she was all better. Next to that picture, draw a picture of yourself when you heard that part of the story."

Mrs. Frolli plans to continue the use of the critical response journals with her first graders. Later in the year they will write their responses, but for now, she wants them to think about their feelings related to the stories they are reading and become aware that other critical issues should be addressed when reading.

CONCLUSION

Mrs. Frolli has found ways to include the study of critical reading in her first-grade classroom. Introducing critical reading to young readers is important and can be done through oral reading and discussion. Students learn early that their experiences and knowledge are important in making sense of reading materials. Critical reading journals can be introduced to young children through the use of illustrations and then expanded as the students are more able to write and express themselves. Reading comprehension is greatly enhanced as students learn more about ways to involve their vast store of background and intertextual knowledge.

REFERENCES

Arnold, C., & Hewett, R. (1999). *Baby whale rescue: The true story of J.J.* New York: Troll.

Burmeister, L. E. (1978). *Reading strategies for middle and secondary school teachers.* Reading, MA: Addison-Wesley.

Pearson, P. D., & Johnson, D. D. (1978). *Teaching reading comprehension.* New York: Holt, Rinehart, and Winston.

24

IMAGINATION, IMAGES, AND INTERACTION

Creating and Describing Mental Pictures

Focus on English Learners

English learners may need to both draw and label the images they create. The English labeling will assist them in verbalizing their conceptualizations.

Comprehension is one of the most important learning skills that our students need to do well academically and perhaps even in life. Thus, they must be taught comprehension skills that they can use for themselves during the process of reading text. Einstein said, "If I can't picture it, I can't understand it." If one of the greatest minds of our times recognized imagery as the basis for his thinking, what more evidence do we need to demonstrate the value of teaching individuals to integrate language with imagery? Students need to be encouraged to create mental images of the text they are reading and to verbally describe the images they have created from the text (Pressley, 1995).

The mental images assist students in ordering and sequencing the information they are processing in reading. By verbally interacting with the conceptual images they have created, they are incorporating the vocabulary connected with the textual concepts and further internalizing the material. They are encouraged to create relationships among the images, the text, and their past experiences with similar or related material and prior knowledge (Linden & Wittrock, 1981). Imaging and discussing stimulates significant gains in reading comprehension, oral language expression, and paragraph writing.

The most consistent theory and practice regarding the mechanisms of language comprehension are related to the human brain's ability to use two primary neurological coding mechanisms: mental imagery and language. Research in the last few decades has culminated in some significant findings:

- Humans vary widely in their abilities to create mental representations (Kosslyn, 1994).
- The brain's facility in integrating language and images is related to its ability to comprehend oral and written language. The activation of these two coding systems, verbal and imaginal, simultaneously serves to strengthen intellectual ability to aid in reading comprehension (Paivio, 1971). The ability to comprehend language can be explicitly stimulated or taught, and educators can learn to use specific techniques in the classroom or special education environments (Bell, 1991).

The power of this strategy is enhanced by the fact that it can be taught to students quickly and easily. By beginning with sentence imaging and proceeding to short paragraphs, the students can easily be led through the process. Once they have mastered the technique, they will increase their ability to recall information, detect inconsistencies within the text, construct inferences, and make predictions (Gambrell & Jawitz, 1993).

Now that some of the complexities of how to make sense of our universe are demystified, individuals can be directly taught to comprehend language.

STEP BY STEP

The steps in teaching students to create and describe mental images are:

STEP 1   CHOOSING APPROPRIATE TEXT

The teacher selects or creates a single sentence including elements that are easily imaginable and visually oriented. For example:

The dog chased the cat up a tree.

STEP 2   DISCUSSING THE VISUAL IMAGES

The teacher presents the sentence to the students. He asks them to close their eyes and imagine what the situation might look like if they were seeing a picture of it. The "pictures" they see will not look exactly the same. The teacher asks students to share with the class what they see in their pictures. He encourages them to elaborate on the pictures they see and asks them to relate those images to current or past experiences. He may even ask them to draw a picture of what they see.

STEP 3   REINFORCING THE IMAGING CONCEPT

The teacher repeats the process with a few more individual sentences. The sentences contain strong visual references so that students connect the ideas to clear visual images. If appropriate, the complexity of the sentences may be increased to encourage more intricate imaging. For example:

The dog chased the cat up the tree.

John's big black dog chased Lucy's calico kitten up the huge oak tree.

STEP 4   EXPANDING THE TEXT

The concept of using individual sentences may now be expanded into larger pieces of text, like short paragraphs. The teacher takes care to be certain that students are creating appropriate images based on the text prior to engaging in the use of more expanded reading material. The development of imaging skills is a gradual process that must not be rushed or shortcut. Some students will acquire the skill rather rapidly, while others may need significantly more reinforcement and follow-up activities. See figure 24.1 for suggested follow-up activities.

APPLICATIONS AND EXAMPLES

 On File 24 of the accompanying CD, Mr. Smith provides an example of teaching imagery to second-grade students.

In teaching his fifth-grade class about the early formation of the colonies in the New World, Mr. Alden enjoys focusing on many of the individuals responsible for leading the way for setting this new land. He particularly likes introducing the students to many of the more picturesque characters. Ethan Allen is a prime example.

The use of vivid characterizations allows and encourages his students to conceptualize visual images of the characters and surrounding events leading to their contributions to the formation of this new nation. Mr. Alden has chosen to use Joy Hakim's *From Colonies to Country* (1993), a part of the series, *A History of US,* to present much of the colorful, living history of the formation of the new American

FIGURE 24.1 Suggested follow-up imaging activities.

GRADE LEVEL	TEXT LEVEL	ACTIVITY
Primary	**Basic Sentence**	
K–third	*The dog chased the cat up the tree.*	Arrange pieces on a flannel/magnetic board. Draw picture.
	Expanded Sentence	
	John's big black dog chased Lucy's calico kitten up a huge oak tree.	Add to or modify pieces on flannel/magnetic board. Add details to picture.
	Short Paragraph	
	One sunny day, John took his dog for a walk. Lucy brought her new calico kitten over to show to John. John's big black dog chased Lucy's calico kitten up a huge oak tree.	Create a picture for each sentence and display them in the proper sequence on the wall. Retell the story from the pictures.
Intermediate	**Basic Sentence**	**Activity**
Fourth–eighth	*Abraham Lincoln was a tall, skinny man.*	Draw a picture. Think of a present-day person who reminds you of Abraham Lincoln.
	Expanded Sentence	
	Abraham Lincoln was a tall, skinny, bearded man who wore a stovepipe hat.	Add details to picture. Make a stovepipe hat and a beard.
	Short Paragraph	
	Abraham Lincoln was a tall, skinny, bearded man who wore a stovepipe hat. He stood in front of the large podium and delivered his famous speech, the Gettsyburg Address. As he spoke, he gestured broadly with his huge hands.	Create a storyboard, a series of pictures showing the sequence of the scenario. Reenact the scene described in the paragraph as depicted in the storyboard.

union. This particular text gives students many opportunities to add visual imagery connections to their understanding of the historical contexts presented.

Mr. Alden asks his students to look at the picture of Ethan Allen on page 76 and to silently read the first two paragraphs found there. The students are then asked to discuss the descriptions of Ethan Allen given in the text and to clarify new words and definitions of terms used to characterize Allen.

Once these comparisons and characterizations have been shared, Mr. Alden asks students to close their eyes and visualize what they think Ethan Allen might look like, especially in comparison to other typical men of the period.

"He sounds like a real rough guy, foul-mouthed and always looking for a fight," Tommy suggests.

Robert agrees but reminds the class that, "He just seems, like, kind of a really independent person, an individual who isn't going to be pushed around and told what to do."

Mary Sue defends his character, saying, "Well, in the picture he looks like a really nice gentleman."

Ramona reminds her, "Yes, but in the paragraph it tells us that he was a giant of a man, famous for his strength. And his language was rough and rowdy."

At this point, Mr. Alden interjects that it is important then to read the information contained in the paragraph to get a clearer mental picture of what the man really was like. What we see in an illustration might not give us an accurate representation of the "whole man." He asks students if they have ever had a mental image of a person that changed after they met the person or found out more information about him or her. Several students share how when they finally met people after hearing about them or talking to them on the phone, their mental image had been totally different than the actual people. They agree that the combination of information and visualization provides a clearer picture of the total person or event.

Mr. Alden now instructs the class to continue reading the balance of chapter 15 and to stop whenever necessary to visualize the text and discuss the images with the rest of their group. He also encourages them to draw illustrations and diagrams, if they like, to help clarify events in the text. Finally, he asks the students to use small sticky notes he has provided to mark the places in their texts where they stop to visualize the images contained in the text. This will assist him later in leading a discussion with the group as to why they chose to stop at certain points in the text and what sort of images were created. It will also point out to the students that not everyone visualizes in the same manner or in the same quantity.

As a follow-up to the reading, Mr. Alden asks each group to create a storyboard showing the sequence of events and the role that Ethan Allen played in the revolution and the early colonization of what is now known as New England.

CONCLUSION

The use of visual imaging is a powerful tool for students to use in solidifying their comprehension and understanding of often complex material. It allows them to sequence and form mental pictures of concepts, events, and personalities as they read both narrative and informational text. The early development of this skill is essential in developing and strengthening their comprehension processing from the individual-word level through the summarization of entire sections of text. It also provides students with ways to integrate their background knowledge and experiences into the interpretation of new material and ideas.

REFERENCES

Bell, N. (1991). *Visualizing and verbalizing for language comprehension and thinking*. San Luis Obispo, CA: Gander Educational Publishing.

Gambrell, L., & Jawitz, P. (1993). Mental imagery, text illustration, and children's story comprehension and recall. *Reading Research Quarterly, 28*, 265–276.

Hakim, J. (1993). *From colonies to country*. New York: Oxford University Press.

Kosslyn, S. (1994). *Image and brain: The resolution of the imagery debate*. Cambridge, MA: Massachusetts Institute of Technology.

Linden, M., & Wittrock, M. (1981). The teaching of reading comprehension according to the model of generative learning. *Reading Research Quarterly, 18*, 44–57.

Paivio, A. (1971). *Imagery and verbal processes*. New York: Rinehart and Winston.

Pressley, M. (1995). *Cognitive strategy instruction that really improves children's academic performance*. Cambridge, MA: Brookline Books.

SUGGESTED READING

Denman, G. A. (2000). Poetry in the classroom: Reading a poem well. *The California Reader, 33*(2), 12–14.

Hibbing, A. N., & Rankin-Erickson, J. L. (2003). A picture is worth a thousand words: Using visual images to improve comprehension for middle school struggling readers. *The Reading Teacher, 56*, 758–770.

McKenzie, G. R., & Danielson, E. (2003). Improving comprehension through mural lessons. *The Reading Teacher, 56*, 738–742.

HOLISTIC COMPREHENSION

Understanding the whole text—the plot, characters, problem, and resolution in narrative text and the basic concepts and interrelated ideas in expository text—is the ultimate goal of reading. This section focuses on strategies for supporting deep meaning in readers. Often, it is the discussions, dramatization, or creation of scripts related to the text that leads to true understanding. Until a reader has gone beyond reading the text to explore the interactions among the ideas or characters, the comprehension of the text can be superficial. Section IV focuses on active learning strategies to support readers in active engagement with text. In the process of dramatizing, writing scripts from narrative text, or writing reports from expository text, students must explore the deeper meaning of vocabulary and reflect on the interaction and relationships among characters and ideas in the text.

In the process of active engagement with text, readers create connections in their minds that support their deep understanding of the meanings and nuances of vocabulary, expression, and situations. Techniques that involve readers in creating scripts from text require them to explore character motivation and modes of expression. These types of activities require reflection and interactive discussion as well.

Also included in this section are strategies for encouraging collaborative exploration of meaning. Often a reader feels that his or her interpretation of text is the only valid one. By using collaborative discussion and creation of shared meaning, students are exposed to the ideas and perceptions of others. When teacher scaffolding encourages students to explain and support their perceptions, students begin to realize that different past experiences often support different interpretations of text, both narrative and expository.

This section is intended to provide strategies so that students and teachers working together can explore meaning to its fullest, sharing ideas, perceptions, and interpretations. In this process, students learn about all the factors that contribute to true understanding.

25

KWL CHARTS

Supporting Comprehension into, through, and beyond Reading

Focus on English Learners

English learners benefit greatly from the use of graphic organizers. This strategy assists them in approaching and interpreting text by organizing the process in a clear, sequential manner.

KWL charts (Ogle, 1986), with which students explore what they know, what they want to know, and what they learn about a topic, have been widely used in thematic unit studies. Typically the teacher divides a large piece of chart paper into three vertical sections, labeling *K* in the first section for what we KNOW, *W* in the middle section for what students WANT to learn about, and *L* in the last section for what students LEARN during the course of studying the material. The teacher asks students to think of all the things they know about the topic. As they respond orally, she lists their responses in the section labeled *K*. The teacher then asks students what they want to know about the topic and lists their responses in the *W* section, the second column. As the students read and study the topic, their newly acquired information is listed in the *L* section, the third column. Students explore resources to locate the answers to the questions generated and listed under the *W* section of the chart. These answers are also listed under the *L* section of the KWL chart.

This same format can be used to support students as they read content-area text. The teacher supplies an individual blank KWL chart to each student. The teacher gives a brief introduction to the topic to be explored in the reading assignment and asks students to list all the information they already know about the topic under the column marked *KNOW*. The teacher then provides a brief walk-through of the material to be read. As she walks the students through the material, she calls attention to the headings and subheadings found in the material. She asks the students to complete the *WANT TO KNOW* section of the KWL chart with questions they have about the topic or questions they feel they may be able to answer by reading the material. As the students read the material, they note any answers they locate or interesting information gained under the section marked *LEARNED*. Because the students are interacting with the KWL chart on an individual basis, they are actively engaged in the reading act. They activate their own personal background knowledge, predict about the information they expect to find in the reading material, and take notes related to information gained. Each of these tasks supports their comprehension as they prepare to read, as they read, and after they read. See figure 25.1 for an example of a blank KWL chart.

FIGURE 25.1   KWL chart.

K	W	L
(What we **KNOW**)	(What we **WANT** to know)	(What we **LEARNED**)

STEP BY STEP

The steps in implementing individual KWL charts are:

STEP 1   INTRODUCING THE KWL CHART IN A GROUP SITUATION

If students are unfamiliar with the KWL chart, the teacher introduces the use of the chart in a group lesson. A three section chart labeled *K* (Know), *W* (Want to Know), and *L* (Learned) is displayed. The teacher introduces an informational book by asking the students to predict what the book will be about by looking at the title and the front cover. She then asks the students what they know about the topic and writes their responses under the label *K* in the first section. She writes all responses, even if they are incorrect, because they will be able to correct misconceptions after the reading by entering their new understanding under the LEARNED section. The teacher then walks the students through the book pointing out the headings and subheadings and asking them what they think they will learn from reading this book. The students are asked to formulate questions about things they would like to learn or things they think they will learn by reading this book. The teacher writes their questions under the section on the chart labeled *W* (Want to Know). For the purpose of demonstrating the strategy, the teacher then reads the book aloud. As she reads, she stops whenever the answer to one of the questions on the chart is encountered. She asks students to state the answer to the question, and she writes their statements under the section on the chart labeled *L* (Learned). If there were erroneous statements made under the *K* section, the correct information is noted under the *L* section and the correction is discussed.

STEP 2   TEACHING THE USE OF THE KWL CHART IN INDIVIDUAL READING

The teacher distributes blank individual KWL charts to the students. She gives a brief introduction to the topic to be studied and assigns the reading to be accomplished. She then asks students to jot down any information they know about the topic under the column marked *K* on their chart. The teacher encourages students to think about any experiences they have had in the past that relate to the topic and any other reading material they have read that provided them with information about the topic. Even if they have limited knowledge about the topic, they should be encouraged to note that information on their charts. The students are then encouraged to look through the reading material and to formulate questions that they have about the topic. These questions should be written in the column marked *W*. The teacher then gives the students instructions to follow as they read the material. The students should be focusing on the information they are gaining as they read the material. They should be noting any new information they gain under the column headed *L*. They should be looking for answers to the questions they generated under the *W* column but also writing down any other new information they are gaining. They should be instructed to underline any new information they gain that corrects a misconception they had before the reading.

After the students have worked their way through the process, the teacher leads a discussion in which the students share their experience and have an opportunity to see that all the KWL charts are different. The teacher leads the discussion related to the ways in which we gain knowledge: through reading, through experiences, and through hearing other people's experiences. She asks students to share the items they listed under the *K* section of the chart and how they gained that knowledge. Any misconceptions identified should be discussed and the clarifications celebrated.

STEP 3   PRACTICING THE USE OF THE KWL CHART

The strategy should be practiced several times using new reading material and blank KWL charts. The teacher may need to provide support for any students experiencing difficulty with the procedures. Each time the strategy is used, the follow-up discussion should focus on new knowledge being obtained and refining the use of the strategy.

STEP 4   APPLYING THE KNOWLEDGE LEARNED

Once the individual KWL strategy is practiced, the teacher can extend its use by teaching the writing of informational reports based on the new information being gained. She might also help students to prepare to interview experts in the fields being studied, based on the information they have gained, or create posters, overhead transparencies, or other visual materials demonstrating their newfound knowledge.

APPLICATIONS AND EXAMPLES

 Frogs are at the center of study in Mrs. Trivet's kindergarten classroom. See how she uses a KWL chart with these young scholars on File 25 of the accompanying CD.

Mr. George's fifth-grade class is embarking on a study of the American pioneers by tracing the paths of those who crossed the historic Oregon Trail. As an introduction to the unit, Mr. George is having his students read, from the *Cornerstones of Freedom* series, a book entitled simply *The Oregon Trail* (Stein, 1994). He reminds students about how they have used KWL charts in the past to help them organize their thinking in preparation for a unit of study. He tells them that they will be creating their own individual KWL chart this time to assist them in reading the assigned text. He passes out the individual KWL charts and instructs them to fill in the first column, the *K* column, with what they know (or think they know) about the Oregon Trail. He emphasizes that students should put just what they know themselves about the Oregon Trail and should not be talking with their neighbors or asking them what they know. While Mr. George is circulating around the room monitoring the progress of the students, he notices that some students have very little to put in the column while others are including quite a bit of information. One student in particular, Michael, seems to have quite a bit of information to list in the *K* column.

"How did you come to know so much about the Oregon Trail, Michael?" Mr. George asks.

"Well, for Christmas I got this cool computer game that is like going on the Oregon Trail yourself," Michael says. "You go through all the problems and stuff that the pioneers went through, and then when you make different decisions, you get to see how things come out. I guess I learned a lot of stuff that I didn't know about before."

"Well, it looks like you certainly did, Michael. That's great. And we are going to be using that simulation here in class with our computers too, so maybe you can be my class assistant with that activity," suggests Mr. George. He continues monitoring the class until it appears that all the students have completed filling in as much information as they can in the *K* column.

"Now we're going to look at just what it is that you want to know about these early settlers and their hard journey. So I want you to look at the picture on the front of the book and tell me a few things that you would like to know about what you see in that picture."

Jenny says, "I see some children working really hard, so I'd like to know what kind of work the children had to do. And did they get to play at all, and what kinds of toys they had, and did they have to go to school and stuff?"

"Whoa, Jenny," says Mr. George. "That's really great! You're coming up with a lot of questions just from that one picture. Now, I would like all of us to look through the book at the pictures and charts and see what questions we might want to answer when we start reading the text. And now tell me where on our chart are we going to write the questions that we *want* to learn more about?"

"Under the *W*," responds the class.

"That's right," agrees Mr. George. "And when we finish reading the text, we will return to the chart and test some of the things we listed under the *K* column and add something to the *L* column to show what we have learned about these brave souls who worked so hard to cross the prairies in search of a new life."

After the students have formulated their questions and listed them on their individual charts, Mr. George instructs them to begin reading the text to search for some of the answers to the questions they have and to see what new things they can learn about the hard life of the settlers.

Once the students complete reading the text and entering information on their own KWL charts, Mr. George guides the class in a discussion of the questions they generated and the information they gained from reading the text and scanning the charts and pictures. Michael engages in the conversation by pointing out that even though he already knew a lot about the farmers and settlers from having played the computer simulation game of *The Oregon Trail*, he learned a lot more about how the trail came to be and about all the other people associated with the westward movement.

"That's right, Michael, we can really learn a lot from our books as well as from our computers," Mr. George replies. "You have all learned a great deal from this reading strategy and now we are going to expand that learning by taking you on a virtual trip across the Oregon Trail. I have installed the computer simulation in our computers, and we will be dividing up into teams to see who can match the accomplishments of these brave settlers."

He again points out that by doing a little prethinking and preparation, the text becomes more meaningful and actually easier to understand and follow.

CONCLUSION

The use of prereading planning is an effective strategy for increasing comprehension, especially when approaching material for which the students may not have a strong preexisting schema. Developing the students' ability to preplan and strategize their approach to reading is an important tool in preparing them to meet the challenge of reading for information and learning. It also helps students to realize that, in most cases, they have preexisting knowledge about the content and that through previewing the material and organizing their thought processes, they can activate existing knowledge, make predictions, and thereby enhance their ability to comprehend and internalize the text.

REFERENCES

Ogle, D. M. (1986). K-W-L: A teaching model that develops active reading of expository text. *The Reading Teacher, 39,* 564–570.

Stein, R. (1994). *The Oregon Trail (Cornerstones of Freedom)*. Danbury, CT: Children's Press.

The Oregon Trail. (Computer software). Cambridge, MA: The Learning Company.

26

DATA CHARTS

Organizing Information to Aid Comprehension and Recall

Focus on English Learners

Developing text-surveying skills that can be used prior to reading helps English learners to anticipate what will be included in the text.

Data charts (Tompkins, 1998) are a form of graphic organizer generally used to keep track of information gathered from several sources on a given topic. Their use can be adapted to organize information gathered while reading informational text. In their adapted form, data charts work well to help students identify big ideas and supporting detail. They also provide a succinct, one-page summary of vital information to enable students to study for tests, write reports, or give organized oral reports. See figure 26.1 for the standard format of a data chart.

Data charts serve to support comprehension by encouraging students to survey the text before reading by looking over the table of contents, chapter headings,

FIGURE 26.1   Data chart.

Topic _____

Questions → Sources ↓				

subheadings, illustrations, and charts and graphs to get a general idea of what the text conveys. Students then have the opportunity to formulate questions they have in connection to the topic being studied before they read. As they begin to read the text, they can write brief answers to the questions. Following the reading, they identify the main points and supporting details. All of this information is entered onto the data charts for future referencing. Data charts are also extremely helpful in encouraging the gathering of information from multiple sources to deepen the understanding of topics of study.

STEP BY STEP

The steps in implementing the use of data charts to support comprehension are:

STEP 1   SELECTING TEXT SUITABLE FOR DATA CHARTING

The teacher usually chooses content-based informational text as most suitable for the technique of data charting. This charting of information will help students remember facts and relationships found in the text.

STEP 2   EXPLAINING AND MODELING DATA CHARTING

The teacher introduces the data chart by sharing a chart created by a previous class on a reading from similar content material. He walks them through the text, pointing out the various cues that students might draw on to provide information for the data chart. He displays a blank chart on the overhead projector and has the class help him fill in a few areas of the chart as they scan the text together.

STEP 3   PROVIDING GUIDED PRACTICE

The teacher should walk the students through the first section of the text being studied, locating answers to the questions he and the class have generated. They will also be looking for important facts or concepts to be charted. As facts or concepts are located and charted, the teacher should ask questions to help students reflect on the selections they are choosing to chart. The questions the teacher asks can also relate to the thought process the students are using to make selections of items to chart. Such questions as "Why do you think that part is important to remember?" helps students begin to evaluate the choices they are making. Once the teacher and students have completed the charting of a section of the text and the teacher is satisfied that students are using the process effectively, the students can continue to chart independently.

STEP 4   PROVIDING INDEPENDENT PRACTICE

The teacher then divides the class into small groups to look for answers to questions, main concepts, and important facts, continuing to chart the rest of the text. Each group is given a section of the text to read, analyze, and chart. As the groups are working, the teacher circulates around the room, facilitating questions and providing support as needed. He asks why students choose to list some facts and concepts on their charts and why they omit others.

Step 5   Reporting Back, Discussing the Process, and Sharing Knowledge Gained

Once the groups have charted their sections of the text, the teacher brings the class back together to report their findings and discuss the process. Each group should bring forward its transparency, display its data, discuss the answers to questions they located in their section, and share the important concepts and facts they found. The teacher should ask questions related to the reasons for their choices and related to any facts or concepts that they chose to omit from their chart. After reviewing the main concepts and facts located in each section of the text, the teacher can instruct the students in ways to use the data chart created to study for a test to be given or to write a report on the topic.

Applications and Examples

 File 26 of the accompanying CD shows an example of the use of data charts in an eighth-grade class to introduce research and report writing.

Shortly after Thanksgiving, Mr. Velasco and his third graders are beginning a study of explorers. Mr. Velasco decides to introduce his students to data charting as an approach to support their comprehension of informational text. He finds a grade-appropriate text entitled, *Explorers: Searching for Adventure* (Thompson, 1998), which he will use to introduce the data-charting strategy.

"This morning," Mr. Velasco begins, "we will learn a way to read and organize information so that we can begin to learn how to give exciting oral reports. What we will learn to do is called data charting. We will use a chart like this one." Mr. Velasco shows the students a blank data chart on the overhead projector. "Let's look through the book we will be using to see what we think we will learn by reading it."

Mr. Velasco distributes copies of *Explorers: Searching for Adventure* to each of the students, and they page through the book looking at the pictures and talking about what they think they will learn by reading the book. After examining the book, Mr. Velasco asks the students to suggest some questions that they would like to be able to answer after they read the book. The group suggests the following questions:

What is an explorer?

Why do explorers go looking for things?

What have explorers discovered?

How did the early explorers find their way without computers?

How did the early explorers live on ships for such long periods of time?

If the explorers thought the world was flat, why did they sail off to new places?

Mr. Velasco writes the students' questions on the transparency of the data chart and models the use of the data chart by reading the first section of the book aloud, stopping to discuss information found in the text and writing answers to questions on the transparency as they are found. After the first section is read aloud, he challenges the students to read their books to find answers to each of the questions. He divides the class into six small groups and has each group read a section of the text to look for answers to the questions and other interesting facts. He gives each student a copy of a blank data chart to use as they read. As the students read and list answers to the questions on their data charts, Mr. Velasco circulates around the room making sure that everyone is engaged in the reading and writing activity.

Once the groups have read their sections, Mr. Velasco encourages them to discuss what they have written on their charts. He asks each group to appoint a spokesperson, and the groups report their findings. As each group spokesperson reports to the class, Mr. Velasco adds their discoveries to the data chart. When the groups are finished reporting, the class data chart looks like the one in figure 26.2.

FIGURE 26.2   Data chart on explorers.

Topic _____ Explorers _____					
Questions → Sources ↓	What is an explorer?	Why do explorers go looking for things?	What have explorers discovered?	How do they find their way?	Other interesting facts
Explorers Searching for Adventure by Gare Thompson	travelers to faraway places	treasure	7 continents	maps	Columbus was looking for Asia when he discovered America.
Explorers Searching for Adventure by Gare Thompson	someone who wants to learn about different places	adventure	oceans	charts	Magellan made the first trip around the world.
Explorers Searching for Adventure by Gare Thompson		curiosity	science of navigation	compasses	

Mr. Velasco and his students review and discuss each section of the reading and the main concepts and facts identified by the groups. He gives them a final task related to their data chart: "Now I would like each group to use your text and the data chart you created to design a poster. The posters will be displayed in our classroom to help us recall what we have learned in our study of explorers."

As the student groups get busy creating their posters, they take the concepts and facts from the data chart and use the text for ideas of illustrations they can use on their posters. The result is a colorful display of facts and pictures about the explorer book they have read.

Mr. Velasco then presents another group of books about explorers and says, "Now that you know how to do data charting, you might want to read more about the explorers mentioned in this first book. These books can be read and charted in the same way. When you have read several more books about explorers, we will learn how to use our data charts to write explorer reports."

CONCLUSION

As Mr. Velasco has demonstrated, data charting is an effective way for students to learn to gather and organize important concepts and facts from informational text. By the use of the charting process, analysis of the information being read, and decision making related to choosing the most important aspects of content text, students experience a process that supports their understanding of the whole text. The whole text becomes more cohesive by breaking it into understandable chunks and providing a structure through which connections can be made between the chunks of information gathered. The fact that the data chart provides relatively small boxes in which to write the information gathered discourages the copying of large amounts of text onto the chart. The students quickly learn to write succinct bits of information instead of whole sentences. This naturally supports the needed ability to paraphrase.

REFERENCES

Thompson, G. (1998). *Explorers: Searching for adventure*. Austin, TX: Steck-Vaughn Publishers.

Tompkins, G. (1998). *50 literacy strategies step by step*. Upper Saddle River, NJ: Merrill/Prentice Hall.

27

DRAMA CENTERS

Building Comprehension through Active Processing

Studies have been undertaken that provide information on the relationship between dramatic play and literacy behaviors (Pellegrini & Galda, 1993; Rowe, 1998; Wolf, 1994). Those who advocate for the increased use of classroom drama stress the students' active construction of meaning and their affective engagement in making meaning of text. The use of drama centers in the classroom provides opportunities for more improvisational interaction with text as opposed to the more formal scripting of activities such as reader's theater and play production. At the centers, students are given the opportunity to reenact text that they have previously read, thereby increasing their understanding and comprehension of the reading. They can interpret characters, improvise dialogue, and physicalize the content of text to make it more meaningful to themselves. A variety of forms may be used in drama centers for students. See figure 27.1 for suggested formats for drama centers.

Teachers may choose those forms that are most appropriate for their students, introduce the forms to students in a directive group lesson, and then give students opportunities to explore literature and informational text through reenactment at the drama centers. Students may also be given the opportunity to perform their

FIGURE 27.1
Suggestions for drama center formats.

Narrator–mime	One student retells the story in his/her own words while the other student/s act out the retelling.
What's my mime?	A small group pantomimes the text and other students identify what they are portraying as they act it out.
Character interviews	One student acts as a news reporter and interviews other students who have taken on the various character roles in the selected text. The students being interviewed must respond as the characters they represent.
Mock trial	The character who has caused the conflict in the story is put "on trial" by other students. A mock courtroom scene ensues with lawyers, witnesses, judge, and jury.
Argue–resolve	Students may take sides related to a conflict within the story and debate the issues.
Improvisation	Students assume roles from the story and improvise a retelling of the story using action, dialogue, and props.

text-centered improvisations should they desire to do so. Providing them with a variety of resources at the center further encourages a deeper exploration of the text and motivates students to a higher level of involvement and interpretation.

Step by Step

The steps in implementing drama centers are:

Step 1   Identifying a Dramatization Format

The teacher chooses a piece of literature or informational text that will be used at the drama center. She then selects a dramatization format that best matches the text she has chosen for demonstration purposes.

Step 2   Explaining and Modeling the Format

The teacher explains to the students that they will be working at a center at which they will act out the text they have been reading for the past several days. She enlists the help of several students depending on the requirements of the chosen text and brings them forward to assist with the demonstration. She walks them through the process of reading, stopping to discuss how the text can be acted out, assign roles, and improvise dialogue. She reminds them that there will be materials made available at the center and that they are free to use whatever materials they need to create their reenactment.

Step 3   Making Expectations Clear

The teacher must clearly explain to the students that, though this is a fun activity, certain things must be accomplished at the center to make the activity complete. See figure 27.2 for a drama center expectations chart.

She goes through the list of expectations on the chart and explains clearly what each step of the process requires of the students. She encourages questions from the students to clarify their center tasks.

Step 4   Allowing Time for Creative Play and Practice

The teacher sets aside a time during the day when students have an opportunity to work in small groups at the drama center. This may be done during regular "center time" or during a special time set aside for all the students to work on various proj-

FIGURE 27.2   Drama center expectations chart.

1. Reread the book/text provided.
2. Decide what roles are needed.
3. Assign roles.
4. Discuss actions.
5. Decide if props are needed.
6. Gather any materials needed.
7. Practice the action and dialogue.
8. Work together.
9. Present your work to the teacher.
10. Decide if you want to perform for others.
11. Fill in the feedback form.

ects related to the text being explored. These projects might include working with the provided materials to produce props or minimal costumes to use during the improvisations. Research indicates that in order for students to get maximum results out of the activity, sufficient time must be made available for them to participate in the exploration of the text (Christie, 1990).

STEP 5   PROVIDING OPPORTUNITIES FOR PERFORMANCE

Students may be given the opportunity, on a voluntary basis, to share their improvisations with the rest of the class or others. The teachers may also videotape their reenactment and allow the students to view their own completed project. This provides yet another opportunity for the students to revisit the text and thereby increase their comprehension of the material.

STEP 6   SELF-MONITORING

The teacher explains to the students that they are responsible for completing the feedback form at the end of the activity. She explains the importance of reflecting on whether or not the activity was complete or incomplete. Did the group work well together? Did they accomplish their objective? Did the students discuss the various elements of the story, and did everyone in the group have a clear understanding of the text following the activity? See figure 27.3 for a suggested feedback form.

FIGURE 27.3 Drama center feedback form.

Date: _____

Group Members: _____
_____

Title of Story: _____

We: (check off each one completed)	Problems we had:
☐ 1. Reread the book/text provided	
☐ 2. Decided what roles were needed	
☐ 3. Assigned roles	
☐ 4. Discussed actions	
☐ 5. Decided if props were needed	
☐ 6. Gathered any materials needed	How we solved them:
☐ 7. Practiced the action and dialogue	
☐ 8. Worked together	
☐ 9. Presented our work to the teacher	
☐ 10. Decided if we wanted to perform for others	
☐ 11. Filled in feedback form	
	How well did we understand the story?
	☐ Very well
	☐ OK
	☐ There are still some things some of us are not sure about

APPLICATIONS AND EXAMPLES

For an example of drama center use in a first-grade classroom, see File 27 of the accompanying CD.

Mrs. Cowart's eighth graders have been reading Esther Forbes' (1943) exciting novel tracing the exploits of Johnny Tremain, a young apprentice locksmith during passionate times in Boston just before the Revolutionary War. "Now that we have completed our reading of *Johnny Tremain*," says Mrs. Cowart, "I want you to have a chance to act out your favorite scene from the book. We are going to use our drama center to accomplish this, so pay attention now and let me explain what you can do there. For example, in chapter 5, the scene where Johnny is in court could be presented in several different ways. One person in your group could narrate the chapter while the remaining members choose roles and pantomime the action as it is described. Another way would be for the whole group to pantomime the action and let other class members try to discover what scene you are doing and what is happening in it. A third way would be to choose roles and actually improvise the scene, creating your own dialogue and actions to fit what is happening. You want to work very hard on these scenes because I'm going to be videotaping them for you to look at and, if I have your permission, to show during our next open house for your parents. I'm also hoping that some of you will be willing to present your work to the whole class so we can use that as a review of the contents of the book as well, but I will leave that up to your individual groups."

Mrs. Cowart reviews the chart of expectations (figure 27.2) and reminds them that each group will be completing a self-evaluation form (figure 27.3) at the conclusion of the conclusion of the activity. She also points out the materials available in the center for making props and/or simple costumes.

"These materials will help you clarify your roles and will help others understand what you are trying to convey in the scene," she comments. "So, let's have a lot of fun with this, but remember that what we are trying to do is to clarify his role in the prerevolutionary days and to increase our comprehension and understanding of the activities leading up to the Revolutionary War."

CONCLUSION

Drama centers provide an opportunity to get students actively involved in reading material. By acting out roles and situations they are given multiple exposures to the text on several different levels and at different times. They are provided with an opportunity to explore the problems introduced in books in a relatively low-risk environment. It gives them a chance to analyze the text, calling on life experiences to make choices in voice, action, and connections with others. They can shift viewpoints and step into the shoes of a character, if only for the briefest of time (Wolf, 1994).

REFERENCES

Christie, J. (1990). Dramatic play: A context for meaningful engagement. *The Reading Teacher, 43,* 542–545.

Forbes, E. (1943). *Johnny Tremain.* New York: Bantam Doubleday Dell Books.

Pellegrini, A., & Galda, L. (1993). Ten years after: A reexamination of symbolic play and literary research. *Reading Research Quarterly, 28,* 162–175.

Rowe, D. (1998). The literate potential of book-related dramatic play. *Reading Research Quarterly, 33,* 10–35.

Wolf, S. (1994). Learning to act/acting to learn: Children as actors, critics, and characters in classroom theatre, *Research in the Teaching of English, 28,* 7–41.

28

STORY RETELLING BOXES

Using Props to Reenact Stories

Focus on English Learners

Using props to retell stories provides English learners with experiences using new book language in creating oral presentations.

Story reenactment (Herrell & Jordan, 2004) is a strategy that requires students to retell a story in sequence with the use of simple costumes and/or props. Story retelling boxes are used to store the constumes and/or props students use to retell the story, either by dressing up in costumes and portraying the action or by using small props to retell the story and demonstrate the action. Story reenactment requires students to remember the sequence of the story, use some of the verbal interactions within the story to make characters come alive, and comprehend the main ideas in the story to portray the action.

Teachers can be creative in assembling props for the story retelling boxes. Clay made from flour, salt, and water can be used to construct sturdy props, or flannel figures or laminated pictures with magnetic tape on the back can be used. Reviewing the story to create the list of props needed is a part of the strategy. Students may be involved in choosing the stories for which prop boxes are to be made, listing the props needed, and even creating the props and decorating the boxes. Once the props are created and the stories reenacted, the prop boxes are available for additional retellings and make interesting literacy centers.

STEP BY STEP

The steps in implementing story retelling with prop boxes are:

STEP 1   PRACTICING THE RETELLING OF STORIES

The teacher introduces the concept of story retelling by engaging the whole class or a small group of students in the retelling of a story they have read. He walks the students through the story using the illustrations as prompts and asking, "What happened after that?" to keep the sequence going. If the story being retold fits into a beginning, middle, and end structure, he can help the students to see that dividing the story into the parts, or "scenes," that occur in each section helps them to remember the major events of the story.

STEP 2   ## SUGGESTING OTHER WAYS TO RETELL STORIES

The teacher introduces the concept of story retelling boxes by suggesting that it might be interesting to practice retelling stories in some new ways. He enlists the help of the students in selecting a favorite story from the stories they have read recently. The teacher asks the students to name all the ways they could retell the story. This might include:

- using costumes and acting it out
- using puppets
- using small props
- using mime

STEP 3   ## LISTING THE PROPS AND/OR COSTUMES NEEDED

As a group, the teacher and class decide on one of the approaches from their list. Together they brainstorm a list of simple costumes they would need for the first method. Students are assigned to bring items from home or locate items available in the classroom to put in the costume box. The teacher may want to gather a variety of costume-like pieces from which the students may choose items. He rereads the story, stopping at each page as the class brainstorms all the props needed to tell that part of the story.

STEP 4   ## MAKING PROPS FOR A STORY RETELLING BOX

The teacher makes a batch of flour, salt, and water clay, and the students each choose a prop from the prop list to make from the clay. See figure 28.1 for the recipe for this clay.

After the students have made the props from the clay, they bake the clay and allow it to cool. The props are painted with a mixture of half tempera paint and half Elmer's glue and are allowed to dry. The props are then placed in an appropriately decorated shoebox, and the story retelling box is complete.

STEP 5   ## PRACTICING RETELLING WITH THE PROP BOX

The teacher models the retelling of the story using the small props. Students can make a story retelling board depicting the setting of the story for use in future retellings. After the teacher models the use of the props, students are encouraged to try the

FIGURE 28.1   Recipe for making flour, salt, and water clay for story retelling boxes.

4 cups flour (NOT self rising)
1½ cups water
1 cup salt

Mix ingredients together. Mixture will be stiff.
Knead for 10 minutes.

Make desired shapes, separate by thickness (poke holes in thick pieces).
Bake at 325–350 degrees (½ hour per ¼ inch of thickness)
Cool.

Paint to resemble figures in the storybook.
Use acrylic or tempera paints mixed with Elmer's glue (half and half).

Other suggestions for prop boxes:
Paper doll figures, flannel board figures, magnetic tape on the back of pictures, overhead transparency pictures, actual dress-up clothes, and larger props.

retelling with props. Once students are comfortable using the props, the box is placed in a literacy center for use by all students in retelling the story.

STEP 6   PRACTICING RETELLING WITH THE COSTUME BOX

Once the costumes are collected for the costume box, the teacher gathers a group of students together to retell the story in costume. One student can act as the narrator and the others act out the story in mime, or the students may choose to speak the characters' lines. The teacher places the costume box in the retelling center for use by other students as well.

STEP 7   ADDING OTHER STORY RETELLING BOXES TO THE LITERACY CENTER

As the students read other books, props are made to provide ongoing practice in story retelling. Flannel boards with figures and props cut from felt work well for story retelling boxes. Other possibilities include laminated illustrations with magnetic tape on the back that can be used for retelling on the side of a filing cabinet.

STEP 8   USING STORY RETELLING IN ASSESSMENT

Student comprehension can be assessed by having students use the props to retell a story and evaluating the completeness of their story retelling. See chapter 48 for formats used in scoring story retelling assessments.

APPLICATIONS AND EXAMPLES

 Ms. LeMeisure's second-grade class is involved in story retelling on File 28 of the accompanying CD.

After Mr. Bernard's sixth graders have completed the reading of *The Witch of Blackbird Pond* (Speare, 1958), he wants to get them actively involved in reenacting the story. He assigns small groups to specific chapters in the book and explains the activity. "Each group will reenact the story by creating transparency pictures to use on the overhead projector. The group will decide on the appropriate scenes to use in order to move the story forward. Obviously, you can't include every scene in the book. Select the scenes you need to describe or act out. You will draw and color the pictures on transparency film and cut them apart so that you can move them around on the glass."

"How will we retell the story?" asks Steven.

"That's up to the group," replies Mr. Bernard. "Just make sure that the group works together to select the scenes that are most important to the story. Create the illustrations you need to tell the story and then you can practice retelling your part of the story. Since this book has no illustrations, you will have to read your sections carefully for descriptions of the clothing and people you're drawing. I have a book here that has some pictures of the types of clothing worn during this period of history. You can use that for ideas, too."

The students get together to reread their assigned chapters. They make a list of the illustrations they need and assign people to draw the pictures. Some of the groups plan to present their scenes in dialogue taken from the book. Others will have a narrator and several people from the group to move the illustrations around on the glass. One of the students has a costume at home that she plans to wear to set the tone of the presentation. Another says he has a small stuffed blackbird at home that can be used in retelling the chapter they are preparing. They have lots of good ideas and work busily preparing their scenes.

On the day of the presentations, Mr. Bernard introduces each group and they present their scenes. The students applaud for each group, and Mr. Bernard then explains that the illustrations, props, and costume pieces they have created will be stored in a shoebox in a literacy center. "The overhead projector will be in the center along with the transparencies you made to retell the story. I'll put the illustrations into envelopes with the chapter numbers on them so you can go into the center in small groups and practice retelling the story using the transparency illustrations. During your center time, you may also want to create some illustrations like this for other books you are reading. The materials will be there for you to use."

CONCLUSION

Story retelling prop boxes are helpful to support students as they become more proficient in retelling stories. The use of props is often motivational. Some students are eager to dress up in costume and take a role, but others find the use of small props much less intimidating. Having a variety of ways to make the props is important. Some students are good at making clay props, while others like to draw their props. Retelling entire stories requires that students identify the main ideas and themes in a story and choose the scenes most pertinent to the story. Story retelling is also good oral language practice. Students tend to use a lot of the language from the book as they retell stories, and this often expands their spoken vocabulary and gives them practice in using a greater variety of words.

REFERENCES

Herrell, A., Jordan, M. (2004). *Fifty strategies for teaching English language learners* (2nd ed.). Saddle River, NJ: Merrill/Prentice Hall.

Speare, E. G. (1958). *The witch of blackbird pond*. New York: Dell.

SCRIPT WRITING

Investigating and Analyzing Text

Focus on English Learners

Script writing provides English learners with opportunities to discuss the meaning of text and create dialogue based upon a storyline.

Script writing involves the careful examination of text in order to translate it into interactive material suitable for theatrical presentation. It supports comprehension by encouraging students to carefully analyze the words in a text, deciding which words can be translated into dialogue, which words can be spoken by a narrator, and which words are best illustrated through actions.

Placing students in small heterogeneous groups provides an ideal situation to accomplish script writing. It adds the benefit of verbal interactions among several readers discussing the contextual meaning of words and possible ways of translating them into a script format. Considerable research supports the importance of this type of interaction. Verbal discourse plays a vital role in the development of language skills, especially among English language learners. The small, heterogeneous group offers rich opportunities for these exchanges.

Students discuss setting and interactions among characters, formulate actions and reactions, and design props when necessary. The entire process serves to deepen understanding of both the original text and the importance of understanding characters, time sequences, and actions and their impact on the plot.

Based on their newly discovered understandings of the characters' expressed thoughts and agendas, groups may be encouraged to explore possibilities for alternative solutions or outcomes of the conflicts and dilemmas presented in the text. Moving students to this higher level of thinking is a natural outgrowth of their increased understanding and comprehension gained through the text analysis and verbal interaction of the group script-writing process.

STEP BY STEP

The steps in teaching script writing are:

STEP 1   CHOOSING THE TEXT

The teacher selects reading material that offers students opportunities to analyze interactions among the characters, to translate active verbs into stage directions and movement for the performers, and to investigate and illuminate problematic situations. The selection might often include instructional textual material, poetry,

Primary-Level Books

Title	Author
Frederick	Leo Lionni
Something from Nothing	Phoebe Gilman
Stone Soup	Marcia Brown
Ira Sleeps Over	Bernard Waber
Who Will Help?	Rozanne Williams (adaptation)

Also traditional folktales such as:

Jack and the Beanstalk
Little Red Riding Hood
The Three Bears
Little Red Hen
Cinderella

Upper-Grade-Level Books

Bridge to Terabithia	Katherine Paterson
The Sign of the Beaver	Elizabeth George Speare
The Giver	Lois Lowry
Catherine Called Birdy	Karen Cushman
Onion John	Joseph Krumguld
Island of the Blue Dolphins	Scott Odell
Holes	Louis Sachar

Secondary-Grade-Level Books

Most novels being read at this level can be scripted. It is suggested that the class begin with scripting scenes and then connect the scenes into larger productions.

and music. It may contain unfamiliar language and/or vocabulary to challenge students and to give them the opportunity to explore language in an unfamiliar context. See figure 29.1 for examples of text appropriate for beginning script-writing experiences.

Step 2   Reading and Discussing the Text

Depending on students' reading levels, the text is read aloud by the teacher, read independently, or read in small groups by the students. When they finish reading, students engage in a grand conversation relating to the setting, characters, and plot. In this way, students prepare to write their scripts.

Step 3   Modeling the Writing of a Script

The teacher walks through the steps used to translate the text into script form.

1. Identify the characters by creating a chart of characters with a listing of their attributes based on information gained from the text, prior knowledge, and their role in the scenario.
2. Identify dialogue in the text that is directly transferable and place it into the correct script format. See figure 29.2 for an example of translating dialogue to script format.
3. Identify actions in the text that translate into expression and/or stage movement. After these actions are identified, discuss the need for specific directions related to exactly how, when, and where characters would move on the stage.

FIGURE 29.2 Model script describing process.

Step 1 *Convert text to script format.* This model is based on *Make Way for Ducklings* (McCloskey, 1941).

Text:

Mr. and Mrs. Mallard were looking for a place to live. But every time Mr. Mallard saw what looked like a nice place, Mrs. Mallard said it was no good. There were sure to be foxes in the woods or turtles in the water, and she was not going to raise a family where there might be foxes or turtles. So they flew on and on.

Script:

NARRATOR: Mr. and Mrs. Mallard were looking for a place to live.

MR. MALLARD: This looks like a good place.

MRS. MALLARD: No, there might be foxes or turtles in the woods. I can't raise a family with foxes or turtles nearby. They might eat our eggs or babies.

Step 2 Add stage directions.

Script:

(Mr. and Mrs. Mallard enter stage left. They flap their wings and look from side to side as they move to center stage.)

NARRATOR: Mr. and Mrs. Mallard are looking for a place to live.

MR. MALLARD: *(Pointing stage right with his right wing)* This looks like a good place.

MRS. MALLARD: *(Shaking her head from side to side)* No, there might be foxes or turtles in the woods. I can't raise a family with foxes or turtles nearby. They might eat our eggs or babies. *(She turns left and flaps her wings as she moves stage left. Mr. Mallard turns and follows her.)*

Step 3 Heighten conflict in dialogue and action.

Script additions to heighten conflict:

(Mr. and Mrs. Mallard enter stage left. They flap their wings and look from side to side as they move center stage.)

NARRATOR: Mr. and Mrs. Mallard are looking for a place to live.

MR. MALLARD: *(Pointing stage right with his right wing* **and nodding his head vigorously***)* This looks like a **great place to live. Look at all the big trees and blue ponds.**

MRS. MALLARD: *(Shaking her head from side to side* **and placing her wings on her hips***)* No, Mr. Mallard. This is NOT a great place! There might be foxes or turtles in the woods. I simply CAN'T raise a family with foxes or turtles nearby. *(She stamps her right foot)* They might eat our eggs or babies. *(She turns and flaps her wings as she moves stage left.)*

MR. MALLARD: *(turns and follows her shaking his head.)* We'll NEVER find a place to live!

4. Teach basic stage directions and translate identified actions into stage directions within the script. See figure 29.3 for a description of basic stage directions and a teaching activity.
5. Place the actions into the proper stage-directions format within the script. See figure 29.2 for an example of translating actions to stage directions.

FIGURE 29.3   Basic stage directions.

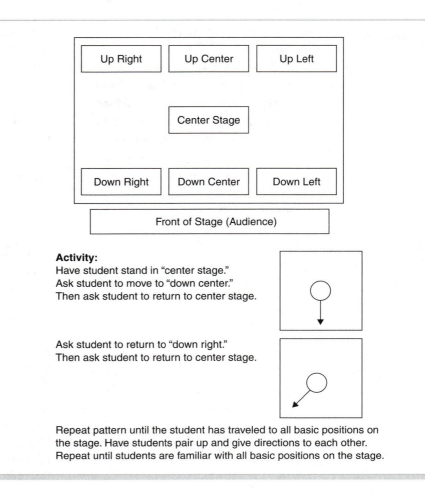

6. Identify and discuss conflicts within the text: conflict between the character(s) and nature, between the character(s) and society, between characters, or within a character (Tompkins, 2000). Discuss with students the importance of conflict in conveying the ideas and agendas of the text. Refer students back to the model script to identify and enhance, if necessary, the evident conflict. Conflict may be enhanced by adding stronger words (verbs, adverbs, adjectives, etc.) and/or action(s) to the existing dialogue and stage directions. See figure 29.2 for examples of heightened conflict in dialogue and action.

STEP 4   SELECTING THE APPROPRIATE METHOD OF ENACTMENT

Depending on the developmental level of the students and their background related to theatrical performance, the appropriate level of enactment might vary from something as simple as reader's theatre (see chapter 30) to a more elaborate, fully staged production. See figure 29.4 for examples of methods of enacting the script.

STEP 5   GROUPING THE STUDENTS FOR SCRIPT WRITING

First of all, the groups should be small enough so that everyone can participate in script writing. The use of assigned tasks within the group may be used to facilitate the process. According to Cohen (1994), "The use of roles alleviates problems of nonparticipation or domination by one member" (p. 87). For example, one student

FIGURE 29.4   Production formats.

Format	Positive Factors	Considerations
Reader's Theatre	Minimal preparation time	Individual reading levels
	Extensive group participation	
	No memorization necessary	
	Opportunity for individualization of parts	
Puppet Plays	Shy children tend to participate more freely	Puppet creation takes time
	Integrates art and visual creativity	May need a puppet stage
	Puppets can be reused in a variety of plays	
Video Productions	Students can view and critique their performances	Equipment needed
	Copies of tapes can be shared with parents	
Minimally Staged Productions	Few props and costumes needed	Time for creation of props/costumes
	Time commitment is minimal	
Fully Staged Production	Students find it easier to assume roles and	Time commitment is heavy
	develop characters fully	Additional costs

might serve as a facilitator to keep the group on track and refer them to the model script when the group is straying off task or is stalled in the creative process. Another member of the group might serve as a recorder to write down the actual dialogue and stage directions produced by the group. The number of assigned tasks used within a group might be the deciding factor in determining the size of the group, but not necessarily. Each member of the group may be assigned a crucial role in the scriptwriting process so that all students are an essential part of the undertaking and all are contributing to the final product at their individual level. Additional task assignments might include:

1. Materials manager—gathers materials the group needs to create props, scenery, and costumes.
2. Illustrator—creates figures and illustrations needed to convey the visual effects of the script. This student might, for instance, design the set and/or set pieces, costumes, and lighting.
3. Reader—reads the text aloud to provide the model for the script being written.

When assigning tasks within the group, the teacher must make sure that members understand what each member of the group has been assigned to do and that all students have the authority to carry out their duties.

STEP 6   MOVING THE SCRIPT FROM THE PAGE TO THE STAGE

Groups must be given time to follow the procedures that have been modeled in the script-writing process. This may (and usually does) require that longer blocks of time be allotted within the daily schedule. During the time the teacher becomes a group facilitator, assisting groups in the writing procedure, she must take care to refrain from interfering in the creative process in which the students are engaged. The teacher has delegated the authority for writing the script to the individual groups and now must step back and allow the process to evolve. Students should not be turning to the teacher for constant direction and assistance, but should use the existing skills

FIGURE 29.5
Appropriate teacher
interventions during group
work.

Problem	Intervention
A group is having trouble getting organized.	Remind them of the rules and roles. Suggest that the facilitator discuss what needs to be done. Make a list. Prioritize the list. Assign duties. Remind them you will be back to hear results of discussion.
A group gets stuck on a problem.	Ask open-ended questions to redirect group discussion. Leave the group to discuss the questions.
Group is not sharing materials cooperatively.	Ask them to review cooperative norms. Have them discuss conclusions and decide what they should do about it. Tell them you will return to hear their decisions.
Group is struggling with difficult text.	Point out key parts. Check for understanding of what is being asked. Fill in missing parts of their knowledge only to the point necessary for them to move on.
Group has not read directions.	Tell them not to touch the materials until they can tell you what they are supposed to be doing. Give them time to read the directions. Return and ask them to verbalize the task.
Group finishes early.	"Open" the task further by asking for additional analysis. For example: *Is there another way to . . . ? How can you apply this to . . . ?*

Source: Adapted from E. Cohen, 1994, *Designing Groupwork*, New York: Teachers College Press.

within their own group. The teacher's role is to remind students of the need for interacting with their peers and for returning to the task at hand as quickly as possible. During this time the teacher also monitors group progress and makes mental or written notes about individual contributions that can be shared later with the whole class. See figure 29.5 for appropriate teacher interventions during group work.

STEP 7   REPORTING OUT—A TIME FOR SHARING

This is a time for the students to share their script and to reflect on the group writing interactions. Students may explain the steps followed during the creation of the script and some of the challenges they faced during the activity. They may field questions from fellow students related to the group accomplishment. The teacher may use this as an opportunity to report on successes achieved during the writing. She may assign status to individuals for specific task-related accomplishments or recognize groups for their problem-solving approaches. Difficulties observed during the group work might also be addressed at this time, either on an individual group basis or for the class as a whole.

APPLICATIONS AND EXAMPLES

Mr. Gustar introduces script writing to his seventh-grade on File 29 of the accompanying CD.

Ms. McCloskey's kindergarten class is listening to her read *Where the Wild Things Are* by Maurice Sendak (1963). As she finishes reading the book, Ms. McCloskey asks the children, "Who are the characters in this book?"

Jeremy raises his hand quickly and says, "Max is the little boy."

Ms. McCloskey smiles and nods her head. "You are right, Jeremy. Max is the little boy in the story." She writes the word *Max* on the white board. "Who else is in this story?"

Maria raises her hand very tentatively. "His mother tells him he is a wild thing."

"Yes," replies Ms. McCloskey. "Max's mother is in the story, too." She writes *Max's mother* on the white board next to the word *Max*.

"There are wild things in the story!" states Chan emphatically.

"You are right, Chan," replies Ms. McCloskey. "How many wild things are in the story? Let's count them."

The students count aloud with Ms. McCloskey as she shows the pictures in the storybook, and the students agree that they see five different wild things in the pictures. Ms. McCloskey adds *Five wild things* to the list of characters on the white board.

"We can write a play about Max and the wild things," suggests Ms. McCloskey. "Then we can make puppets and act out our play."

"Yeah! Puppets!" the students respond.

Ms. McCloskey reads the first two pages of the book again and asks the students to tell her what is happening.

"Max has a wolf suit on and he's acting like a wild thing," says Juanita.

"Yes, that's what is happening," replies Ms. McCloskey. "We can have someone say that in our play so that everyone will understand what is happening. Ms. McCloskey stands and writes on a large piece of chart paper with a marker. As she writes Juanita's words, she sounds them out so the students can see the connection between the sounds she is making and letters she is writing.

"Let's read this together," Ms. McCloskey says. "The first word is *NARRATOR*. That's someone who tells the story while the puppets act it out." The students read along with her as she moves her hand along under the words. "Max has a wolf suit on and he's acting like a wild thing."

"Why didn't we read the first word?" asks Jeremy.

"That word just tells us who is talking," Ms. McCloskey says as she points to the word *NARRATOR*. "One of you will be the narrator and this word tells you that it's your turn to talk."

"What do you think Max is saying as he acts like a wild thing?" asks Ms. McCloskey.

"Gr-r-r," says Sandra.

"We'll write Max's words like this," says Ms. McCloskey as she writes, "MAX: Gr-r-r," on the chart paper.

Ms. McCloskey walks the students through the story, taking their dictation as they retell the story and modeling the writing of the script. The students get many chances to reread the words she writes as they decide what to write next. Because the wild things don't actually talk in the text, the students are imaginative in creating unique sounds for each of the five wild things.

Their completed script looks like this:

NARRATOR: Max has a wolf suit on and he's acting like a wild thing.

MAX: Gr-r-r

MOTHER: Wild thing!

MAX: I'll eat you up!

MOTHER: That's it. You're going to bed without any supper!

NARRATOR: That night a forest grew in Max's room. The trees and vines got really big and an ocean came by. Max got into a boat.

MAX: I'll sail away for days and days and weeks and weeks.

NARRATOR: Max came to the place where the wild things are.

WILD THING 1:   Aaaaaaaaaaarrrrrrrrgggghhhhhh! Aaaaaaaaaaarrrrrrrrgggghhhhhh!

WILD THING 2:   Screetch! Screetch!

WILD THING 3:   OOOOOOOOOOOOOOh-h-h-!

WILD THING 4:   Whoooooooooooooo-o-o!

WILD THING 5:   Brrrrrraaaaaaaapppppppp! Brrrrrraaaaaaaapppppppp!

MAX: BE STILL!

NARRATOR: The wild things were scared and they stopped making noise. They made Max the king.

MAX: Let the rumpus begin!

NARRATOR: The wild things and Max danced and climbed and made lots of noise. But soon Max was tired and wanted to go back home.

MAX: I will go back home now.

WILD THINGS: Oh no! We love you so!

NARRATOR: But Max got into his boat and sailed home. When he got to his room he found a surprise.

MAX: My dinner! And it's still hot!

Once the class finishes writing the script, the students make stick puppets for the characters and Ms. McCloskey prints the script on a piece of paper and makes copies to attach to the backs of the puppets. The students take turns playing the different parts in the play. They read and reread the script as they play with the puppets and act out the story. Ms. McCloskey also notices the students rereading the script from the large chart, pointing to the words with a yardstick as they read. See figure 29.6 to see the way Ms. McCloskey attaches the scripts to encourage the rereading of the script.

FIGURE 29.6 Stick puppet with script attached.

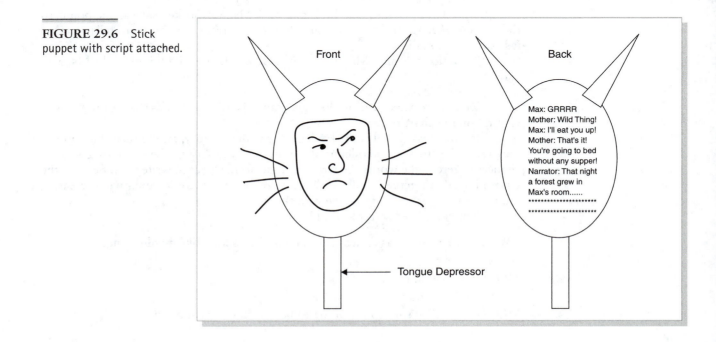

CONCLUSION

Ms. McCloskey has found that the use of script writing enhances her students' comprehension and enjoyment of reading. The students examine the text carefully in the process of writing scripts. Because Ms. McCloskey's students are not actually reading and writing independently, she reads the book aloud and takes the students' dictation as they write the script. This kindergarten example demonstrates that even 5-year-olds can be engaged in script writing and benefit from the experience. Older students benefit from careful examination of the text and the translation of the story into dialogue, movement, and conflict. Although it is not always necessary to take script writing on to the next step—production of the script, doing so adds more opportunities for reading and translating the words into actions and dialogue. Thus, it further expands the comprehension process.

REFERENCES

Cohen, E. (1994). *Designing groupwork*. New York: Teachers College Press.

McCloskey, R. (1941). *Make way for ducklings*. New York: Penguin Putnam.

Sendak, M. (1963). *Where the wild things are*. New York: HarperCollins.

Tompkins, G. (2000). *Literacy for the 21st century*. Upper Saddle River, NJ: Merrill/Prentice Hall.

30

READER'S THEATRE

Using Active-Reading Processes to Enhance Comprehension

Involving students with enjoyable and exciting active-reading procedures provides the key to fluency and higher levels of comprehension gained through a natural process of repeated readings and interactive transactions with language. A natural and fun process for providing students with these interactions is a strategy of theatrical interpretations of valued text commonly referred to as *reader's theatre*.

Reader's theatre is an interpretive presentation of text by a group of readers in a nonthreatening, controlled, and prepared setting. Typically, a group of students reads prepared scripts of interesting and important literature and/or curricular materials. These readings provide students with an opportunity to explore the text itself and to become involved with the process of rehearsal and repeated readings, thereby increasing fluency and comprehension.

The method of presentation in the classroom may vary greatly in relation to the confines and capabilities of the setting itself. Students may sit or stand, in formal or informal arrangements, communicating primarily through the use of vocal inflection, gestures, and facial expressions. Scripts are written so that as many students as possible are involved in the presentation singly, in pairs, or in small groups. Those not directly involved become the audience members whose listening skills can be emphasized and reinforced to enhance their later involvement in the presentation.

Reader's theatre provides classroom teachers with an opportunity to involve students with an interactive, interpretive process without the constraints of typical theatrical endeavors involving elaborate props, costumes, memorization of lines, lengthy rehearsals, and scenery. Although these elements are not entirely necessary for the success of the presentations, the use of minimal props and costumes might enhance the students' interest and enjoyment of the process. The creation of such additional elements can be used to give students not directly involved in the presentation an opportunity to display individual creative skills.

Reader's theatre need not be limited to stories or literature, but might include appropriate works of poetry, music, informational content, or character and civic education themes. See figure 30.1 for suggested uses of reader's theatre.

FIGURE 30.1 Suggested uses of reader's theatre.

Categories	Focus	Special Considerations
Narrative Stories	Vocabulary	Adapting for student reading levels
	Sequencing events	Writing narration to clarify action
	Characterization	Practicing to develop fluency and expression
	Fluency and comprehension	
	Self-discovery	
Informational Text	Writing	Researching
	Grasping "big ideas"	Summarizing
	Fluency and comprehension	Scripting
Poetry	Vocabulary	Practicing to develop fluency and expression
	Poetic structure	Understanding poetic rhythm
	Fluency and comprehension	
	Appreciation of poetic language	
Culminating Activity	Reviewing concepts	Scripting to include major concepts
	Script writing	Locating related poetry, music, and visuals
	Related forms of text	
	Fluency and comprehension	
Literature	Adaptation for student reading levels	Practicing to develop fluency and expression
	Interpretation	Adapting for student reading levels
	Vocabulary	Interpreting universal human themes
	Fluency and comprehension	Examining parallels with contemporary problems
		Staying true to author's intent

STEP BY STEP

The steps in implementing reader's theatre are:

STEP 1 CHOOSING THE TEXT

The teacher may draw text from materials that fulfill requirements of the classroom curriculum, but it should contain elements of high interest to students. The selection should not necessarily be limited to literature; it might also include instructional textual material, poetry, and music. The text may contain unfamiliar language and/or vocabulary to challenge students and to give them the opportunity to explore language in an unfamiliar context. Reader's theatre offers a nonthreatening and supportive environment for students to practice repeated reading and develop the fluency so vital to increased comprehension.

STEP 2 WRITING THE SCRIPT

Although commercially produced reader's theatre scripts are readily available, they are not difficult to write and students benefit greatly when involved in the writing project. The process is simplified somewhat when the teacher chooses text that contains direct dialogue, necessitating only minor interjection of narration to clarify the

FIGURE 30.2   Converting text to reader's theatre scripts.

Test as It Appears	Scripted Version
Direct conversion:	
"A stone?" said the little old lady. "What will you do with a stone? You cannot eat a stone!"	
"Ah," said the young man. "I can make soup from a stone."	
Now the little old lady had never heard of that. Make soup from a stone? Fancy that.	

From:
Stone Soup by Ann McGovern (1968)

Text as It Appears	Scripted Version
Adapted conversion:	
Now, one day the king announced that he would give a ball and that all the ladies of the land were invited.	
Cinderella's stepsisters set about choosing what they would wear.	
All day they ordered Cinderella around as they made their preparations.	

From:
Cinder Edna by Ellen Jackson (1994)

story action. The characters of the presentation must first be identified, and their dialogue is taken directly from the text. The amplification of the story through narration is a good way to challenge strong readers; the story line may even be divided between two narrators. The dialogue should be adapted to the appropriate age level of the students with consideration given to providing a variety of skill levels to meet the needs of individual students. The goal should always be one of creating a high degree of success for those students involved in the presentation. See figure 30.2 for examples on converting text to scripts.

STEP 3   PREPARING THE SCRIPTS

Scripts may be attached to the inside of simple file folders for added strength. This protects the scripts and makes it easier for students to handle them during the presentation. One folder is created for each character. The folder contains the entire script with the lines of the individual character highlighted with a neon marker. The highlighting helps students in following the dialogue. Two copies of each script should be made so that students have the opportunity to take one home for individual study and rehearsal. See figure 30.3 for a portion of a script.

STEP 4   ORGANIZING FOR PRESENTATION

The class may be introduced to presentation skills through a whole-class-participation exercise. For the purpose of skill building, scripts are distributed containing a two- or three-character story or a simple poem with parts highlighted in

FIGURE 30.3 Example of highlighted script.

> **One Misty, Moisty Morning**
>
> **Highlighted for girls' part:**
>
> Girls: One misty, moisty morning,
>
> Boys: When cloudy was the weather,
>
> Girls: I chanced to meet an old man,
>
> Boys: Clothed all in leather.
>
> Girls: He began to compliment
>
> Boys: And I began to grin,
>
> Girls: How do you do?
>
> Boys: And how do you do?
>
> ALL: And how do you do again?
>
> *Anonymous*

different colored neon markers. Students are divided into groups according to highlighting colors and instructed to read in chorus only those parts highlighted in their assigned color. Through appropriate teacher modeling, students are encouraged to engage in expressive reading. After a few repetitions, the students will develop the skills necessary to successfully participate in reader's theatre presentations. The class is then divided into appropriately-sized heterogeneous groups, depending on the requirements of the chosen scripts. Roles are preassigned in each group based on the needs of the students, and scripts are distributed accordingly.

Daily practice times are a necessary part of the success of reader's theatre presentations. Students need to be given time on a regular basis to read, reread, and discuss their presentations. Additional time may be given for the production of minimal props, costumes, and sets if these are to be included in the presentation. If all groups are presenting the same material, then the production of props and related materials is divided among the groups, thereby creating a shared workload and more efficient use of time.

STEP 5   PRESENTING READER'S THEATRE

Students may stand or sit in the presentation area, carrying scripts in hand. The actual style of presentation may be relatively free-flowing or may be carefully orchestrated. A more free-flowing presentation might resemble an expressive extemporaneous reading in a small group. A more carefully orchestrated reading provides students with specific instructions on movement, positioning, or style of presentation. If sitting, characters may stand for their readings and sit when not reading. If standing, they may step forward for readings and then return to their original position when not reading. The narrator(s) are usually located on the extremities of the group and offer amplification of the story to the character readings.

Students who are not participating in the actual presentation are participating as audience members. They must be instructed on the roles and expectations of being good active listeners. The teacher prepares students to develop an understanding of the important role that an audience plays in a presentation along with appropriate etiquette and behavior expectations. It is also important to introduce a real audience to the presentation. Be sure to invite administrators, parents, and other classes to view the group's work. The anticipation of presenting to a real audience increases the importance of practice readings to the students, elevating them to the level of rehearsals for public performance. Students take a great deal of pride in their efforts and should be allowed to share their accomplishments with a broader audience.

STEP 6   CONTINUING THE LEARNING

Following the presentation, students return to their theatre groups to discuss their experiences and insights gained through active participation in the presentation of contextual material. The discussion should focus on such areas as:

- the meaning of the text in relation to the role of the characters
- new vocabulary
- interaction of the material presented with other curricular areas
- changes in previously held ideas about the text

The groups are then brought together for a broader discussion in which students are asked to compare and contrast their outcomes and understandings gained through participation in the activity.

Scripts, props, and costumes are gathered together and placed in a literacy center. Here, students can continue repeated readings and reenactments, exchanging roles and obtaining new understandings and insights while increasing fluency and comprehension.

APPLICATIONS AND EXAMPLES

See File 30 of the accompanying CD for an example of reader's theatre in a third-grade unit on weather.

Mrs. Arenas's eighth-grade social studies class is studying the United States Constitution. Because several of her students read below eighth-grade level, she is concerned that they will not be able to understand the language of the document and the history related to its origin. As she is planning the Constitution study, she looks for books that are easy to read and give interesting information about the events leading up to the Constitutional Congress and the lives of the men who were involved in writing the Constitution. As a culminating event, Mrs. Arenas plans to involve her students in the writing and presentation of a reader's theatre script that reviews all that the students have learned.

As a whole group the class reads chapters from *A History of US* (Hakim, 1993) and discusses the beginning of the formation of the American government. They build a time line that identifies the vital sequence of events between the end of the American Revolution and the beginning of the third Constitutional Congress. Once the time line is complete, the class generates a KWL chart (see chapter 25) about the writing of the Constitution. The information students want to know includes:

- Why was a Constitution necessary?
- Why was a convention needed to write the Constitution?
- Who were the delegates to the convention?
- How were they chosen?
- How long did it take to write the Constitution?
- What problems did the delegates encounter?
- How has the Constitution changed since it was originally written?

After this preliminary work, Mrs. Arenas assigns the students to collaborative reading groups and gives students in the groups different books about the Constitution, written at appropriate reading levels for the students. The groups are given time each day to read their books, discuss what they are reading, and complete the LEARNED section of their KWL charts based on what they are finding. Once the groups have completed their reading tasks, students are called together to share what they have learned and to work on the reader's theatre script for their culminating activity.

"We will need a narrator to tell the story," suggests Joann. "We can have the delegates speak for themselves but we'll need someone to connect the pieces."

"I think you are right," replies Mrs. Arenas. "We may even need more than one narrator."

"I have a great idea," chimes Raymond. "Since women, blacks, and Native Americans were all left out of the process, maybe we can have narrators who tell the story from the white man's perspective, the woman's perspective, the black perspective, and the Native American perspective."

"It's also important to explain why the states had decided to have a Constitution linking them together as United States," added Luis.

"I really didn't understand that," admits Pieturo. "They had the Articles of Confederation. Why did they need a Constitution?"

"There were things that weren't working," replies Marcos. "The states didn't have the authority to collect the taxes from their citizens. No one was taking the states' powers seriously."

The discussion of the issues surrounding the Constitutional Convention brings out an interesting discussion, and the class agrees on a format for the reader's theatre script. Each group is assigned a scene to write, and the students reconvene their groups to work on their assigned scenes. Because the groups have a number of different resources to study in creating their scripts, they discover personal stories about the delegates and create some exciting verbal interchanges among the delegates. The group writing the scene demonstrating the length of time it took to bring the delegates together introduces several delightful sequences. James Madison, the first delegate, arrived 11 days early. Patrick Henry stayed at home stating that he "smelt a rat" (Fritz, 1987) and refused to attend. George Washington arrived with a headache and upset stomach, and the first meeting had to be adjourned because only two states were represented. By using a large calendar prop, the students show the passage of time.

The students present their reader's theatre production to a group of parents and administrators as the culmination of their study. Mrs. Arenas invites the other eighth-grade social studies classes to attend the production the next day, since the first performance is such a rousing success. The unit test she gives on the Constitution unit proves successful, too. The students not only are able to explain the language of the Constitution, they are familiar with the three branches of government because of the discussions included in the reader's theatre production and the reading they did to write the script.

Raymond's idea about presenting the perspectives of the nonrepresented groups proves to be popular and helps students to understand the need for the constitutional amendments. After the completion of the unit, Mrs. Arenas asks the students to discuss what they have learned.

"I never knew there was so much controversy about the Constitution," says Marcos. "I always pictured a group of old men sitting down one afternoon and writing this paper."

"Most people think of it in exactly that way," replies Mrs. Arenas. "What did you find the most helpful in what we did?"

"All the different books we used helped me," says Joann. "They each gave us a little bit of information, but we had to talk to each other to get the whole picture."

"Working as a group and talking about the questions helped me to understand it all better," says Raymond. "My book, *Shh! We're Writing the Constitution* [Fritz, 1987] was pretty easy but it had some of the best information in it. I really didn't understand the words in the Constitution itself until we started reading about the problems they had agreeing on things. Then the words made more sense."

"I liked the part where we had to find some of the actual words the men spoke in order to create dialogue for our script," says Theresa. "I never knew that we had so much information about what went on at the convention. That was a long time ago. It shows me how important it is to have a historian. James Madison was very wise to write down all the conversation that took place."

Mrs. Arenas is pleased with the increased comprehension displayed by her students in their study of the Constitution. The students developed a new repertoire of skills for understanding and interpreting text. She immediately begins planning other ways to include reader's theatre into her curriculum.

CONCLUSION

As Mrs. Arenas demonstrated with her reader's theatre project, students benefit from presenting material orally and writing scripts. To present material fluently, students must read it many times. To present it expressively they must understand the meaning of the words they are speaking. To write a script, students must examine closely the texts on which they base the script. Working in groups provides opportunities for discussion of word meanings, the best way to express ideas, and the logical sequence in which to present events. All of these experiences work toward increasing reading comprehension.

Students from a variety of diverse backgrounds and age levels can be given the opportunity to experience repeated readings of text, exploration of characterization and expression, discovery and illumination of new vocabulary, and event sequencing through reader's theatre presentations and script writing. These activities lead to and strengthen reading, oral fluency, and comprehension.

REFERENCES

Fritz, J. (1987). *Shh! We're writing the Constitution.* New York: G. P. Putnam's Sons.

Hakim, J. (1993). *A history of US: From colonies to country* (vol. 3). New York: Oxford University Press.

Jackson, E. (1994). *Cinder Edna.* New York: Lothrop, Lee & Shepard Books.

McGovern, A. (1968). *Stone soup.* New York: Scholastic.

SUGGESTED READING

Martinez, M., Roser, N., & Strecker, S. (1999). I never thought I could be a star: A reader's theatre ticket to fluency. *The Reading Teacher, 52*(4), 326–334.

Tompkins, G. E. (2000). *Literacy for the twenty-first century.* Upper Saddle River, NJ: Merrill/Prentice Hall.

Worthy, J., and Broaddus, K. (2002). Fluency beyond the primary grades: From group performance to silent, independent reading. *The Reading Teacher, 55*, 334–343.

31

STORY STRUCTURE STUDIES

Recognizing and Building on Narrative Story Elements

<table>
<tr><td>

Focus on English Learners

Providing a predictable structure for text assists English learners in making more accurate predictions and provides a comfortable "scaffold" for making reading more comprehensible.

</td></tr>
</table>

Teaching students the elements of narrative stories enables them to integrate the narrative being read into a predictable structure. If they understand that certain stories follow a predictable pattern such as beginning, middle, and end, each containing predictable elements, their ability to comprehend the story and even write stories following the pattern is greatly increased (Tompkins, 2000).

Students must recognize that not all stories follow the beginning, middle, and end pattern. Several standard patterns must be introduced, explained, and experienced before students can begin to look for patterns and predictable events in stories they read. Direct instruction of story structures is valuable in supporting students' comprehension, but students also must recognize that some stories may veer from the standard structure.

Learning to recognize story structure and the common elements of characters, setting, problem, details, and problem resolution will serve students well in their ability to understand and remember the whole story, the main idea, and supporting details (Davidson, 1982).

STEP BY STEP

The steps in implementing story structure instruction are:

STEP 1 SELECTING A STORY STRUCTURE AND EXEMPLARY BOOK

The teacher chooses a story structure to be studied and chooses a book that serves as a good example of the structure. See figure 31.1 for the three main story structures and example books that can be used with elementary school students.

FIGURE 31.1 Basic story structure books.

Beginning, Middle, and End	Circular	Cumulative
Wilfred Gordon McDonald Partridge By Mem Fox	If You Give a Mouse a Cookie By Laura Numeroff	The Napping House By Audrey Wood
Grandpa's Teeth By Robert Clement	If You Give a Moose a Muffin By Laura Numeroff	This Is the House That Jack Built By Pam Adams

STEP 2   ## READING AND DISCUSSING THE BOOK

The teacher reads the chosen book aloud, discussing the illustrations and events as a part of the presentation.

STEP 3   ## TEACHING THE STRUCTURE AND ELEMENTS OF THE STORY

The teacher introduces the structure of the story and returns to the book to illustrate the main elements. Depending on the structure being taught, the following elements should be explained and illustrated by returning to the text and reading the parts that exemplify each of the elements.

Beginning, Middle, and End Structure

The characters, the setting, and the problem are introduced in the beginning.

The problem gets worse, or more interesting, and we learn more about the characters in the middle.

The problem is resolved in the end.

Circular Structure

The story begins and ends at the same point.

As the story progresses, it moves from point to point until it ends up where it began.

There is a logical connection between each segment in the story.

Cumulative Structure

The story builds in a cumulative fashion, piece by piece.

When new pieces are introduced, they are added to the existing structure and then repeated each time another new piece is added.

STEP 4   ## RETELLING THE STORY WITH THE USE OF A GRAPHIC ORGANIZER

The teacher supports the students in retelling the story, using a graphic organizer to enable the students to visually picture the story's structure. As each part of the story is retold, the organizer is constructed using the events, characters, and elements of the story. See figure 31.2 for sample graphic organizers that support narrative story structures.

FIGURE 31.2 Story structure graphic organizers.

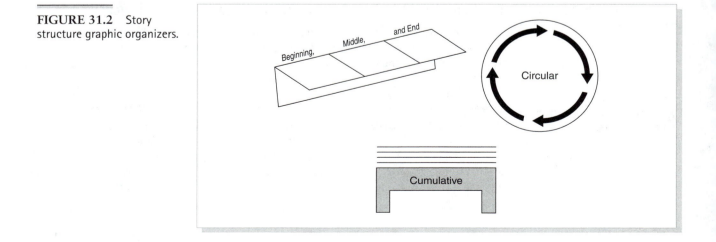

STEP 5   EXTENDING STUDENTS' UNDERSTANDING OF NARRATIVE STRUCTURE

The teacher uses the narrative story structure graphics that were introduced in the lesson to provide additional practice in the identification of key elements of the story. This can be done in a literacy center where blank story structure forms are available for students to use in writing the main elements of selected stories (see figure 31.2). The forms can be used to aid oral retelling of the main elements of selected stories, using a tape recorder. A pocket chart activity can be used to support students' practice of retelling stories. The teacher and students build the graphic by placing the sentence strips into the correct sequence, including them in the graphic format to represent the story structure. In all cases, the story being graphically represented should first be read and discussed.

APPLICATIONS AND EXAMPLES

File 31 of the accompanying CD shows the use of story structure study in a sixth-grade remedial reading class.

As Ms. Frederick reads aloud *Wilfred Gordon McDonald Partridge* by Mem Fox, she stops periodically to discuss Julie Vivas's colorful illustrations and to make sure that her second-grade students are understanding the story. When she finishes reading the book, Ms. Frederick asks, "How do you think authors decide what things to put into their stories?"

"You have to have characters," states Jeremy seriously.

"Yes, Jeremy," responds Ms. Frederick. "You are right. When does the author introduce the characters in the book?"

"You almost always meet the main character right away," says Barbie. "Like in this book. We met Wilfred Gordon on the first page."

"Yes, we did," replies Ms. Frederick. As she says this, she takes out a large piece of construction paper and folds it in half lengthwise. "If I fold this piece of paper in half and then again into three sections, thirds, I can show you how Mem Fox organized this book into the beginning, middle, and end sections." Ms. Frederick quickly makes the folds in the piece of construction paper and labels each part of the flap book she uses to demonstrate the story elements of beginning, middle, and end. See figure 31.3 to see how she folded the paper and labeled each section.

"In the beginning of the story, Mem Fox introduced the main character, Wilfred Gordon McDonald Partridge. She also told us about where the story takes place. Do you remember what that is called?"

"The setting!" responds the class in chorus.

"Exactly! The setting in this story is very important, isn't it?" Ms. Frederick says with a smile. "If Wilfred Gordon had not lived right next door to an old folks' home, he probably wouldn't have gotten to know all the old folks."

"And that's the next thing that happens in the beginning of the story. We meet all the old folks. Do you remember what the problem is?" she asks as she adds the word PROBLEM to the flap book under *Beginning*.

"Miss Nancy has lost her memory," says Maria solemnly. "It's very sad."

"Yes, Maria, you are right. She did lose her memory and it was sad," responds Ms. Frederick.

FIGURE 31.3 Beginning, middle, and end flap book.

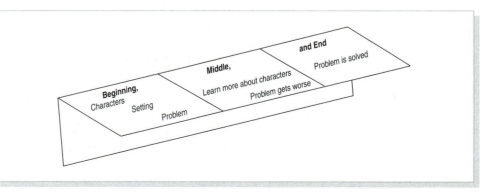

Ms. Frederick continues to walk the students through the book, adding the elements of story to the flap book. After they have completed listing the elements to the flaps of the book, Ms. Frederick goes back to the beginning of the story. She asks the students to respond briefly to questions related to each of the elements listed on the flaps, making sure they understand exactly what each of the terms means. As she does this, she lifts each flap and takes the students' dictation about each element in relation to the story of Wilfred Gordon. When they have reviewed the story elements of beginning, middle, and end, Ms. Frederick says, "I am placing some flap book paper in the writing center today. I am also putting some of our favorite books at the center. You can use the flap book paper to make flap books for one of your favorite stories. Make sure you write the parts of the story under the correct flap. Put the characters, setting, and problem under the beginning flap, the parts about new things you learn about the characters and the problem under the middle flap, and how the problem was solved under the end flap."

"Ms. Frederick!"

"Yes, Josef," responds Ms. Frederick.

"May we write our own beginning, middle, and end story on the flap book paper?"

"Of course, Josef," exclaims Ms. Frederick with a smile.

CONCLUSION

The use of predictable structures in stories provides a comfortable "scaffold" for students in their ability to make reading more comprehensible. Teaching students to recognize the basic story structures gives them insights into the type of story they are reading and allows them to formulate more accurate predictions based on their knowledge of the elements contained in the structures. It allows them to grasp the "big picture" of the text more readily in that they have the structural elements to use in deciphering the overall plot and interaction of the basic elements in the text. Visualization of the story structures is extremely important to some students and enhances their ability to use the structures to "make sense" of the text. Once they have established a foundational understanding of predictable story structures, they can use these elements in identifying and working with more advanced and intricate structures.

REFERENCES

Adams, P. (1989). *This is the house that Jack built*. London: Child's Play International.

Clement, R. (1998). *Grandpa's teeth*. New York: Harper Collins.

Davidson, J. (1982). The group mapping activity for instruction in reading and thinking. *Journal of Reading, 26*, 52–56.

Fox, M. (1985). *Wilfred Gordon McDonald Partridge*. New York: Cane/Miller Books.

Numeroff, L. (1991). *If you give a moose a muffin*. New York: HarperCollins.

Numeroff, L. (1992). *If you give a mouse a cookie*. New York: HarperFestival.

Tompkins, G. (2000). *Literacy for the 21st century*. Upper Saddle River, NJ: Merrill/Prentice Hall.

Wood, A. (1984). *The napping house*. New York: Harcourt Brace.

SUGGESTED READING

Manz, S. L. (2002). A strategy for previewing textbooks: Teaching students to become THIEVES. *The Reading Teacher, 55*, 434–435.

Newman, G. (2002). Comprehension strategy gloves. *The Reading Teacher, 55*, 329–332.

TEXT MAPPING

A Traveler's Guide to Comprehension

A text map is a visual or textual display of ideas that represent the key elements of text. The organizational arrangement of ideas and concepts in a story or text often provides the key to understanding for the reader. Developing the skills necessary to interpret these organizational patterns is an essential element in the enhancement of students' abilities in comprehension. Some students have a sense of story structure when they first come to school, but many do not. Although this story sense probably will be developed or enhanced through natural exposure to the many stories read in school, it should not be assumed. Teaching students about structural elements enables them to anticipate the type of information they should be looking for as they read and strengthens their recall of story events, main ideas, or content. Text mapping provides one way of assisting students in visualizing and internalizing these organizational arrangements.

The concept of text mapping may take a variety of formats, all equally valid within the context of the reading selection being explored. Several formats will be explored here for the purpose of providing maps that might be employed in an assortment of reading genres.

One major purpose for mapping is to assist teachers in planning and conducting reading instruction. Therefore, in preparing students to read a selection, it is recommended that teachers analyze the structure of the selection and create a map. The process of creating such a map helps teachers determine what is important enough about a story to be emphasized in class. For example, the theme often indicates background knowledge that students will need to use to comprehend new material, and this can become the focus of a prereading discussion. This is a crucial part of the planning and preparation prior to presenting text to students.

A map is a diagram or symbolic representation of the reader's personal response to text. Young readers often make pictures when asked to map; older readers tend to use lines, arrows, or other symbols to represent their thoughts. Mapping activities may be accomplished in small groups or individually, as appropriate for age and developmental levels. A few words may be used to label portions of a map. The first time students map, the teacher can help them understand the concept with directions such as, "If you were going to retell this story to someone, what main ideas would you want to be sure you included in the retelling? You can use circles, boxes, or arrows. If you like, try to show your ideas without using too many words. Don't worry about a 'right' way to map; there isn't any." This detailed explanation won't

Focus on English Learners

Visualizing the organizational arrangement of text can be the key to opening the door to strengthening English learners' increased comprehension.

32

151

be necessary after students' initial encounter with mapping; when they see the variety of responses, the concern about being "right" soon diminishes.

Students' maps need not be detailed or perfect; in fact, making one should take only a few minutes. Mapping allows the reader to synthesize his or her response to the text, but its real purpose is to provide a framework for the discussion that follows. That discussion typically allows students to develop further insights into what they have read and realize that text interpretations often differ.

STEP BY STEP

The steps in implementing text mapping are:

STEP 1   ANALYZING THE STRUCTURE OF THE SELECTION

To prepare for teaching the selection, the teacher prereads the text and determines the underlying organization and structure of the material. He may decide to construct a teaching map to assist in leading a prereading discussion, emphasizing activating prior knowledge as it relates to contextual elements and construction.

STEP 2   PREPARING THE STUDENTS TO READ

The teacher leads a prereading discussion, focusing on prior knowledge and the structure of the text. Students are guided at this point to use previous knowledge and known vocabulary to further their understanding of the selection.

STEP 3   READING AND MAPPING

Following the reading of the text, the students are engaged in a discussion as to the main ideas found in the selection. During this discussion, the teacher models how the ideas offered might be expressed in a visual format on a "text map." This might take the form of illustrations, main idea words, grouping from context, or even outline-like structuring. See figure 32.1 for examples of mapping structures.

After students have had several opportunities to see how the major elements of the story can be represented in a map, provide experiences for the students to become active participants in creating and using them. In this way students will become directly aware of how knowledge of text structure will help them understand what they read. As an initial introduction to this skill, a group mapping activity may be chosen. In this model the students work in small groups, reading the same text and discussing, planning, and executing the map style they have chosen to use for their presentation to the class.

STEP 4   DISCUSSING AND COMPARING MAPS

After reading, students create maps, either in groups or individually, which are then shared and explained to others. It provides an opportunity for questions or comments that generally prompt continued discussion of the text. Children show genuine interest in each other's maps, and the discussions that accompany sharing can be fascinating. Consistently discussing stories in their logical sequence will strengthen students' sense of the important story elements and thus increase their ability to comprehend stories they will read in the future. This is an important step in building comprehension bridges because it helps readers recall and retain text information while providing them with a means to respond personally to what they have read.

FIGURE 32.1 Examples of text mapping.

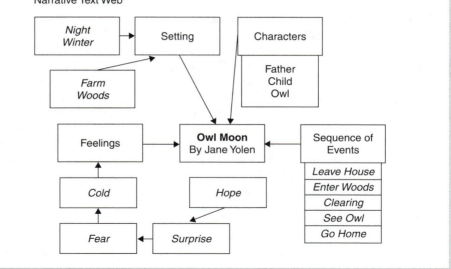

Narrative Text Web

| Night Winter | → | Setting | | Characters |
| | | | | Father Child Owl |

| Farm Woods | | | | |

Feelings	→	**Owl Moon** By Jane Yolen	←	Sequence of Events
				Leave House
				Enter Woods
Cold		Hope		Clearing
				See Owl
Fear	←	Surprise		Go Home

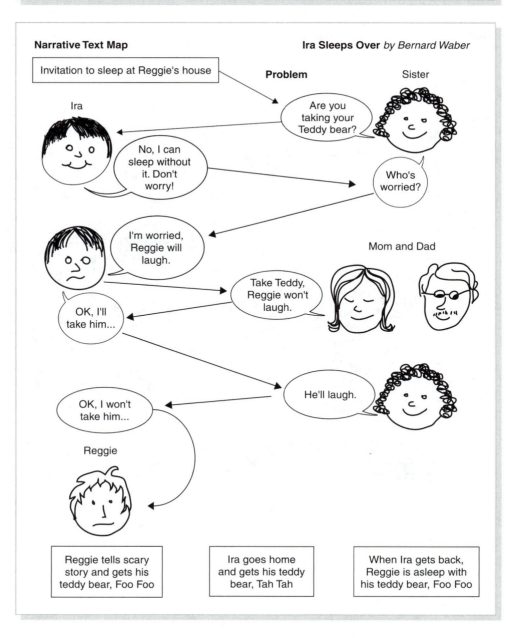

Narrative Text Map   **Ira Sleeps Over** by Bernard Waber

Invitation to sleep at Reggie's house

Problem   Sister

Ira

Are you taking your Teddy bear?

No, I can sleep without it. Don't worry!

Who's worried?

I'm worried, Reggie will laugh.

Mom and Dad

Take Teddy, Reggie won't laugh.

OK, I'll take him...

He'll laugh.

OK, I won't take him...

Reggie

| Reggie tells scary story and gets his teddy bear, Foo Foo | Ira goes home and gets his teddy bear, Tah Tah | When Ira gets back, Reggie is asleep with his teddy bear, Foo Foo |

APPLICATIONS AND EXAMPLES

An example of text mapping in first grade, using both narrative and informational text, can be found on File 32 of the accompanying CD.

Ms. Williams's 10th-grade English class is beginning a study of Shakespeare's *Romeo and Juliet*. They have discussed the plot line of the play, and now Ms. Williams wants students to construct a text map of the major events that occur during the course of the play. They are divided into groups, with each group assuming a family name (the House of Capulet, the House of Montegue, etc.) They are allowed to create names that would be appropriate to the period and setting. Each group is provided with a map of the city of Verona, and Ms. Williams instructs them to create labels for various points on the map that show the events in the play. She instructs them to number the labels to indicate the sequence in which the events occurred. Each group is then asked to report their findings and to show how they have chosen to label their maps relative to the text.

The first group to report is the House of Adige. In talking about the events as they saw them take place in the play, the students also mention that they have noticed an interesting relationship among the events. Marcia "Adige" says, "It looks

FIGURE 32.4   The House of Adige map.

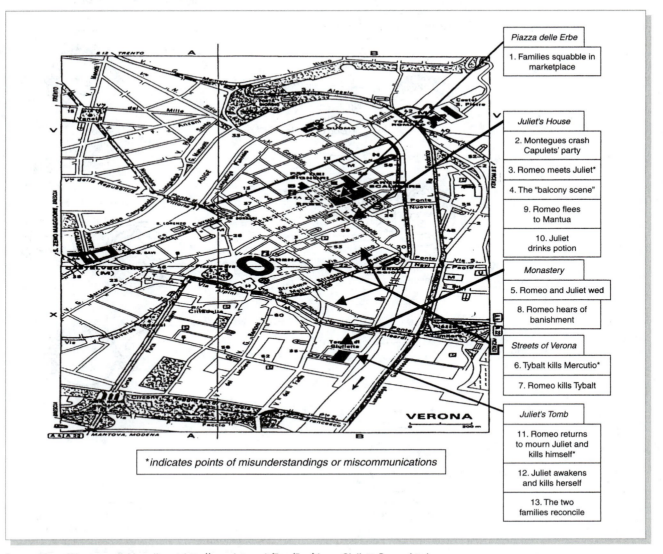

indicates points of misunderstandings or miscommunications

Piazza delle Erbe
1. Families squabble in marketplace

Juliet's House
2. Montegues crash Capulets' party
3. Romeo meets Juliet*
4. The "balcony scene"
9. Romeo flees to Mantua
10. Juliet drinks potion

Monastery
5. Romeo and Juliet wed
8. Romeo hears of banishment

Streets of Verona
6. Tybalt kills Mercutio*
7. Romeo kills Tybalt

Juliet's Tomb
11. Romeo returns to mourn Juliet and kills himself*
12. Juliet awakens and kills herself
13. The two families reconcile

Source: Map of Verona available online at *http://www.intesys.it/Tour/Eng/VeronaGiuliettaRomeo.html*

like a lot of the problems came about because of misunderstandings between a lot of the people involved. So, we marked on our maps where things happened and numbered them to show the order they happened in. Then we also put down some of the misunderstandings that took place in those locations." See figure 32.4 for an example of using an actual map to create a text map.

The House of Adige presentation includes some interesting discussion related to how miscommunications and misunderstandings create many of the conflicts that exist in the play. It leads to an informative reflection on the importance of understanding issues completely before reacting to them.

CONCLUSION

This classroom example shows the variety of purposes for which text mapping may be used. As schools and school districts become more and more accountable for meeting published standards, text mapping is a valuable tool in assisting students and teachers in accomplishing these standards in an integrative program of literacy and writing. By adjusting the format of the text map, students can be guided toward a fuller understanding of the skills addressed in normative grade-level standards. The text map can illustrate such concepts as main ideas and supporting details, sequences of events, text structure, settings, character development, or cause and effect. Because the discussion that follows the construction of the text maps encourages students to exchange ideas, text maps serve to increase oral interaction, communication skills, and comprehension.

SUGGESTED READING

Barton, J., & Sawyer, D. M. (2003). Our students *are* ready for this: comprehension instruction in the primary grades. *The Reading Teacher, 57*, 334–347.

Davidson, J. (1982). The group mapping activity for instruction in reading and thinking. *Journal of Reading, 26*, 52–56.

SUMMARIZATION

Identifying the Main Idea and Supporting Details

Focus on English Learners

Focus on English Learners

This process calls on English learners to review many strategies related to comprehension. The discussions, rewriting, and selection of appropriate details serve to strengthen and support their increased knowledge and use of language.

Instruction in summarization is necessary for students to be able to identify the main concepts encountered in a text and the supporting details that are essential to the full understanding of the meaning (Rinehart, Stahl, & Ericson, 1986). Teaching students to summarize requires an organized, sequential approach. Students must first be taught to identify the main idea of the passage and then to select only the details that are necessary to convey the full meaning. Five steps are contained within the sequence of teaching summarization. The students are taught:

1. to identify and select main information
2. to delete trivial information
3. to delete redundant information
4. to relate main and important supporting information
5. to identify samples of good summaries

In some cases a checklist of these steps has been found to be helpful to students in learning the process. Comprehension of the text is enhanced through the rereading that becomes necessary when students examine the details and supporting elements of the text and their relationship to the main idea.

STEP BY STEP

The steps in implementing summarization instruction are:

STEP 1 — IDENTIFYING THE MAIN CONCEPT CONVEYED IN THE PASSAGE

To prepare students for summarizing, the teacher must first instruct them to state the gist of the passage. She can help them practice a one-sentence respose to the question, "What was the story about?" Students may be given opportunities for practice by having them answer this question with familiar stories. The class can create a chart of main ideas for familiar stories. See figure 33.1 for an example.

FIGURE 33.1 Main ideas for familiar stories.

STORY	MAIN IDEA
Cinderella	A hardworking stepdaughter goes to the ball, meets the handsome prince, falls in love, and lives happily ever after.
Three Little Pigs	Three pig brothers work together to defeat the Big Bad Wolf.
Owl Moon	A small child explores the mysteries of the night forest with father in search of the elusive great horned owl.

FIGURE 33.2 Details from Cinderella.

Details	Unnecessary Details
Cinderella's mother died	~~Cinderella's mother died~~
Her father remarries	~~Her father remarries~~
Her stepmother had two daughters	~~Her stepmother had two daughters~~
The stepsisters were ugly	~~The stepsisters were ugly~~
Cinderella did all the housework	Cinderella did all the housework
Her stepsisters ordered her around	~~Her stepsisters ordered her around~~
She never had any new clothes	She never had any new clothes
The king gave a fancy ball	The king gave a fancy ball
He invited everyone in the kingdom	~~He invited everyone in the kingdom~~
Cinderella wanted to go to the fancy ball	~~Cinderella wanted to go to the fancy ball~~
She had no fancy ball gown to wear	She had no fancy ball gown to wear
She helped her stepsisters dress for the ball	~~She helped her stepsisters dress for the ball~~
After they left, she sat down and cried	~~After they left, she sat down and cried~~
Her Fairy Godmother (FG) appeared	Her Fairy Godmother (FG) appeared
FG turned Cinderella's ragged clothes into a beautiful ball gown	FG turned Cinderella's ragged clothes into a beautiful ball gown
FG creates a beautiful carriage to take Cinderella to the ball and warns her that the magic goes away at midnight	FG creates a beautiful carriage to take Cinderella to the ball and warns her that the magic goes away at midnight
Cinderella goes to the ball	Cinderella goes to the ball
She dances with the handsome prince	She dances with the handsome prince
He falls in love with her	He falls in love with her
Cinderella hears the clock begin to strike midnight	Cinderella hears the clock begin to strike midnight
She runs from the ballroom, dropping one of her glass slippers	She runs from the ballroom, dropping one of her glass slippers
The Prince picks up the slipper and vows to find her again	The Prince picks up the slipper and vows to find her again
He travels from house to house in search of the one who's foot fits the slipper	~~He travels from house to house in search of the one who's foot fits the slipper~~
He finds Cinderella and they live happily ever after	He finds Cinderella and they live happily ever after

STEP 2   LEARNING TO DELETE TRIVIAL INFORMATION

Again using a familiar story, students should brainstorm a list of all the things they can remember about the story. For example, a list of details for Cinderella might look like the list in figure 33.2. After the list is generated, the teacher encourages students

FIGURE 33.3
Eliminating redundancy and revising for fluency.

Initial Statement of the Main Idea

Cinderella goes to the fancy ball, meets the prince, and lives happily ever after.

Supporting Details (with redundancy removed)

Cinderella lived with her father and mean stepmother who made her do all the housework. ~~She never had any new clothes.~~ The king gave a fancy ball. She had no fancy ball gown to wear. Her Fairy Godmother (FG) appeared and turned Cinderella's ragged clothes into a beautiful ball gown. FG created a beautiful carriage to take Cinderella to the ball and warns her that the magic goes away at midnight. Cinderella goes to the ball, ~~She dances with the handsome prince. He falls in love with her. Cinderella hears the clock begin to strike midnight. She runs from the ballroom, dropping one of her glass slipppers. The Prince picks up the slipper and vows to find her again. He finds Cinderella and they live happily ever after.~~

Revising for Fluency

Cinderella lived with her father and mean stepmother who made her do all the housework. The king gave a fancy ball, but she had no fancy ball gown to wear. Her Fairy Godmother appeared and turned Cinderella's ragged clothes into a beautiful ball gown. Her Fairy Godmother created a beautiful carriage to take Cinderella to the ball and warned her that the magic would go away at midnight. Cinderella went to the fancy ball, met the prince, and lived happily ever after.

to cross out any details that are not necessary to convey the story in a way that someone can understand. The deleted list is also shown in figure 33.2.

STEP 3   DELETING REDUNDANT INFORMATION

The teacher now guides the students in writing in narrative form the main idea and supporting details left on the list they created. Once this is accomplished, they look at the narrative they wrote together and eliminate any redundant information. This often results in the revision of the narrative and a rearrangement of the sentence sequence to make the narrative flow more smoothly. See figure 33.3 for an example of this process.

STEP 4   RELATING THE MAIN IDEA WITH SUPPORTING INFORMATION

In this last step, the narrative must be reread and rewritten, if necessary, to make sure that the relations among the main concept and the supporting details are clear. See figure 33.3 for an example of how this is done.

STEP 5   RECOGNIZING GOOD SUMMARIES

After the students have walked through the steps in creating a good summary, they should be exposed to several summaries of the same passage so that they can select the best summary and identify the reasons why the summary is considered to be good. See figure 33.4 for an example of three summaries for the same story and a checklist that can be used to evaluate them based on the steps taught in the first part of the summarizing lesson.

APPLICATIONS AND EXAMPLES

See File 33 of the accompanying CD for an example of a seventh-grade summarization lesson.

Mr. Costa is reading the story *Owl Moon* (Yolen, 1987) to his third graders. Once he has completed the oral reading of the book, he asks the students, "What was this story about?"

George responds, "It's about a little child who goes owling with his father." Hee Wan says, "I think it's about walking in the woods on a snowy night."

FIGURE 33.4 Three story summaries with evaluation checklist.

Summary 1
Noni and his dog were stuck on an ice island. Noni threw his knife and it stuck in the ice. A pilot saw light reflected off the knife and rescued them.

Summary 2
Noni and his dog floated off on an ice island by themselves. They loved each other a lot. They didn't have any food to eat. They were very hungry and Noni thought about eating his dog. When he tried to kill the dog with his knife, he found that he couldn't do it. Afterwards the dog growled and came toward Noni and he was very scared. The dog just licked Noni and they lay down together to die. Later, a plane rescued them because the pilot saw a flash of light, a reflection from Noni's knife.

Summary 3
Noni and his dog floated off on an ice island by themselves. They were very hungry and Noni thought about eating his dog. When he tried to kill the dog with his knife, he found that he couldn't do it. He flung the knife away and it stuck in the ice. Later, a plane rescued them because the pilot saw a flash of light, a reflection from Noni's knife.

Summary Evaluation Checklist
Does the summary make sense?
Are there any redundant (repeated) pieces of information that can be eliminated?
Does the summary have enough information so that you get a clear understanding of the text?
Are there any sentences that can be combined?
Does the summary leave you with any unanswered questions?
Does the summary provide a clear and complete picture of the text?

Mr. Costa writes both the sentences on the chalkboard and asks, "Can you tell me everything that happened in the story?" As the children suggest events from the story, Mr. Costa lists them on the chalkboard. Soon the board is full of the students' suggestions. The board looks like this:

It's about a little child who goes owling with his father.

It's about walking in the woods on a snowy night.

They go walking at night.

The moon is very bright.

They hear a train.

The dogs are howling.

They walk into the dark, dark woods.

It is very cold and they have to blow on their hands to keep them warm.

They have to be very quiet.

The dad makes hooting sounds.

He is trying to call owls.

For a long time they don't see any owls.

Father hoots many times trying to call the owls.

All of a sudden, they hear an owl hooting.

They hear the owl flying over their heads.

The father shines the flashlight on the owl.

The owl sits in the tree and stares at them.

It seems like they are staring at the owl for a long time.

The owl flies away.

The child and the father walk back home.

Even though they could talk now, they are still very quiet.

Once the class had helped to create the list, Mr. Costa asks the students, "Which main idea statement do you think works the best for this story?"

The students look at the first two sentences. Holly says, "I think there's important information in both sentences. Can we use some of each?"

"What do you have in mind?" asks Mr. Costa.

"How about, 'The child and the father went looking for owls in the woods one snowy night'" replies Holly.

"That's great," responds Mr. Costa. "Now, let's look at the list of events from the story and see which ones are not really necessary to understand what happened." After much discussion, the students help Mr. Costa to delete some details. Their new list looks like this:

> They went walking at night.
> The moon is very bright.
> ~~They hear a train.~~
> ~~The dogs are howling.~~
> They walk into the dark, dark woods.
> It is very cold and they have to blow on their hands to keep them warm.
> They have to be very quiet.
> The dad makes hooting sounds.
> ~~He is trying to call owls.~~
> For a long time they don't see any owls.
> Father hoots many times trying to call the owls.
> All of a sudden, they hear an owl hooting.
> ~~They hear the owl flying over their heads.~~
> The father shines the flashlight on the owl.
> The owl sits in the tree and stares at them.
> It seems like they are staring at the owl for a long time.
> The owl flies away.
> The child and the father walk back home.
> Even though they could talk now, they are still very quiet.

Mr. Costa says, "Now let's read what we have left. See if you think this tells the important parts of the story." Mr. Costa and the students read the story together.

> The child and the father went looking for owls in the woods
> one snowy night.
> They went walking at night.
> The moon is very bright.
> They walk into the dark, dark woods.
> It is very cold and they have to blow on their hands to keep them warm.
> They have to be very quiet.
> The dad makes hooting sounds.
> For a long time they don't see any owls.
> Father hoots many times trying to call the owls.
> All of a sudden, they hear an owl hooting.
> The father shines the flashlight on the owl.
> The owl sits in the tree and stares at them.
> It seems like they are staring at the owl for a long time.
> The owl flies away.

The child and the father walk back home.

Even though they could talk now, they are still very quiet.

"I think we can leave some of the sentences out," suggests Federico. "We said some things twice."

"Good thinking," replies Mr. Costa. "Which sentences can we leave out?"

"They went walking at night," says Federico. "We already said that."

"The dad made hooting sounds," suggests Dan. "We say that again later."

"Do you want to eliminate any more?" asks Mr. Costa. "No? Well, let's read it again and see what you think."

Mr. Costa and the students read again,

The child and the father went looking for owls in the woods
one snowy night.

The moon is very bright.

They walk into the dark, dark woods.

It is very cold and they have to blow on their hands to keep them warm.

They have to be very quiet.

For a long time they don't see any owls.

Father hoots many times trying to call the owls.

All of a sudden, they hear an owl hooting.

The father shines the flashlight on the owl.

The owl sits in the tree and stares at them.

It seems like they are staring at the owl for a long time.

The owl flies away.

The child and the father walk back home.

Even though they could talk now, they are still very quiet.

"I think we can leave out, 'It is very cold and they have to blow on their hands to keep warm,'" suggests George. "That's not that important."

"OK," agrees Mr. Costa. "Anything else?"

"For a long time they don't see any owls," says Holly. "I think that when we say father hoots many times, it tells you that they didn't see the owls right away."

"Good thinking," replies Mr. Costa as he crosses out the two sentences. "Now, let's see if we can write the sentences so they don't sound so choppy." He and the students work together to combine sentences until they have created a summary that reads smoothly. Then they read the summary together.

The child and the father went looking for owls in the woods one snowy night. The moon is very bright. But they have to be very quiet so they don't scare the owls. Father hoots many times trying to call the owls until, all of a sudden, they hear an owl hooting. The father shines the flashlight on the owl as it sits in the tree and stares at them. It seems like they are staring at the owl for a long time before he flies away. Even though they could talk as they walk home, they are still very quiet. You have to be quiet when you go owling.

"I think you did a great job of summarizing the story," says Mr. Costa. "You even managed to keep the quiet feel of it in your summary."

CONCLUSION

As Mr. Costa explains, models, and guides the students through the steps in learning how to write and recognize good summaries, they are also reviewing many strategies related to reading comprehension. The details and topic statements that the students and teachers create must be reread and analyzed for content. Often sentences are rewritten to more clearly represent the events in the text. The connections between and among details are made clear by combining sentences with appropriate connectives. All of the steps in the process of selecting details to be included in a summary support the students in their growing knowledge of vocabulary, connections among concepts and events, and the rewriting and rereading of a paragraph to create a cohesive narrative. The discussion that takes place as the class makes decisions about which sentences to include and which to delete often sheds light on the meanings and nuances contained in the reading material. Once the process of writing a class summary is repeated several times, students have a much clearer idea of what to include in a good summary. In addition, they also know how to reread to clarify meaning, how to make connections among the sentences in text, and how important attention to sequence and detail becomes in understanding the text.

REFERENCES

Rinehart, S. D., Stahl, S. A., & Ericson, L. G. (1986). Some effects of summarization training on reading and studying. *Reading Research Quarterly, 21,* 422–438.

Yolen, J. (1987). *Owl moon.* New York: Scholastic.

SUGGESTED READING

Oczkus, L. (2003). *Reciprocal teaching at work: Strategies for improving reading comprehension.* Newark, DE: International Reading Association.

Rogers, L. K. (2003). "A Report in a can." *The Reading Teacher, 56,* 734–735.

34

NIPS

An Interactive Support Strategy for Comprehending "Tough" Text

NIPS (noting, interacting, prioritizing, and summarizing) is a group strategy that combines several techniques for using individual reading and small group interaction to support students' understanding of informational text. This strategy combines the use of the dialogue journal and a discussion technique developed by Carolyn Burke (Rasinski & Padak, 2000). Burke's technique, "Save the Last Word for Me," involves a group discussion of informational text that is introduced by a designated group member who then has the responsibility of bringing the discussion to a close by summarizing the discussion and decisions made by the group.

> **Focus on English Learners**
>
> Incorporating a variety of approaches to text provides English learners with multiple opportunities to process text. They come away with a more complete understanding of the material and how the material was presented.

NIPS is particularly effective in supporting comprehension because it incorporates several approaches to informational text. The students begin by reading and taking notes, identifying what they see as the most important parts of the chapter they are reading. They then meet in small groups to discuss the reading and compare their notes with the notes taken by others. The group discussion serves to clarify important points and review the content read. The group then works together to prioritize the information gathered from the reading, deciding which of the notes qualify as main ideas and which are supporting details. As the group time comes to a close, the designated leader summarizes the group's decisions, providing one more review of the material that was read and discussed. Because the informational material is reviewed several times during this process, students come away from the group with more complete understanding of the material. They also have multiple opportunities to ask questions of other members of the group if there is anything they don't understand.

STEP BY STEP

The steps for using NIPS are:

STEP 1   TEACHING OR REVIEWING NOTE TAKING

The teacher presents a brief lesson or review on note taking (see chapter 38 for detailed steps in teaching note taking). The students can use note cards, sticky notes, or journal entries to take notes. The teacher should make it clear that the notes to be taken should contain only the most important facts the readers find as they read the material. One good way of clarifying this is to instruct students to note any facts they would need to include in explaining the reading material to someone. The teacher should also stress that notes are not complete sentences, just words or brief phrases that help to recall important information.

STEP 2   PROVIDING BACKGROUND KNOWLEDGE

If the text to be read is related in any way to content that has been studied in the past, the teacher reviews this information so that readers have some background knowledge on which to build. If the reading material is new, unrelated to past studies, the teacher may want to provide some background information in the form of a brief video, a short oral introduction, or the exploration of some visual materials such as photographs or realia. If the reading contains vocabulary that will not be comprehensible through context clues, the teacher should teach this vocabulary.

STEP 3   ASSIGNING THE READING

The class is given the reading assignment. In the process of assigning the reading, the teacher should make it clear that students will also be working in groups to discuss the material after the reading and note taking. They should be told in advance that their notes will help them in the group activity where they will work to identify the most important facts and concepts contained in the reading material.

STEP 4   GROUPING AND EXPLAINING THE ACTIVITY

After the students have read the material or a short section of the material, the teacher assigns them to groups of three to five students, designating a group leader. The group meets together, sharing their notes and discussing the content they read. The group is given the task of prioritizing the facts and concepts they have noted in the reading material. They do this by deciding which of the facts or concepts are the most important to be understood and remembered and which are of secondary importance. Based on this prioritization, their task is then to identify which of the facts and concepts would be main ideas and which would be termed supporting details. The group then creates a list of the main ideas in the reading material and arranges the supporting details under the main idea they support.

After the group chart is created, the group leader must summarize the work the group did and the decisions that were made. The group leader practices this summary with the group so that everyone in the group agrees that the leader is relating the information in the way it occurred.

STEP 5   PROVIDING TIME FOR GROUP INTERACTION

The teacher gives the groups time to meet together and complete their tasks. The reading material can be divided into sections so that students read short passages, meeting together to compare notes, prioritize, and summarize several times throughout the reading of the entire chapter. However, the teacher may decide to have the groups meet just once, after the material is read. This decision will be based upon the ages and reading levels of the students and the length and complexity of the reading assignment.

STEP 6   BRINGING THE CLASS BACK TOGETHER

At the conclusion of the activity, the teacher brings the class together again to compare the charts created by the groups and to do a final review. Each group leader briefly summarizes the group's work, and the reading material can be discussed one last time so that all students have a clear understanding of the information it contains. The teacher can create a class summary list as the groups present their lists. This allows her to combine and merge the ideas of the groups.

APPLICATIONS AND EXAMPLES

An eighth-grade writing class provides another example of using NIPS on File 34 of the accompanying CD.

Mr. Lewis's fifth graders are studying the westward movement. Mr. Lewis has discovered a wonderful book that clearly explains the way pioneer families accomplished their building, farming, and all other tasks they had to do. Because Mr. Lewis has established "Then and Now" as the theme for the year, he feels that this particular book, *A Pioneer Sampler,* by Barbara Greenwood (1994), will support his students' understanding of the way things were done on pioneer farms.

Mr. Lewis begins his introduction to the NIPS activity by reviewing note taking. He demonstrates the technique by reading the first section of the Greenwood book aloud, thinking aloud as he reads. He does his note taking on the overhead projector so that the students can see that he is not writing whole sentences every time. He also uses small sticky notes to mark important ideas in the text so that he can return to those sections as important ideas are charted in the NIPS group. Because the book is fairly lengthy, Mr. Lewis decides to assign different sections of the book to different groups so that each group can provide information to the entire class about their reading. He groups his students in threes, making sure that each group contains a strong reader, and then posts a chart that states the tasks the students are complete. The chart reads:

1. Read your section silently.
2. Take notes as you read. Note important facts and concepts.
3. Meet with your group and discuss the notes you took.
4. Make a chart of the most important facts and concepts in your section (prioritize).
5. Use poster paper if you need to draw diagrams of anything in your section to make it clear.
6. Help your leader to practice what he/she will say when the group reports.
7. Raise your hands if you need help.

As the groups complete their tasks, Mr. Lewis monitors them to make sure that they have a clear idea of what they will be reporting to the class. He then provides time for the groups to make their reports and display their visuals. The final discussion reflects the class theme, "Then and Now." The students talk about how the things shared in the book are done differently now with the use of technology and new farming machinery. As they discuss the differences they found, Mr. Lewis fills in their findings on a double-column chart entitled "Then and Now." See figure 34.1 for the comparison chart they created.

CONCLUSION

Having students actively analyze the text with which they are working assists them in identifying and recalling important concepts. By searching the text for important ideas and supporting evidence, they are learning the skills necessary for clear processing and understanding of reading material. This process also gives them multiple opportunities to interact with the processing done by other students. That allows them to clarify their thinking in light of discussions entered into with others who have read the same material. It gives them the opportunity to compare their notes

FIGURE 34.1
Comparison chart for "Then
and Now."

	THEN	NOW
Schools	All grades met in one room with one teacher	Each class in a separate room with a separate teacher
Houses	Built from stones and logs cleared from the fields	Various building materials, power tools, high-tech construction
Bathrooms	Outhouses with lye thrown into the holes to control odor	Indoor plumbing and modern bathrooms
Making Syrup	Sap collected from maple trees and boiled in iron kettles over an open fire	Modern collection techniques and syrup made in factories
Measuring	Horses measured by "hands" Fabric measured by "cloth yards," which was the distance from your nose to the length of your arm	Standard measurements of inches, feet, yards, etc.
Fences	Horse high, hog tight, and skunk proof were the standards. Fences made from splitting logs and placing tree stumps	Variety of fencing styles and materials, some wood, some metal, some masonry
Clearing the Land	Harrows, plows were pulled by oxen, with farmer walking behind	Implements pulled by heavy machinery, driven by farmer

and prioritization strategies with others. This variety of interactive approaches to informational text is particularly effective in supporting comprehension.

As Mr. Lewis has shown, NIPS is a sequence of tasks used to support students in reading and comprehending tough text. This strategy can also be adapted to teach specific skills. NIPS is especially effective in supporting comprehension for several reasons. It requires students to practice note taking for a specific purpose that tends to help them to focus on particular facts and concepts. By interacting with other members of the group, comparing and discussing their notes, the students have a chance to discuss and clarify their understanding of the passage read. The task of prioritizing the importance of facts and concepts helps students to differentiate between main ideas and supporting details. Preparing a summary of the reading encourages an additional look at the vocabulary, facts, and concepts that were read and previously discussed. In addition, students can build on their understanding of the text by employing the skills they explored through the process.

REFERENCES

Greenwood, B. (1994). *A pioneer sampler: The daily life of a pioneer family in 1840.* Boston: Houghton Mifflin.
Rasinski, T., & Padak, N. (2000). *Effective reading strategies: Teaching children who find reading difficult.* Upper Saddle River, NJ: Merrill/Prentice Hall.

SECTION V

SELF-MONITORING STRATEGIES

Strategies for supporting readers to monitor their own understanding are vital for developing strategic readers, readers who know what to do to support themselves in making sense of text. It is not enough for readers to simply recognize that they do not understand what they have read. This is only the first step, but it is a very important one. Strategic readers are constantly monitoring their understanding and building their repertoires of techniques for supporting their own processing and integrating of meaning.

Section V provides a series of strategies that can be taught to create an understanding in readers that they are responsible for monitoring and supporting their own comprehension as they read. Instruction in self-monitoring strategies also provides a series of expectations in readers. Good readers expect to be actively engaged in the reading act. Strategic readers expect to have times when they must employ strategies to make sense of text. Reflective readers expect to think about the meanings of what is being read and to relate the meanings to past experiences, knowledge of books, and vocabulary. Teaching self-monitoring strategies encourages readers to approach reading as an active, rather than a passive endeavor, a thinking person's pastime.

Without the strategies included in sections I through IV, section V would be extremely limited. Section V focuses on the use of self-monitoring to make sense of text, while sections I through IV provide strategies that can be employed to support comprehension once the reader recognizes that understanding is not occurring. Good readers employ strategies explained in all five sections. They use these strategies in an automatic fashion, in response to self-monitoring and the realization that understanding is lacking. Without self-monitoring, readers stumble forward through text, getting more and more lost in the forest of words and concepts with no idea of how to find their way.

35

CROSS-CHECKING
Self-Monitoring at the Sentence Level

**Focus on
English Learners**

It is important to identify which cueing systems English learners are using in order to support their use of balanced cueing, which is vital to deep comprehension.

The cues that readers use when they decode text involve processing the text in several different ways (Clay, 1993). As readers sweep their eyes across lines of text, they look at the letters in sequence and connect those letters to the phonological system. This use of visual cues from written letters is one cueing system. Readers' knowledge of the grammar and word order of the language is another system that is used for cueing. That cueing system is called *syntactic* or *structure*. The third cueing system is the meaning that is attached to the words, phrases, and/or illustrations that are printed on the page. That cueing system is called *semantic* or *meaning*. A fourth cueing system is also sometimes used. The *pragmatic* system is involved whenever the words or phrases have a different connotation based on social, regional, or cultural issues (Tompkins, 2000). Good readers use all these cueing systems in a balanced manner. They not only use the cueing systems but they use them to monitor the accuracy of their own reading. When readers use several cueing systems to check on the accuracy and meaning of their own reading, it is called *cross-checking*.

Cross-checking is introduced to young children at the beginning of their introduction to literacy. Students are taught to use phonics, sentence structure, and meaning to make sure that the word calling they are doing actually makes sense. Even though this concept is usually introduced early and maintained throughout instruction in reading, some students need more structured instruction almost all the way through their reading experiences. Some students get false impressions of the mechanics of reading and tend to want to over-rely on phonics without consistently cross-checking for meaning. These readers sound the words out or guess according to the first sound of the word and read without paying attention to the fact that the words they are saying do not make sense. Other readers over-rely on meaning and almost seem to be making the story up as they go along. They read some words but seem comfortable improvising without making sure that the words they are saying are actually printed on the page, as long as their version makes sense.

Teachers identify the cueing systems the students are using by examining the words they are saying. By paying close attention to the types of errors readers make, the teacher can identify which of the cueing systems are being used and then provide instruction in the use of the others. Reading instruction should emphasize the balanced use of multiple cueing systems. Cross-checking is taught as a way to monitor one's own reading accuracy and understanding. It is relatively simple to understand but must be used consistently to be effective.

STEP BY STEP

The steps in teaching the use of cross-checking are:

STEP 1   ASSESSING STUDENTS' USE OF CUEING SYSTEMS

- The teacher listens to the student read a passage of text between 100 and 200 words long. This passage should be at an appropriate reading level for the student. The student should be able to read the passage fairly comfortably, making relatively few errors. The teacher notes the errors the student makes and analyzes the record by asking the following questions:
  - Does the word that was misread make sense in the sentence?

    Example: "The lady opened the door" instead of "The woman opened the door."
    This student is using meaning cues but not cross-checking with phonic cues.

  - Does the word that was misread look something like the word that was read?

    Example: "The boy says the cat ran away" instead of "The boy saw the cat run away."
    This student is using minimal phonic cues without cross-checking for meaning and accuracy. (In some cases the inaccuracy of the reading may not be apparent until the reader attempts to read the next sentence.)

  - Does the word that was misread fit into the sentence structure of the language?

    Example: "The car was running fast" instead of "The car was moving fast."
    The reader is substituting one verb for another without cross-checking for phonic cues.

The most precise way of determining cueing system use is done by using a system of marking a record of the student's reading called a *running record*. Running records are described in detail in Marie Clay's book, *An Observation Survey for Early Literacy Achievement* (1993). Teachers can get a good idea of students' cueing use by listening carefully to their oral reading and noting the mistakes they make. In any case, the solution is to teach the balanced use of cueing systems and cross-checking.

STEP 2   TEACHING STUDENTS TO CROSS-CHECK

The teacher introduces the cues that the students can use when they read. She talks about the cues as if the students were detectives trying to solve a crime. Detectives must use all the clues they find or the wrong person may be put in jail. Readers must use all the cues or they may misunderstand what the sentence is saying. The teacher introduces the concept of cross-checking as an important tool for making sure that the words you read are exactly what the author intended you to read. This is an important time to remind students that it is important for them to be monitoring their own reading for accuracy and understanding. The idea that misreading words sometimes causes the sentence to mean something different can be modeled. The teacher uses examples of sentences that are read incorrectly and the change the misreading makes in the meaning to demonstrate this. She teaches students to stop and ask themselves, "Does that make sense?" If the sentence does not make sense, students should reread, slowing down and making sure that each word matches the word being said and focusing on phonic cues.

STEP 3   GUIDING STUDENTS IN THE PRACTICE OF CROSS-CHECKING

As students practice their reading, they stop briefly to ask themselves, "Does that make sense?" If the sentence doesn't seem to make sense, they then cross-check using phonics cues to make sure that the words they have read match those printed on the page. If the reading and meaning are flowing well, readers don't have to stop and self-question. Only at times when the sentence seems to be causing confusion should the cross-checking be done overtly. This self-questioning is done orally and overtly to make sure that students understand the process but, of course, should be silent and automatic as they become more proficient in using it.

STEP 4   DOCUMENTING AND CELEBRATING THE USE OF CROSS-CHECKING

After the teacher guides the student through the use of cross-checking several times and is confident that the student understands the process, the student should be given a way to mark the text indicating that cross-checking was done. The student can be given highlighting tape or small sticky notes so that cross-checking to correct confusion can be marked. After the reading is completed, the student conferences with the teacher and shows her the places where cross-checking was done. They discuss and celebrate the student's self-monitoring and use of the cues to make sense of the text. This conference provides the teacher with additional information for future teaching that may need to be done.

APPLICATIONS AND EXAMPLES

The use of cross-checking instruction in a seventh-grade remedial reading class is illustrated in File 35 of the accompanying CD.

Mrs. McPhillips's first graders are making good progress in their reading skills. She meets with them in small groups each day for guided reading and introduces a small soft-backed book at the group's instructional level and then coaches them individually on cueing use and self-monitoring as they all practice their silent (not so silent!) reading. As she listens to the students read, Mrs. McPhillips monitors their cueing use and frequently asks questions to alert them to miscues. If a child substitutes one word for another, Mrs. McPhillips says, "Look at that word again." Most of the time the student is able to return to the word and cross-check using phonics cues. Mrs. McPhillips then has the student reread the entire sentence fluently, and she often asks, "Does that make sense now?" She knows that the questions she is asking the students daily are creating a script in their heads that will serve them well as they begin to read independently. She constantly reminds them, "I'm not always going to be sitting beside you when you are reading. You need to be asking yourself questions like, 'Does this make sense?'"

One of Mrs. McPhillips's students, Josh, seems to be having great difficulty with self-monitoring and cueing use. His kindergarten teacher used a commercial phonics program that focused on beginning sounds very heavily. Mrs. McPhillips is not sure whether or not this program is the cause of Josh's problems. Josh seems content to call words based upon their initial sounds. He may read the sentence "The boy walked down the street" as "The ball went down the sewer." Although the individual sentence may make sense, in the context of the story and the illustrations on the page, it doesn't fit.

Mrs. McPhillips decides to focus on two things with Josh. She is going to extend the use of his phonics cueing beyond the first sound in the word and she's going to help him use cross-checking employing all the cueing systems, with a focus on meaning. Teaching Josh that both the illustrations and the story line are meaning cues is an important understanding he must gain.

Beginning with the sentence he read as "The ball went down the sewer," Mrs. McPhillips says, "Look at the picture, Josh. Does that match what you see in the picture?" Josh shakes his head.

"Let's go back to the sentence. Look at this word again," Mrs. McPhillips says as she runs her finger under the word *boy*.

She says, "/b/ /oy/" sounding it out slowly. (Note: The use of a slash on either side of a letter or letters indicates the sound of the letter is being voiced rather than the name of the letter.)

"Oh," says Josh. "The boy went . . ." As he says *went*, Mrs. McPhillips puts her finger under the word *walked* and keeps it there. "Look at this again," she says. "What is the boy doing in the picture?"

Josh glances quickly at the picture and then back to the word. Mrs. McPhillips covers up the *ed* on the end of the word *walked* and slowly moves her finger under the root word as Josh sounds it out. Then she uncovers the *ed* and he adds the *d* sound.

"Now start at the beginning," she says.

Josh reads, "The boy walked down the /st/../r/../ee/../t/."

"Very good!" says Mrs. McPhillips with a smile. "Now read the whole thing."

"The boy walked down the street," reads Josh confidently.

"Good for you, Josh," says Mrs. McPhillips. "You used all the cues. You looked at the picture and the whole word that time. That's exactly what you have to do."

Mrs. McPhillips will work with Josh many more times, teaching him to use all the cueing systems and to ask himself questions as he reads. He started out with a heavy reliance on one cueing system and must begin to use them all, both to figure out unknown words and to cross-check and make sure that his reading is making sense.

CONCLUSION

In the beginning of reading instruction, the teacher asks questions constantly to support the students' understanding that they must be self-monitoring. As students read aloud to teachers, the teachers ask, "Does that make sense?" whenever they make an error that affects meaning. Whenever the student misreads a word, the teacher says, "Look at that word again." When these questions and reminders are consistent in the early stages of reading instruction and the students are taught to use the cueing systems for cross-checking, students are more successful in understanding their need to self-monitor and use the cues they have for correcting their own errors.

With older readers, teaching cross-checking can be more problematic and the teacher may meet with more resistance. The teacher can use modeled think-aloud, demonstrating how she uses cross-checking to monitor her own reading. The teacher asks questions as a way to model the questions students should be asking themselves. Making this clear to the reader often reduces the student's anxiety, which often serves to worsen the problem.

The use of highlighting tape and/or sticky notes to document and celebrate the use of cross-checking often serves to motivate the reader. This is seen as something unique and, especially when followed by celebration of the mastery of a new technique, can be very positive.

Cross-checking is a basic reading strategy. When students are struggling with comprehension, teachers must make sure that they understand cross-checking and have the opportunity to refine its use. The ability to use and combine the cueing systems is vital to reading comprehension. The strategy, as is true with most reading skills and strategies, is most easily taught in the beginning stages of reading instruction. Once students have struggled with reading comprehension, they are more resistant to teaching. The teacher must find ways to motivate students to develop new habits. The practice and refining of cross-checking often serves as a great breakthrough to older struggling readers and so it is well worth the effort it takes to teach it to them.

REFERENCES

Clay, M. (1993). *An observation survey for early literacy achievement*. Portsmouth, NH: Heinemann.

Tompkins, G. (2000). *Literacy for the 21st century*. Upper Saddle River, NJ: Merrill/Prentice Hall.

SUGGESTED READING

Brown, K. J. (2003). What do I say when they get stuck on a word? Aligning teachers' prompts with students' development. *The Reading Teacher, 56*, 720–733.

Short, R., Kane, M., & Peeling, T. (2000). Retooling the reading lesson: Matching the right tools to the job. *The Reading Teacher, 54*, 284–295.

36

PERIODIC PARAPHRASING

Monitoring Your Own Understanding

Focus on English Learners

Giving English learners tools and techniques for monitoring their own progress while reading offers them approaches to problem solving with text.

Periodic paraphrasing is a method of self-monitoring that allows the reader to perform self-checks for understanding while in the process of reading text. Thus there are several different methods of noting the main ideas and supporting details in text, the purpose of this strategy is to actively engage the reader with the text. The reader chooses natural stopping points and briefly reviews what has been read up to that point. If the reader cannot recall the information that has been read or finds that the information does not make sense, the reader can use *fix-up strategies* (see figure 36.1 and chapter 40 in this text) to attempt making sense of the passage. The reader is expected to keep track of the difficulties encountered in the text and the methods used to support understanding. After the reading of the text, the paraphrasing and strategies employed to make sense of the text are read aloud to the group and a comparison of the variety of strategies used is made and celebrated. This final sharing enables all students in the group to hear about a wide range of possible solutions to difficulties encountered.

STEP BY STEP

The steps in implementing periodic paraphrasing are:

STEP 1   MODELING PARAPHRASING

The teacher reads a short section of the text aloud and then stops and paraphrases orally.

STEP 2   EXPLAINING PARAPHRASING

The teacher explains that telling the main idea in your own words is called *paraphrasing*. The teacher explains that paraphrasing is a way to check to see if you really understand what you are reading. He further explains that discovering that you have difficulty explaining what you read in your own words should send a signal that you need to do something to help you to better understand.

FIGURE 36.1 Examples of fix-up strategies for increasing comprehension.

Rereading	Going back and reading the text for a second time
Reading and restating one sentence at a time	Reading the paragraph sentence by sentence, pausing after each sentence to restate the sentence in the reader's own words
Looking up words	Using a dictionary, glossary, or similar reference materials to research words that are unknown or unclear to the reader
Writing down key words and then restating based on the key words	Identifying and writing down the most important words and restating the text based on these words

STEP 3   ## PRACTICING PARAPHRASING

Simple paragraphs from a piece of text are distributed to the students to read silently. The paragraphs should be numbered in the order in which they appear in the text. Students are asked to read their paragraphs silently, cover them up, and then tell in their own words what their paragraph said. After all students paraphrase their paragraph, the teacher relates the new paragraph to the information already shared in previous paragraphs. The teacher can also paraphrase the words of the student to show that a single piece of text can be restated in several ways.

STEP 4   ## BRAINSTORMING FIX-UP STRATEGIES

The teacher asks the group, "What can you do to help yourself when you discover that you cannot paraphrase the paragraph?" The students are asked to brainstorm a list of possible strategies they could employ to revisit the paragraph to understand it and be able to tell the main ideas in their own words. See figure 36.1 for a list of possible fix-up strategies and their definitions.

STEP 5   ## PRACTICING FIX-UP STRATEGIES

Each of the fix-up strategies should be explained, modeled, and practiced so the students know exactly what to do if they find it difficult to paraphrase a paragraph.

STEP 6   ## DOCUMENTING STRATEGY USE

The students can be given strips of paper or sticky notes to use as markers. They should be instructed to practice orally or write a brief paraphrasing after each paragraph. They should be instructed to place a marker or sticky note at each point in the text where they used a fix-up strategy and to note which strategy they used at each point.

STEP 7   ## DISCUSSING AND CELEBRATING PARAPHRASING AND USING FIX-UP STRATEGIES

After the text is read, students should be brought together to discuss the paraphrasing they did, the problems they encountered, and the fix-up strategies they employed. Unique solutions to problems encountered should be celebrated and students should be encouraged to try out some new strategies as they read in the future.

APPLICATIONS AND EXAMPLES

File 36 of the accompanying CD provides an example of periodic paraphrasing instruction in an eighth-grade classroom.

Mr. Bellacorte's fourth graders are reading a chapter about Cesar Chavez in their social studies text (Billings & Billings, 1999). Mr. B. knows that a number of his students are familiar with this folk hero and wants to use this opportunity to teach the students how to monitor their own understanding of passages they read.

"I want to read the first paragraph of this chapter aloud to you today. Listen very carefully because I will teach you a new reading strategy after I read aloud."

Mr. B. reads the first paragraph aloud and then stops and says, "I am going to do something different now. I'm going to tell you, in my own words, what this paragraph says. When I use my own words to tell about something I read, it's called *paraphrasing*. This paragraph says that Cesar Chavez was poor all his life. His parents were from Mexico and they were farmers. They lost all their money and had to work on other people's farms, moving from place to place following the crops that needed to be harvested. Although they worked hard, they never made much money because the farmers didn't pay the workers a fair wage. If workers complained, they were fired. There were a lot of workers who needed work and who would work for very little money.

"Now I'm going to give each of you another paragraph from this same chapter. I want you to read your paragraph to yourself and then I will ask you to tell, in your own words, what your paragraph says."

After Mr. B. gives the students time to read their paragraphs to themselves and think about what they are going to say, he asks them to tell about their paragraphs. When a student has difficulty paraphrasing, Mr. B. asks, "What can you do to help yourself?"

The students give suggestions to each other, and Mr. B. writes their suggestions on the chalkboard. The list grows slowly as the students suggest rereading, reading and restating one sentence at a time, looking up words, and writing down key words and then restating based on the key words.

Once he is sure that the students understand the process, Mr. B. asks them to open their social studies book to the next chapter. He passes out small sticky notes to each student and says, "I want you to practice using paraphrasing as you read this next section in your book. Stop after each paragraph and think of how you would explain the paragraph to someone who has not read it. Use your own words. If you find it hard to paraphrase a paragraph, look at the list on the chalkboard and try one of the strategies listed there. Once you have tried the fix-up strategy, paraphrase the paragraph and see if it is easier. Use your sticky notes to mark any place where you use a strategy. Just write the number of the strategy you used on the sticky note. We'll talk about the paraphrasing and use of the fix-up strategies once you have finished reading the passage."

Mr. B. circulates around the room as students practice paraphrasing and fix-ups. If he sees a student having difficulty, he stops to help. He occasionally asks students to paraphrase orally. Once the students have completed the reading of the passage, Mr. B. pulls the groups together and they share the problems they had and the strategies they used. Mr. B. then has the students share their paraphrasing for the first few paragraphs and they discuss how many different ways they found to restate the meanings of the paragraphs.

"It's almost like each of us is telling it in a different way," says Jorge. "I didn't know you could say the same thing so many different ways."

"Did hearing the different ways of paraphrasing help you to understand the passage?" asks Mr. B.

"Yeah, it did. Sometimes people said things in a way that helped me to understand better," replies Jorge with a smile. "This is good."

CONCLUSION

The usefulness of teaching paraphrasing to assist readers in self-monitoring comprehension of reading materials is evident in the discussions stimulated by these classroom activities. Students begin to recognize the value in rethinking and restating the text. This leads them to recognize their own ability to conceptualize the meanings found in readings and to recognize how much they really understand about the text with which they are engaged. Asking students to "tell in their own words" provides a sort of litmus test for checking for understanding. If they have difficulty restating their reading, then these strategies should assist them in identifying the problem and fixing it.

REFERENCES

Billings, H., & Billings, M. (1999). Cesar Chavez: Uniting farm workers. In *Heroes* (2nd ed.). Lincolnwood, IL: Jamestown Publishers.

SUGGESTED READING

Buettner, E. G. (2002). Sentence by sentence self-monitoring. *The Reading Teacher, 56,* 34–44.

37

SELF-MONITORING THROUGH IMAGING AND INTERACTING

Demonstrating Understanding

The importance of students' ability to check their own understanding of the text they are reading has led to the development of a series of self-monitoring strategies they might use. In the forefront of these strategies is the ability to create mental pictures and then to verbalize the imagery they have chosen. The use of mental images is such an effective structure for connecting details within the text that students must be strongly encouraged to develop these skills and to incorporate the use of imagery into their repertoire of self-monitoring strategies.

The strategies for teaching and developing imaging, imagination, and interaction skills can be found in chapter 24 of this book. The purpose of this chapter on demonstrating understanding is to reinforce the direct application of the skills developed in chapter 24 in situations where students will recognize and identify with the importance of being able to visualize and discuss the imagery they assign to the text. As with all metacognitive strategies, students need to recognize the importance of their active involvement with making sense of the text. They need to develop and implement the skills for identifying checkpoints, or logical stopping points at which they need to analyze the images. Most importantly, students must realize that their level of comprehension is directly related to the level of active involvement they have with the text. In order to develop a consistent system of self-checking, they must learn to stop and review images they have created and to recognize that the difficulty of the text may drive the frequency of the stops and checkpoints. This may require that checkpoints be chosen once every paragraph, after a specific sentence, or maybe only one each page or so. Again, the level of understanding exhibited by students determines the frequency with which they choose to stop and monitor. They need to be reviewing constantly with themselves their comprehension of the text and adjusting the imaging process to meet their individual needs.

STEP BY STEP

The steps in demonstrating understanding through imaging and interacting are:

STEP 1   REVIEWING THE IMAGING AND INTERACTION PROCESS

The teacher briefly discusses and models for the students the processes presented in chapter 24.

STEP 2   DISCUSSING IMAGING AS A SELF-MONITORING STRATEGY

The teacher gives examples of inaccuracies that might result from misinterpretation of the text. She uses examples from curriculum and/or literature currently in use in the classroom. For instance, the following sentence presents an example of word use that might be unfamiliar to many children:

> *Historians say the American Revolution had three firebrands: Samuel Adams, Patrick Henry, and Thomas Paine.*

Asking the students to explain the term *firebrands* might result in several different definitions or none at all. By encouraging them to stop and create images of *fire* and *brands* and to discuss how those two words might be connected to people, students may then make the connection of ways in which people might start a fire or in this case spark a revolution. This combination of imaging and interacting allows them to create meaning and understanding from otherwise incomprehensible text. Then, by reading on in the text, they may be able to confirm the accuracy of their images by comparing them to images in the text that follows. They may also recognize a mismatch between their images and the text and realize the need for further clarification for understanding.

STEP 3   IDENTIFYING LOGICAL CHECKPOINTS

The students must be presented with examples with a variety of logical stopping points. They need to see that the need to stop and create images may occur after a single word, a sentence, a paragraph, or even a whole page. The lack of understanding could be the result of several factors, such as unfamiliar topic, lack of vocabulary, length of sentences, and/or multiple meanings of words. They need to recognize the need to be proactive in looking for areas of misunderstanding and initiating the use of stopping points to take time to create the images necessary to appropriately interpret the reading material. The following example may serve to introduce students to multiple imaging and interaction points for self-monitoring for understanding.

> *Henry stepped into the aisle, bowed his head, and held out his arms. He pretended his arms were chained as he began calmly, "Our chains are forged, their clanking may be heard on the plains of Boston." His voice strengthened as he said, "The war is actually begun. The next gale that sweeps from the north will bring to our ears the clash of resounding arms. Our brethren are already in the field. Why stand we here idle? . . . Is life so dear, or peace so sweet, as to be purchased at the price of chains and slavery?"*
>
> *Then Patrick Henry threw off the imaginary chains, stood up straight, and cried out, "Forbid it, almighty God! I know not what course others may take, but as for me, give me liberty or give me death!"* (Hakim, 1993, p. 62)

Patrick Henry's challenge to his fellow members of the then-dissolved House of Burgesses provides a rich opportunity for students to visualize the context of this speech. Can they see him standing in the aisle of the old church in Richmond, Virginia? Can they visualize the invisible chains he carries on his arms? Can they describe the looks on the faces of his fellows listening to his impassioned outcry? Are they familiar with his colorful choice of words? Could they put his speech into today's vernacular? As the scene unfolds in the text, frequent stops might be necessary to set the stage of the speech and the mood of the fellows meeting secretly in a church, elements of the text that lead to better comprehension and understanding of the importance of the information being presented for the reader.

The teacher has the students pick imaging points in the paragraph that might be appropriate for stopping and creating images that would lead to a better understanding of the text for them. Different students may choose to stop at different points to support their own comprehension. They should be encouraged to stop at those points they feel are necessary to enlighten their own understanding of the text as their personal needs require. The teacher reminds them that there is no set formula for determining these imaging points, but that the choice is under the control of readers as dictated by their need for clarification and comprehension.

STEP 4   PRACTICING AND DISCUSSING THE STRATEGY

The teacher provides the students with a selected portion of text. She directs them to read the text silently and mark their individual imaging points in the body of the text. Then she encourages students to share their selection of imaging points and to discuss the reasons they marked those particular points. This reinforces the concept of the individuality of imaging point selection and the variety of reasons for the need to stop and create images to assist comprehension. Further discussion on reasons for stopping at specific points in the text might help clarify the strategy for students. In this case, the teacher should feel free to facilitate the discussion to lead students to discovering reasons for stopping that may not have surfaced in the individual sharing.

APPLICATIONS AND EXAMPLES

For an example of imaging and interacting instruction in the content of a third-grade literature and history unit, see File 37 of the accompanying CD.

Ms. Cappricio is explaining to her eighth-grade social studies class that much of the version of *Huckleberry Finn* (DeVoto, 1984.) they will be reading is written in a variety of dialects. They will encounter language that may be unfamiliar to them, and they will need to be carefully monitoring their clear understanding of the content as they are reading.

She briefly reviews the imaging processes that they had previously learned, and they proceed to examine the early part of the text to look for possible problem areas.

"Here's a good example," says Ms. Cappricio. "'There was things which he stretched, but mainly he told the truth.' Now what picture does that sentence create in your mind, class?"

Althea raises her hand and says, "He's talking about people stretching the truth—lying, I think."

Lou jumps in and says, "Well, first I pictured him stretching a rope or something, but then when I saw the rest of the sentence, it made more sense to see him as stretching the truth, like Althea said, lying."

"That's great," Ms. Cappricio remarks. "That's just the idea, using what is in the text to inform you about the logic of the pictures you are creating for yourself. Let's see if you can find another example."

"Here's one," says Arlene. "'It was an awful sight of money when it was piled up.' At first I pictured an ugly pile of money, all dirty and wet or something, but then I realized he meant a big pile of a lot of money."

"Good," Ms. Cappricio says. "So now we see that because the author is using a variety of dialects, we may have to do a lot of self-monitoring of our reading using imaging, at least until we get used to the dialects. So what do you think, do we need to stop and self-monitor every sentence, or every paragraph, or what? What do you think, Elsinore?"

"I think we just need to stop whenever we don't clearly understand something. So that might be more in some parts and less in others. It depends on what part of the story we are reading," she responds.

"OK," Ms. Cappricio says, "then for the first five times that you feel the need to stop, I would like you to make a triple-entry journal page on which you put the word or phrase that stopped you on the left side of the page and the image that you pictured in your mind in the middle of the page, and the self-correction, if you were able to decipher it, on the right side of the page. That will help us see what kinds of things are

FIGURE 37.1 Triple-entry journal page example.

Word or Phrase from the Text	Initial Image	Self-Correction
. . . a barrel of odds and ends . . .	a barrel with a lot of different stuff in it	a mixture of food; a stew
I was in a sweat to find out all about him	sitting in a steam room, sweating	I was anxious to find out about him
a tolerable slim old maid with goggles on	skinny old lady with goggles on	reasonably slim, unmarried, with glasses

most confusing for us in this kind of reading and how we can most effectively approach clarifying the text for ourselves. It should look like this." Ms. Cappricio models on the overhead an example for students. See figure 37.1 for her example.

CONCLUSION

Assisting students in developing these self-monitoring strategies is essential to the proper use of imaging and interacting with text. Students must be reminded that first impressions are not necessarily the most correct interpretation of text and that each interpretation must be constantly reexamined in light of the contextual use of the material. In using imaging as a self-monitoring strategy, students need to be comfortable with stopping and creating mental pictures of the ideas and concepts they are unsure of and relating these pictures to the sequence of events as they unfold in the reading. The strength of using this particular strategy is that it requires students to become actively involved in the process of reading and comprehending.

REFERENCES

DeVoto, B. (Ed). (1984). *Huckleberry Finn In The Portable Mark Twain.* (pp. 193–573). New York: Penguin Books.

Hakim, J. (1993). *A history of US: From colonies to country.* New York: Oxford University Press.

NOTE TAKING

Identifying and Monitoring Understanding of Important Information

Taking notes related to the text being read and the lesson being presented has long been considered an important study skill. Research has shown, however, that note taking alone is not the most effective way to employ this self-monitoring strategy. Note taking requires some mental processing of the material being encountered. This in itself implies that readers (or listeners) be engaged in actively processing and monitoring their understanding of the information being read (or heard). Studies on the effectiveness of note taking show that their use is more effective when the notes are used to write slightly longer paraphrased notes immediately after reading the material and taking the notes (Kiewa, 1985a). This step provides an opportunity for readers to test their understanding of the material as well. Another strategy that has been shown to increase the effectiveness of note taking is for the teacher to provide a structure for student note taking that gives main categories or questions to complete as they read. This completing of notes to fill in a structure combined with a review of the notes taken increases readers' knowledge of their understanding and eventually serves to increase student comprehension and learning (Kiewa, 1985b).

Teaching students to take effective notes is made easier when students are looking for certain facts or concepts and completing a note-taking structure. Once students have engaged in this type of note taking, they can be moved into a less structured approach to taking notes because they have had practice in identifying and monitoring their understanding of the main ideas and concepts within a reading passage.

> **Focus on English Learners**
>
> Employing a structure for note taking assists English learners in both creating and reviewing the notes and serves to increase comprehension and learning.

STEP BY STEP

The steps for teaching effective note taking are:

STEP 1 EXPLAINING THE PURPOSE OF NOTE TAKING

The teacher introduces the study of note taking by discussing why people take notes. The usefulness of being able to review and organize short phrases instead of rereading large amounts of text are discussed. The teacher also explains taking notes from several books to combine information when writing a research report. Finally, he discusses reviewing notes as a way of monitoring students' understanding of the material being read.

The teacher introduces the idea that several different methods of note taking can be done for different purposes. Using note cards, for example, is important when preparing notes for a written or oral report. Placing the notes on individual cards that can be organized into categories makes writing a report much easier. If certain information is being sought, the use of a note taking structure makes the process more effective. No matter which note taking system is used, however, notes are an important aid, both in monitoring one's own understanding and in reviewing information.

STEP 2   MODELING EFFECTIVE NOTE TAKING

The teacher models the method of note taking to be used for the reading assignment. If a note taking structure is to be used, he involves the students in making decisions about the type of information that should be gathered to obtain the information that will be useful in completing the assignment for which the notes are being taken. If the students are taking notes in preparation for taking a test, then the main ideas and important supporting details must be identified and written down. If the students are going to complete an assignment in which various species will be compared, the structure should involve taking notes related to certain attributes that can later be compared. Once the teacher and students identify the purpose of the specific note-taking task, they cooperatively construct the structure they will use in taking notes. See figure 38.1 for examples of various note-taking structures. The teacher then models the use of the structure by reading a few pages of the reading assignment aloud and taking notes with the use of the note-taking structure that was designed.

STEP 3   PROVIDING GUIDED PRACTICE IN TAKING NOTES

Once the teacher has modeled the procedure to be used, he walks the students through the reading and note taking of several more pages of text. He asks the students to read the text a paragraph at a time and directs them to take notes. After each paragraph and note taking, the teacher asks students to share what they have written and their choices are discussed. The students are also questioned regarding any techniques, such as rereading, underlining, and consulting dictionaries, they used in the note-taking process to support their understanding of the material. The focus of this discussion should not be identifying the exact words to be written but rather identifying the important facts or concepts and making note of them. It should be emphasized that each reader may actually write different words in his or her notes.

STEP 4   PRACTICING NOTE TAKING

Once the teacher is sure that the students understand the procedures to be used, the students are instructed to complete the reading assignment, taking notes as they read. If the teacher has identified students who need more support to successfully complete the assignment, he gathers these students together and provides more guided practice with them.

STEP 5   USING THE INFORMATION GATHERED

It is essential to provide a use for the notes taken in the early stages of learning to take notes. Only when students must use the notes do they begin to understand the importance of having organized notes, taking down strategic information, and preplanning note taking according to the use the notes will serve. The notes can be used to write oral or written reports, to play informational games such as trivia, or to create

FIGURE 38.1 Examples of note-taking structures.

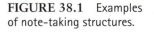

Who?
What?
When?
Where?
How?

Cause ————————▶ Effect

Event Sequence:

Event #1 _____

      Details _____

               _____

               _____

Event #2 _____

      Details _____

               _____

               _____

Event #3 _____

      Details _____

               _____

               _____

Data Chart
Topic _____

Questions ➔
Sources ↓

Comparisons	Example #1	Example #2	Example #3
Descriptions			
Activities			
Notable Attributes			

informational posters, just to name a few uses. In any case, students need to be shown the importance and applicability of taking and using the notes they have collected. They should be taught to reread for clarification whenever they cannot expand on the meaning of the notes. Again we emphasize the importance of research that points out that the simple act of taking notes is not sufficient to increase comprehension.

STEP 6   REPEATING THE PROCESS

Once students have mastered one format for note taking, they should be introduced to others so that they can see the importance of planning the taking of notes to enhance the way they will be used.

APPLICATIONS AND EXAMPLES

In the process of studying ocean animals, Ms. Santos has discovered that her third-grade students are fascinated with whales and dolphins. To capitalize on this interest and teach them basic note taking, Ms. Santos plans to introduce the book *Discovering Whales and Dolphins* (Craig, 1990). Ms. Santos is especially excited

Note-taking instruction in a 10th-grade research project is explained on File 38 of the accompanying CD.

about finding this resource since the book is available in both English and Spanish and several of her students read more successfully in Spanish. She begins the study of note taking by explaining the purpose of taking notes to her students.

"Sometimes when we are going to use information from a book to write a report or create posters, we need to be able to remember exact facts," she tells them. "I'm going to teach you how to take notes as you read this book today. After we read the book and take notes, we will design posters telling about the different kinds of whales and dolphins explained in the book. Now, if we are going to design posters, what kind of information do we need to gather?"

"The different kinds of whales?" asks Mario tentatively.

"Very good, Mario," replies Ms. Santos. "We'll need to remember the different kinds of whales. What else will we need to know?"

"How big they are?" suggests Tomas.

"Yes, Tomas, we will want to know their size," confirms Ms. Santos. "Let's make a form that we can use to take notes. That way we'll be sure to get all the information we need about each whale and dolphin." Ms. Santos writes *name* and *size* on the chalkboard vertically in a column.

"What other information will we need to know?" asks Ms. Santos.

"Maybe anything special about each whale?" suggests Martha.

"Good idea, Martha," says Ms. Santos as she adds the words *special features* to the growing list.

The discussion continues and the list is lengthened by the addition of the terms *food*, *body parts*, *swimming speed*. Once the list is complete, Ms. Santos tells the students to listen as she reads the first two pages of *Discovering Whales and Dolphins* aloud. She copies the list from the chalkboard down the left side of an overhead transparency and stops occasionally during the oral reading to note the information she is gaining. She uses this modeling time to demonstrate that she can take notes by writing just a word or short phrase. She also models rereading for clarification when the students have difficulty deciding what to write.

After Ms. Santos models the taking of notes using the student-generated note-taking structure, she instructs them to read the next two pages, taking notes about the sperm whale just as she did about the blue whale. She first has the students write the note-taking list down the left side of their paper and then they are told to find the information about the sperm whale and note it next to the categories on their paper. She reminds them to reread anytime they can't complete the notes. Since they seem to understand just what to do, she instructs them to finish reading the book, in English or Spanish, taking notes about each of the whales. Since she has two students for whom reading the text is difficult, she pairs each of them with a strong reader and they work together as partners.

Once note taking is complete, Ms. Santos gathers the students together and they discuss the notes they have taken. She finds that the students have written almost the same things on their papers, with slight variations. She congratulates them on a job well done and goes on to explain their next task. "We will use the notes we have taken today to create whale posters for our classroom," she explains. "We will work in six groups since we read about six different kinds of whales. Each group will visit the Internet and find a picture of their whale. You may choose to draw your picture, if you'd rather do that. You will then add the information you have discovered to your poster. Remember, when you make posters, you want the print to be large enough to read easily. Now, let's decide exactly how we want to put the information on the posters."

The students work together to design the format of the whale posters. Ms. Santos assigns them to groups and they work happily from their notes to complete their assignment.

CONCLUSION

Note taking is not an easy strategy to teach. The purpose and application of taking notes must be made clear to students. The use of note taking in metacognition is especially powerful, but students have to be taught to use notes for this purpose. Teaching them to reread for clarification anytime they have difficulty deciding what to include in their notes is a good strategy. Additional strategies such as using a dictionary, paraphrasing, and using contextual clues can be used anytime students recognize that they are not really understanding the material.

The specific note-taking strategy must be carefully matched to the assignment or students may become frustrated with the task. If the strategy is presented logically and modeled well, students can be successful taking notes. Note taking can be powerful in supporting reading comprehension if the notes are discussed periodically during the lesson. The organization of note cards to support the writing of a research project involves another lesson in which modeling and guided practice are necessary. Note taking will only serve to enhance comprehension and recall if it is taught thoroughly and students understand its purpose and power.

REFERENCES

Craig, J. (1990). *Discovering whales and dolphins.* New York: Troll Associates.

Kiewa, K. A. (1985a). Investigating note taking and review. *Educational Psychologist, 20,* 23–32.

Kiewa, K. A. (1985b). Providing the instructor's notes: An effective addition to student note taking. *Educational Psychologist, 20,* 33–39.

39

RECIPROCAL TEACHING

A Cooperative Approach to Comprehension Monitoring

Reciprocal teaching (Palincsar & Brown, 1986) is a strategy in which a small group of students work cooperatively to apply metacognitive strategies while reading and studying informational text. The strategy involves students taking turns presenting sections of the reading passage through a series of steps that enable the group to practice **reading** for a purpose, **summarizing** what has been read, **questioning** the main points to ensure understanding, and **clarifying** points that are unclear. The teacher introduces the procedure by itemizing the series of strategies to be used, modeling the sequence, and reviewing the steps. Students in small groups then take turns being the "teacher," leading members of the group through the steps of reading, summarizing, questioning, and clarifying for one paragraph of the assigned reading material. The "teacher" changes with each paragraph in the reading assignment, and each group member takes a turn leading the group through the steps until the entire reading assignment has been completed.

The power of the group interaction supports comprehension of the reading material by each member of the group. The continual repetition of the sequence of reading, summarizing, questioning, and clarifying establishes a metacognitive sequence that supports individual students as they transfer it to their own reading and studying. See figure 39.1 for an explanation of the sequence of events in reciprocal teaching.

STEP BY STEP

The steps in implementing reciprocal teaching are:

STEP 1   CHOOSING THE TEXT

The teacher chooses informational text that contains some difficult vocabulary or concepts that may cause comprehension problems. Tough text is a good choice for modeling the use of reciprocal teaching since the students will be required to interact and support one another's understanding of the reading material.

FIGURE 39.1   Steps in reciprocal teaching.

Step	What to Do	Learning Strategy
Group formation	Form a group of students to read cooperatively. Choose the sequence of reciprocal teachers (students).	Cooperation
Read	Each member of the group reads the first section of the text.	Silent reading
Summarize	The first student summarizes the section just read.	Summarizing
Question	The first student questions other members of the group.	Questioning
Clarify	The first student clarifies any area of text that presented difficulty to any member of the group.	Comprehension monitoring
Problem solving	The group discusses possible solutions or strategies that could be used.	Cooperation
Prediction	The first student makes a prediction about what is likely to happen in the next section of text.	Predicting Inferring
Read	The group reads the next section silently.	Silent reading

The whole procedure is repeated with the second student in the group leading.

Adapted from A. Herrell, 2000, *Fifty Strategies for Teaching English Language Learners*, Upper Saddle River, NJ: Merrill/Prentice Hall. Used with permission.

STEP 2   FORMING THE RECIPROCAL TEACHING GROUPS

The teacher establishes the groups that will work together in reading the chosen text. It is important to make sure that each group has some strong readers.

STEP 3   MODELING THE PROCEDURE

The teacher distributes a copy of the text to be read to each member of the class. She serves as teacher for the first paragraph of the reading material. Students read the material silently. The teacher then briefly summarizes the most important information in the paragraph and thinks of questions that require readers to be able to provide main-idea types of responses. The students answer the questions formulated by the teacher, and the teacher must clarify any points that are not clear to any of the students. The group can be involved in some problem solving at this point if any students experience confusion. The final step is for the group to predict what information will be contained in the next section of text.

STEP 4   TAKING TURNS BEING THE TEACHER

After the classroom teacher models the sequence of activities, the groups convene and repeat the process with students serving as designated teachers for a paragraph. Each student takes a turn leading the group through the steps of reading silently. Then the designated teacher for an assigned paragraph summarizes, formulates questions, asks the questions of the group, clarifies to ensure understanding, and predicts what will be contained in the next section.

STEP 5   DEBRIEFING AFTER THE ACTIVITY

The teacher calls the whole class back together after the activity is complete. The teacher asks each group to briefly discuss any problems they had or any parts of the reading that still require clarification. The students are encouraged to share their approaches to solving problems and any areas of the reading that cause problems.

APPLICATIONS AND EXAMPLES

For an example of reciprocal teaching in a middle school ESL class see File 39 of the accompanying CD.

In preparation for a field trip to Yosemite Park, Mr. Burton and his fourth graders are reading a series of Native American legends they located on the Internet. Accessing the web site on California Native Americans, Mr. Burton has downloaded a series of stories related to Yosemite and its history and the explanations for the names of the park and other locations within the park (*www.indians.org/welker/ yosemite.htm*).

Mr. Burton decides to use reciprocal teaching to support the students' understanding of the Native American legends since they sound like factual information but are the Native American explanations for natural phenomenon. He divides the students into groups of five and distributes copies of the first legend, *The Origin of Yosemite*.

"I am going to teach you a procedure we call reciprocal teaching. The word *reciprocal* means that we teach each other. I teach you something and you return the favor, or reciprocate, by teaching me something. There are a series of steps we do in reciprocal teaching."

As he names the steps, Mr. Burton writes them on the chalkboard. "First, we all read the first paragraph silently. Let's go ahead and do that." Mr. Burton writes the word *read* on the chalkboard.

When the students have finished reading the first paragraph, Mr. Burton says, "Now, since I am the teacher, I summarize the paragraph for the group." As Mr. Burton writes the word *summarize* on the board, he begins, "Many years ago there was a group of peaceful Indians who lived among the trees of beautiful Oak Canyon. Oak Canyon was a spectacular place. It is now known as Yosemite Valley and it is located in central California."

Mr. Burton then writes the word *question* on the board. "Now, as the teacher, I question the group. What was Yosemite Valley called before it was called Yosemite?"

The students answer in unison, "Oak Valley."

"Very good, class," says Mr. Burton. "Who lived there before the white man came?"

"Peaceful Indians," answers the class.

"Next we clarify the information if there is any confusion," says Mr. Burton as he writes the word *clarify* on the board. "Does anyone need for us to talk about anything in that first paragraph? Is anyone confused?"

"I understand it," says Gina, "but do we know the name of the Indian tribe?"

"Not yet, Gina," answers Mr. Burton, "but maybe it tells us that later in the passage. Now, the last step is to predict what will be in the next paragraph." Mr. Burton writes the word *predict* on the board.

"Who thinks they know what will be in the next paragraph?"

Gina responds, "Maybe they'll tell us the name of the tribe."

"OK, maybe they will," responds Mr. Burton. "We'll have to read and see. Now, you are in your groups and I want you to take turns being the teacher. I'll come around and tap the shoulder of the first teacher in each group, and you'll take turns moving clockwise around the tables. Let's review the steps. First everyone reads the paragraph silently. Then the 'teacher' summarizes the paragraph for the whole group. Next the 'teacher' asks questions of the group. Then the 'teacher' clarifies any confusion for any member of the group who needs clarification. If the 'teacher' needs help in clarifying, he or she can ask the group for help. Then the 'teacher' predicts what will be in the next paragraph. The whole series of activities is then repeated with the next student serving as the 'teacher.' Does anyone have any questions about the procedure? Remember, we will meet together at the end of the reading activity. The purpose of this activity is to make sure everyone in your group understands the information in the reading. This is a Native American legend. Who remembers what that is?"

"It's the Indians' explanation of how things came about," answers Jason.

"So, is it factual information?" asks Mr. Burton.

"Not really," responds Gina. "It's just the Indians' thoughts on how it happened. Some of it may be facts, but some of it is just a story that's been passed down over the years."

"Exactly," says Mr. Burton with a smile. "Now, get to work and help each other make sense of this material."

Mr. Burton moves around the room listening to the students take turns teaching the reading material. He makes notes of particularly good group work and explanations to celebrate with the class when they finish the activity. He knows that reciprocal teaching will take several practice sessions before the students can do it well, but he's pleased with their first attempt.

CONCLUSION

Reciprocal teaching is an exciting way to support students' use of metacognitive strategies. As each student has an opportunity to serve as teacher for the group, she or he has to practice summarizing, formulating questions, finding ways to clarify concepts, and predicting. All of these strategies are helpful later when the students are facing informational text as individuals. Seeing the procedures repeated multiple times helps them to understand the metacognitive strategies and gives them several chances to practice. The discussions that take place in the groups serve to clarify understanding and support the students in seeing that many times people understand concepts in slightly different ways.

REFERENCES

Palincsar, A. S., and Brown, A. L. (1986). Interactive teaching to promote independent learning from text. *The Reading Teacher, 39,* 771–777.

SUGGESTED READING

Hashey, J. M., & Connors, D. J. (2003). Learn from our journey: Reciprocal teaching action research. *The Reading Teacher, 57,* 224–232.

Herrell, A., and Jordan, M. (2000). *Fifty strategies for teaching English language learners* (2nd ed.). Upper Saddle River, NJ: Merrill/Prentice Hall.

Oczkus, L. (2003). *Reciprocal teaching at work: Strategies for improving reading comprehension.* Newark, DE: International Reading Association.

40

FIX-UP STRATEGIES

Knowing What to Do When Reading Doesn't Make Sense

Metacognition, monitoring your own understanding, is a vital part of reading comprehension. Students are involved in making sense of the words they are reading, but they must be monitoring their own understanding in order for the messages in the words to come alive to them. Once they recognize that they are not comprehending, however, they must have a repertoire of strategies to use to clarify the meaning of the text. In addition to having a choice of strategies to use, they need to be able to decide which of the strategies is most likely to clarify the meaning of the text with which they are struggling.

Fix-up strategies are a general name for all the possible strategies students might choose to use to clarify meaning once they recognize that they are not comprehending the text they are reading. Collins and Smith (1980) call these *repair strategies* and recommend six approaches:

1. Ignoring the problem and continuing to read, hoping that something in the following text will clarify the text that's not understood.
2. Suspending judgment for now and continuing to read with the idea that connections will be made clear at a later point in the text (slightly different from the previous approach in that it's the connections between or among elements in the story that are not making sense rather than a particular sentence or phrase).
3. Forming a tentative hypothesis based on information in the text and then continuing to read to confirm or revise your hypothesis.
4. Looking back or rereading the previous sentence.
5. Stopping and thinking about the meaning of the previously read material and rereading it in an attempt to fit it into the bigger picture.
6. Seeking help from resources within the room such as dictionaries, reference materials, and knowledgeable people.

One of the important factors in using fix-up strategies is the practice of stopping at appropriate places in reading the text to check for understanding. Often teachers begin teaching self-monitoring by having the students stop at the end of each paragraph to check for understanding. The students may use self-questioning: What happened? When did it happen? Where did it happen? To whom did it happen? Another strategy is periodic paraphrasing (see chapter 38), in which readers stop and paraphrase the paragraph to make sure they can review what was read in their own words. No matter what method students use to check their understanding, they still need to know what to do once they recognize that they can't answer the questions or can't retell the paragraph in their own words. For some students, simply rereading the paragraph is an effective strategy. This often works as long as they are carefully monitoring their understanding sentence by sentence so that they can clarify meaning at the point at which comprehension breaks down. Sometimes they then move into using resources such as dictionaries or other people in the room.

Teachers must introduce the need to apply fix-up strategies and the variety of approaches available to readers to clarify meaning. Students need to be aware of the strategies they use and whether or not they are using them effectively. If students recognize that they are not always fixing their comprehension problems, they need to try some new strategies to see if they can find some additional ones that rectify the situation.

STEP BY STEP

The steps in teaching the use of fix-up strategies are:

STEP 1   ENCOURAGING STUDENTS TO IDENTIFY THE STRATEGIES THEY USE

The teacher asks the students, "What do you do when you realize you are not understanding the material you are reading?" As the students give responses, the teacher writes them on a chart or chalkboard. He then gives the students some reading material and asks them to read it, stopping periodically to monitor their own understanding. If they find that they need to do something because they didn't understand the material, they should write down exactly what they do to try to clarify the meaning of the text.

STEP 2   DISCUSSING FIX-UP STRATEGIES STUDENTS USE

After reading the assigned text, the teacher encourages students to describe the strategies they use. He probes as necessary to get a full description of exactly what students do and in what sequence. These strategies are written on the chalkboard along with the ones they suggested earlier. If there are repetitions, the teacher tallies them so that it becomes evident which of the strategies are used by many students.

STEP 3   INTRODUCING THE REPAIR STRATEGIES

The teacher then introduces the six repair strategies listed previously and discusses them with students. Together they note the strategies that match the ones used by students and discuss any that were not used. The teacher makes note of the repair strategies that are not currently being used by students and uses them for the first lessons to be taught on fix-up strategies.

STEP 4   TEACHING FIX-UP STRATEGIES

The teacher introduces fix-up strategies, one at a time, and gives the students guided practice in using them. He introduces the strategy and then models using it, thinking aloud as he processes the text, attempts to paraphrase it, and recognizes that he needs to do something to clarify the meaning. Once the teacher models the thought processes involved in identifying a problem with comprehension, he introduces the new strategy and walks the students through the steps, thinking aloud so they can observe the process he uses to clarify meaning. He lists individual steps on the chalkboard as he uses them.

STEP 5   PRACTICING THE NEW STRATEGIES

The teacher then gives students a reading assignment and reminds them to use the new strategy. He walks them through the steps he has listed on the chalkboard and asks them to use the strategy at least once as they read the assigned text.

STEP 6   DISCUSSING THE PRACTICE EXERCISE

Once the students have completed their reading, the teacher encourages them to discuss how they used the strategy. Some students may not have experienced difficulty and would not have had an opportunity to use the strategy but by walking through the steps several times as their fellow students explain their use of it, the strategy will be more familiar to them. The steps for using the strategy should be placed on a chart in the room so that students can use it for reference for awhile as the sequence becomes automatic.

APPLICATIONS AND EXAMPLES

 A fix-up strategy lesson is used in a fourth-grade classroom on File 40 of the accompanying CD.

Mr. Jacowizc is working with a group of 11th graders whose reading scores are low. He is teaching them strategies they can use in their reading to improve their fluency and comprehension. Many of these students are convinced they will never graduate from high school, and they've almost given up on ever learning to read well. Mr. J. is determined that their reading will improve this year. He has chosen a simple book entitled *The Journey of English* (Brook, 1998) to use with his students. He is convinced that understanding how English got so complicated will help the students to realize that the language is difficult and they are not "stupid" because they have difficulty in mastering its reading and writing.

He begins by saying, "There are many times when I am reading that I must stop and try to make sense of what I am reading. Sometimes I reread a sentence or two. Other times I have to stop and look up a word in the dictionary. But the most important thing I do is stop every now and then and make sure I understand what I am reading. I often ask myself questions like, 'Where was he going?' or 'How does he know that?' Those questions may tell me that I need to go back and reread. It is very important that you know the strategies you use when you don't understand what you are reading."

He then says, "We are going to be doing some silent reading for awhile this morning. I want you to stop at the end of each paragraph and work with a partner. One of you should tell the other one, in your own words, what the paragraph was about. If you find you cannot restate the meaning of the paragraph, note what you do to clarify the meaning. Do you automatically reread the paragraph? Do you go back and reread just a sentence or two where you may have had some questions initially? Do you ask your partner what he or she thought it meant? The purpose of this exercise is for you to identify the strategies you use. You may not always use the same ones. If you use a number of different strategies, write them down. When we finish reading this passage, I want you and your partner to be familiar with the approaches you currently use. Then we can begin to learn some new approaches that may help you in the future."

After the students complete their reading of the first four pages, Mr. J. stops them and asks them to share the strategies they find they are using the most. While many of the students report using rereading, Leslie shares an important point. "I think I've used phonics more in this book than I usually do," she says. "So many of the words are hard. I haven't ever seen a lot of them before."

"You have made an important discovery, Leslie. The strategies we use do change according to the reading material. Because this book has a lot of foreign words in it, or at least English words that came from foreign languages, you may have to sound them out or even look them up in the dictionary," Mr. J. says. "Now read an example of what you are talking about."

Leslie reads, "'Going back to prehistoric times, many languages, including English, started near the present border between Europe and Asia.' These aren't foreign words. They're just long words. Pre-his-tor-ic was hard to figure out."

"I think maybe we will review our study of prefixes and suffixes from last year," says Mr. J., almost thinking out loud. "Sometimes breaking the word into smaller parts helps you to figure out how to pronounce it, but also what it means."

"Well, I reread a lot on these four pages. I also used phonics. I also was really glad the book has pictures because they helped me too," says Jerome. "One thing I learned, though, is that English has a lot of words. The book says that helps you to say just what you mean. It also keeps you from understanding if you don't know the words people are using or the words in the books. There are just too many words to learn."

"I hear you saying that we need to work on building your vocabularies so you won't have this problem," answers Mr. J. with a smile.

"Only if you can make it painless. I have had enough pain with reading and writing, already," laughs Jerome.

"The important thing I want you to learn this year is that you can learn to read and write well," responds Mr. J. "We are going to really focus on putting each of you in charge of your own learning. We are going to be learning new strategies for solving problems as you read. The first of these fix-up strategies we are going to practice this morning is called *reading on*. What it means is this: If you don't understand something in a sentence you just keep reading to the end of the sentence. You don't stop. If, by the end of the sentence, the meaning of the confusing part is not clear, you read on through the next sentence. Then, if you still don't understand what the sentences mean, you go back and try to put the pieces together. Let me show you how it's done."

Mr. J. opens *The Journey of English* to the fifth page and reads aloud, "About 3000 B.C., tribes that lived in the area of today's Siberia spoke one language, now called Indo-European." Mr. J. stops.

"Now suppose I don't understand the meaning of the phrase 'in the area of today's Siberia.' I just keep reading on to the end of the sentence. Well, I get the idea that the sentence is talking about a certain place on the map, but I don't really know where it is. I'm not even sure it's important so I go ahead and read the next sentence. 'These tribes kept moving farther away from one another.' So I have read on through the next sentence. I still don't know where Siberia is but I'm beginning to get the idea that it's not that important. The 'tribes moving away' seems to be more important so I am going to continue to read and try to put the pieces together. If I find out later that I need to know where Siberia is, what can I do?"

"You can always look at a map," suggests Donald.

"Exactly!" says Mr. J. "Actually there's a map on this page. It just doesn't have Siberia marked on it. Maybe I am right. Maybe Siberia is not really important to understanding this page."

"Now, for the next four pages, you and your partner are going to practice reading on," Mr. J. continues. "After you both read the page silently, talk to each other about the problems you had and whether reading on helps. After you finish page eight, let's get back together and see how well we do."

As the students practice their new fix-up strategy, Mr. J. moves around the room listening, taking notes, giving encouragement, and answering questions. He has learned a lot about his students during this short lesson. He knows he needs to continue to focus on vocabulary development and structural analysis. He also realizes that he needs to locate more high-level reading material with illustrations to support their reading and comprehending of text. As is usually the case, students will tell you what they need, if you are watching and listening carefully.

CONCLUSION

Supporting students as they learn to monitor their own comprehension involves a constant updating of their strategies for solving their own problems. Teachers must find methods to reveal the strategies their students are currently using as they encounter difficulties. Teaching new strategies must always include modeling and guided practice to make sure that the students fully understand how to use the new strategies but also how to combine strategies for the most effective problem solving.

One of the most important parts in teaching self-monitoring is to help students get into the habit of stopping to check for understanding on an ongoing basis. Some students seem to want to rush through any reading assignment as if they were taking bad-tasting medicine. Teachers have a tendency to blame their poor comprehension on the fact that they rush when they read. The rushing is a symptom, not a cause of the poor comprehension, however. All students need a wide repertoire of strategies to use to help themselves make sense of text. Validating that all readers, even the teacher, occasionally must use fix-up strategies helps struggling readers to understand that knowing how to use strategies is a valuable part of supporting understanding.

REFERENCES

Brook, D. (1998). *The journey of English*. New York: Clarion Books.

Collins, A., & Smith, E. (1980). *Teaching the process of reading comprehension* (Technical report number 182). Urbana-Champaign: University of Illinois at Urbana-Champaign, Center for the Study of Reading.

SUGGESTED READING

Baker, L. (2002). Metacognition in comprehension instruction. In C. C. Block & M. Pressley (Eds.), *Comprehension instruction: Research-based best practices* (pp. 77–95). New York: Guilford.

Massey, D. D. (2003). A comprehension checklist: What if it doesn't make sense? *The Reading Teacher, 57,* 81–84.

SQ4R

Studying for Comprehension and Memory

Metacognitive strategies, used to monitor your own understanding and provide interventions when you don't understand, have been studied for many years (Robinson, 1961; Slavin, 1988; Thomas & Robinson, 1972). One of the best known of the metacognitive strategies is SQ3R (Robinson, 1961), updated to SQ4R by Thomas and Robinson in 1972. The title of the strategy stands for the steps used in studying reading material:

Survey—look through the material quickly, noting main topics and subheadings.

Question—ask yourself questions related to the headings and subheadings.

Read—try to answer the questions you formulated as you read the material.

Reflect—try to make sense of the material by relating it to your prior knowledge.

Recite—ask and answer the questions based on the reading you did.

Review—go over the material, rereading when you find you can't answer the questions you formulated or whenever you realize your understanding is not complete.

The original SQ3R left out the reflection step, but the procedure has remained the same since 1961 with that one addition. Students are taught to employ the sequence of steps when they are reading informational text. The strategy is especially powerful because it combines a number of comprehension processes. The sequence spans the before, during, and after stages of reading. It incorporates the emphasis on expository structure by teaching students to examine the organization of the reading material, especially headings, subheadings, charts, and graphs. The added reflection step encourages students to tap in to their prior knowledge, an important part of comprehension. Finally, the strategy places a focus on monitoring their own understanding and provides support for gaining meaning through a combination of techniques.

STEP BY STEP

The steps in teaching SQ4R are:

STEP 1   INTRODUCING AND EXPLAINING THE STRATEGY

The teacher introduces SQ4R by explaining that the strategy has been used in many settings for 30 or more years but is still good to know. The purpose of the strategy, helping yourself to understand and remember the material you read, especially informational books and textbooks, should be thoroughly discussed. The steps are introduced, and each step is explained and modeled using a familiar textbook.

STEP 2   PROVIDING GUIDED PRACTICE

The teacher gives the students a reading assignment in one of their textbooks and then walks them through each step in the strategy, giving them a chance to practice each step and talk about their discoveries—both the text and their own thought processes. The teacher gives students a chance to ask questions and to talk about any problems or misunderstandings they encounter.

STEP 3   ENCOURAGING INDEPENDENT PRACTICE

The teacher posts the steps in SQ4R on a chart in the classroom and encourages students to use the strategy as they read their textbooks or any other informational books.

STEP 4   DISCUSSING PROBLEMS AND OUTCOMES

After the students have an opportunity to practice the strategy, the teacher leads a discussion in which she asks questions about the reading assignment, their use of SQ4R, and their level of mastery of the material they read. The teacher explores any instances in which the students were able to recognize their own lack of understanding and go back to the reading material to clarify meaning.

STEP 5   REFINING THE USE OF THE STRATEGY

The teacher works with individual students who have difficulty in using SQ4R, giving them additional guided practice in using the strategy. Students who are using the strategy effectively are given a chance to discuss their approach and to refine the reflection step through use of think-aloud (see chapter 19 on think-aloud).

APPLICATIONS AND EXAMPLES

Miss Elsinore's fifth graders are going on a whale watching ship as a field trip. Because they are motivated to learn about the whales they will be watching, she seizes this opportunity to teach them a strategy for reading and remembering factual information. Miss Elsinore prepares a chart listing the steps in the SQ4R study strategy and introduces the sequence through the use of a book entitled *Finding Out About Whales* (Kelsey, 1998).

"The first step in using SQ4R is to survey the book. That means we look through it quickly, not reading the book but looking at the way the book is organized," she tells students. "We want to look at the headings, subheadings, illustrations, and any special features we find. Do you notice anything special about the way this book is organized?"

"Well," starts Karen, "the first part is an introduction and there's a chart showing how big the various whale are in comparison to school buses."

"Good observation, Karen," replies Miss Elsinore. "What do you notice in the next section?"

"There's a page about blue whales and two questions as headings, 'How do we find them?' and 'How do we count them?'" answers Janine. "Oh, and there's a list of research notes. This book has a lot of interesting information about whales."

"The next two pages answer those two questions about the blue whales," says Leonard, "and there are orange circles on each page with more information in them. One tells about what they eat and the next one tells about how scientists

FIGURE 41.1   SQ4R
outline constructed by Miss
Elsinore and her students.

<u>Finding out about whales</u> (Title of the book)
Introduction (Heading)

> *What will we learn by reading this book?* (Student-generated question)

> The sizes of different whales. (Subheading)

Blue Whales (Chapter Heading)

> Research notes. (Subheading)

> *What do researchers know about blue whales?* (Student-generated question)

> How do we find them? (Subheading)

> *Where do they live?* (Student-generated question)

> *What kind of equipment is used to find them?* (Student-generated question)

> How do we count them? (Subheading)

> *What methods do researchers use to count them?* (Student-generated question)

learn about whales from bones they find. I've never seen a book organized like this before."

Miss Elsinore tells the students that they will be using the whole SQ4R sequence to study the book but, for demonstration, she will be modeling the strategies with just the first section of the book, the part about blue whales. She shows the students how to construct a simple outline of the material based on the way it is organized and the questions they are constructing. See figure 41.1 for the outline format Miss Elsinore and the students construct.

She takes the group through the steps of surveying and questioning and then asks them to read the first section with a special emphasis on answering the questions they formulated during the Q step. "You can jot down some brief notes on your outline, if you want to, just to help you remember what you're reading," says Miss Elsinore. The students are engrossed in their reading, and as she walks around the room, she sees a number of them making quick notes.

When the group has finished reading the first section of the book, Miss Elsinore points to the *reflect* section on the SQ4R chart and says, "Now we are going to do the second R, which stands for *reflect*. Reflecting means that you think about the main ideas in the passage and try to relate them to other reading you have done or other experiences you have had. Reflecting means that you make connections between what you are reading and the things you already know or have done in the past. You can jot ideas down on your outline during this part of the strategy, too."

The students talk about some of their experiences going to Sea World and seeing whales and other books they have read about whales. Then Miss Elsinore introduces the third R in the SQ4R sequence, *recite*.

"Work in partners for this part, if you want," she says. "Recite the things you are learning about blue whales in this section. Take turns with your partner, answering the questions you listed on your outline and talking about the information you want to re-member from this section."

She gives the students a few minutes to recite to one another and then talks about the last R, *review*. "In this section you will review what you have learned. Go through the questions and think about the answers. If there is something you can't remember, go back and read that section again and then try to think it through as if you were practicing for an oral report. This is your last step in the procedure so you want to make sure you know the information. When we go out on our trip, you want to be able to understand what's happening and ask good questions. This will help you get ready.

"Now, are you ready to practice SQ4R on your own?" Miss Elsinore asks the class. "There are a lot of steps. I will leave the chart up for you to use but I made something else that I think will help you." She passes out bookmarks to each student with the SQ4R steps printed on them. "Maybe these bookmarks will help you re-member the steps." See figure 41.2 for an example of the bookmark.

Miss Elsinore instructs the students to start the SQ4R sequence again, begin-ning with the second section of the book, Humpback Whales. "Remember to start with surveying, then form your questions so you can answer them when you read. After you read, you reflect, then recite, then review," says Miss Elsinore. "You will all be whale experts by the time we finish this unit."

For an example of SQ4R used in a high school ESL class see File 41 of the accompanying CD.

FIGURE 41.2   Sample SQ4R bookmark.

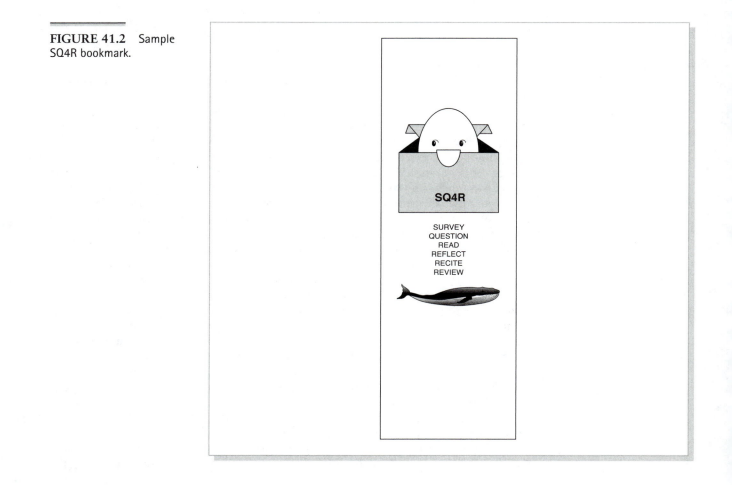

CONCLUSION

SQ4R is a complete strategy to use with informational text any time the teacher wants to make sure that the students are reading, understanding, and remembering content material. The strategy can easily be adapted for use with partners by having the pairs work together for all the steps except the actual reading. When a student cannot read the material independently, the reading can also be done with a partner. The strategy works best when the students have the opportunity to hear it explained and see it modeled. Often students do not comprehend expository text without having a sequence of experiences that include interactions, discussions, and time to reflect on the material and make connections to their prior experiences. This sequence of actions provides a structure for having these supportive interactions with the text.

REFERENCES

Kelsey, E. (1998). *Finding out about whales*. Toronto, Ontario, Canada: Owl Books.

Robinson, F. (1961). *Effective study*. New York: Harper and Row.

Slavin, R. (1988). *Educational psychology: Theory into practice*. Englewood Cliffs, NJ: Prentice Hall.

Thomas, E., & Robinson, H. (1972). *Improving reading in every class: A source book for teachers*. Boston: Allyn and Bacon.

SECTION VI

ASSESSMENT TO INFORM INSTRUCTION

Assessment is vital to effective reading instruction. Teachers should be constantly monitoring students' understanding of the texts they are reading and their use of strategies to support their understanding. A great deal of this ongoing assessment can be done in informal ways; observing, writing simple notes, and taking anecdotal records are all viable methods of assessment in reading. Because the focus of this book is on strategies for supporting vocabulary and comprehension development, section VI focuses on strategies for assessing the effective use of reading strategies.

This section provides a series of assessment strategies that encourage the teacher to "look into the minds" of readers. In an effort to determine the strategies students employ to make sense of text, teachers often get valuable information about the students' self-monitoring strategies, their understanding of vocabulary, and their abilities to draw upon their prior knowledge and thought processes in creating meaning.

This section is in no way an all-inclusive review of comprehension assessment. Many books have been written on assessment in reading. This section provides some assessment strategies that encourage the teacher to look closely at comprehension strategies used by readers. After the assessment is given, the teacher should identify the readers' strengths in relation to their use of strategies to support understanding. In addition, the teacher should zero in on teaching points, areas in which readers would benefit from further instruction. It is easy to identify the fact that students are not comprehending. The more difficult task is to identify the instruction needed to support them in constructing meaning effectively. That is the purpose of the assessment strategies provided here. By using assessment that focuses not just on the level of comprehension but also on the level of comprehension strategy use, the teacher can collect data that informs teaching. The assessment results must, of course, be used to plan future instruction to complete the cycle.

LITERACY OBSERVATION CHECKLISTS

Observing and Conferencing to Document and Set Goals

Focus on English Learners

Literacy observations are especially appropriate for English learners because they allow the observer to see what the student can do rather than relying on purely language-based responses.

As teachers work with groups of students in guided reading, literature discussion groups, and even in content-area classes such as science and social studies, they often have opportunities to observe as students process and discuss text. In these informal assessment situations it is often helpful for teachers to use a checklist of skills, strategies, and reading behaviors to record their observations and thoughts about student strengths and needed instruction.

Literacy observation checklists should include the strategies that have been taught, along with those commonly used by effective readers. The checklists should be appropriate for the ages and grade levels of the students; we don't expect the same levels of problem solving from first graders that we do from high school students. The observation checklist should have space for comments and notes so that the teacher is not confined to the list of strategies and can note any significant reading behaviors. See figure 42.1 for samples of observation checklists.

Literacy observations are unique opportunities to watch students in action. In the more authentic setting of interactions with text that are not identified as "testing situations," the responses and interactions the teacher can observe are often different than those he would see when the student is aware of being tested. Teacher-made checklists allow the teacher to monitor and document strategy use by the students, focusing on the comprehension strategies that are currently being studied (Keene & Zimmerman, 1997).

STEP BY STEP

Steps in using literacy observation checklists are:

STEP 1 PREPARING THE CHECKLIST TO MATCH THE STRATEGIES TAUGHT

The teacher prepares the checklist to include the strategies students are currently studying and those already taught that he wants to monitor. The checklist includes space for comments since the teacher wants to document incidents of unique comprehension strategy use or areas that warrant additional instruction. Many teachers

FIGURE 42.1   Sample literacy observation checklist.

Name _____	Date					Comments
Upper Grades						
Uses background knowledge						
Infers based on illustrations						
Infers based on text						
Asks questions						
Monitors own understanding						
Applies appropriate fix-up strategies						
Visualizes and creates mental images while reading						
Retells including salient points						
Makes text-to-self connections						
Makes text-to-text connections						
Makes text-to-word connections						
Uses knowledge of author to make predictions						
Uses knowledge of story structure to make predictions						
Primary Grades						
Uses background knowledge						
Uses illustrations to support understanding						
Predicts based on illustrations						
Asks questions						
Determines important ideas in text						
Monitors own understanding						
Applies appropriate fix-up strategies						
Visualizes and creates mental images while reading						
Retells including salient points						
Makes text-to-self connections						
Makes text-to-text connections						
Uses knowledge of story structure to make predictions						

find it helpful to use a clipboard to hold the checklist so they can record their observations more easily.

STEP 2   ENGAGING THE STUDENTS IN AUTHENTIC LITERACY SITUATIONS

The teacher plans a literacy activity that enables him to observe students in authentic interactions with text or discussion of text they have read. The activity chosen should give the teacher an opportunity to observe students' literacy behaviors, ask questions to clarify their understanding, and watch verbal interactions among students.

STEP 3   OBSERVING AND MAKING NOTES

The teacher observes students and places plus marks (+), checks (✔), minus signs (−), and comments on the checklist to indicate the effectiveness of the literacy behaviors observed. The teacher also takes this opportunity to note strengths and teaching points for individual students. When observing a group interaction, the teacher should prepare the checklist so that all students are listed and then be careful to observe and document the behavior of all students in the group.

STEP 4   ## MEETING WITH STUDENTS TO TALK ABOUT OBSERVATIONS AND SET GOALS

After the observation or a series of observations, the teacher meets with individual students to discuss the behaviors he has observed. This is a perfect opportunity for celebration and congratulations. Individual conferences are also a good time to talk with students about establishing goals for working on consistent use of comprehension strategies. Some teachers have found it helpful for students to use sticky notes or bookmarks with reminders such as "Stop and check your understanding!" or "Paraphrase after every paragraph" to remind them to practice their comprehension strategies.

STEP 5   ## REPEATING THE PROCESS IN AN ONGOING MANNER

The teacher uses the checklists periodically to monitor the students' progress and their increased use of comprehension strategies. It is sometimes helpful to use the same checklist and make checks and comments in different colored pens/pencils for subsequent observations so that areas of concern are visible and areas of growth are quickly obvious. The teacher uses subsequent conferences with students to share the growth he has been able to document.

APPLICATIONS AND EXAMPLES

Mrs. Rosen prepares an observation checklist to use with her ninth-grade English class. The students have been working on the balanced use of comprehension strategies. Mrs. Rosen has introduced a number of strategies to support her students' use of self-monitoring as they read the literature required by the state language arts standards. Because a number of the readings are challenging for her students, Mrs. Rosen and the students have created a series of charts that are prominently displayed in the classroom. These charts list and briefly explain self-monitoring and fix-up strategies so that students can refer to the charts for strategies to use when they are experiencing difficulty with understanding what they are reading.

Mrs. Rosen gives the students time to read the first 14 pages of *The Old Man and the Sea* (Hemingway, 1952) and moves around the room observing as they read. Because she has taught the students to mark places in the text where they use strategies to clarify, she can see them stop occasionally to attach a sticky note or to turn back and reread. When she observes students marking a place in the text, she allows them time to use their strategy and then she asks, "Which strategy did you use?" Often the students say, "I had to reread to try to figure out the meaning of this word." They also sometimes explain how they arrived at the word meaning through context clues or a combination of context clues and past experience with the word. Mrs. Rosen notes these reports on her literacy observation checklist and then moves on to observe some more.

Once the students have completed their reading, Mrs. Rosen brings them together and asks, "Well, what do you think so far?" Her students are comfortable with "grand conversations" and know they're in charge. Mrs. Rosen asks few questions, and the students talk about the story so far and their impressions of this famous author and their first experience with his works.

Lionel begins, "I can't believe that the old man goes for months on end, rowing out and fishing all day without catching a single fish. He must get very discouraged."

"And the part I found strange was that he thought three fish a week was a lucky week," chimes in Delores.

"I think you're thinking of little lake fish," says Ernie. "Those three fish probably each weighed a hundred pounds. They are talking about Atlantic marlin."

"How do you know that?" asks Delores. "I didn't catch that information."

"Look on page 11," says Ernie. "Where they're talking about the other fisherman laying their fish out and cleaning them. It tells you right here that they're marlin. Besides my grandfather lives in Florida and I've been marlin fishing. Those are really huge fish!"

Mrs. Rosen is listening carefully to the conversation and making notes on her literacy observation checklist. The students are familiar with the purpose of the grand conversation, which is to explore the book, discuss the parts of the story that make impressions on them, and help each other clarify meaning. In the beginning, Mrs. Rosen had to start the conversation with open-ended questions to get them going and occasionally intervene. At first she would ask questions about the ways in which they were constructing their understanding. After a few sessions the students began to take charge and support one another in discovering ways to create meaning. Because she has trained them to mark places in the text where they employ strategies, the students always have a lot to talk about. This allows Mrs. Rosen to use this time to observe and document the strategies her students are using and note the students who still need further instruction.

Delores goes on, "Now I understand the place where the young man says he brought the fish in too green. That didn't make any sense at first. I reread it three times but decided it may not be important so I went on. Now, I get it. Because the fish are so big, the fishermen don't want to pull them into the boat too soon. It talks about how the fish flipped all around. I guess you wouldn't want a huge fish flipping around in the boat."

Mrs. Rosen is getting some good information about her students and the approaches they use. She has noted that Ernie uses a combination of text and experience clues to make meaning. Delores seems to rely more on context clues but does reread to clarify. As the conversation continues, she learns more about all five students in the group. She has purposefully chosen to keep the conversation groups small so that all the students get a chance to talk and she has a chance to observe and note the evidence she is gathering to determine which students need more instruction and specifically what type of instruction they need.

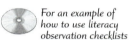

For an example of how to use literacy observation checklists with primary grade students see File 42 of the CD that accompanies this text.

CONCLUSION

Literacy observation checklists allow teachers to monitor and document the students' use of the comprehension strategies that are being taught in the classroom. By using observation, teachers move into more authentic arenas to determine whether or not the instruction they are providing is actually being transferred into practice. Often students understand and can perform strategies under the watchful eyes of their teachers and in the context of being reminded of the strategy that's under discussion and practice. The true test of the students' understanding of the importance of the use of strategies is whether they employ them as situations in reading occur. Teachers continually monitor students' use of strategies with the help of checklists to document behaviors and student conferences to celebrate growth and set new goals. Reminders to students related to strategy use are sometimes needed to encourage students to self-monitor and use fix-up strategies. Although observations and documentation of comprehension strategy use seem to be basic assessment tools, they often support the missing link in comprehension instruction—the use of new techniques for clarification and extension of understanding.

REFERENCES

Hemingway, E. (1952) *The old man and the sea*. New York: Scribner.

Keene, E., & Zimmerman, S. (1997). *Mosaic of thought: Teaching comprehension in a reader's workshop*. Portsmouth, NH: Heinemann.

SUGGESTED READING

Massey, D. D. (2003). A comprehension checklist: What if it doesn't make sense? *The Reading Teacher, 57*, 81–84.

VOCABULARY RATING

Assessing Word Understanding and Use

Focus on English Learners

Beginning English learners can often demonstrate word knowledge by acting out words or pointing to illustrations in books.

This chapter presents a methodology for assessing the reader's understanding and use of new vocabulary. Readers' ability to comprehend text that is being processed is directly related to their understanding of and experience with the words and concepts presented in the text. In order to facilitate the teaching of comprehension strategies, a teacher must be able to analyze the components of comprehension difficulties related to a student's ability to process informational text.

This vocabulary rating system (Jordan & Herrell, in preparation) enables the teacher to determine a student's ability to define words and to analyze their ability to use the words in proper context. This strategy may be used as a prereading assessment to give the teacher information relative to the need to provide experiences or understandings prior to reading the text to increase comprehension. It can also be used as a postreading assessment to check for accuracy of word comprehension and the ability to relate the word to use within the assigned text. Because the words are chosen from a passage to be read, the teacher gets contextual feedback linked directly to the students' prior knowledge related to the text and their ability to comprehend the material being presented.

STEP BY STEP

The steps in implementing a vocabulary rating system are:

STEP 1 SELECTING THE VOCABULARY

The teacher analyzes a piece of text that the students will read as part of their curricular assignment. She then chooses a variety of vocabulary words that are key to comprehending the subject matter being presented.

STEP 2 PRESENTING THE VOCABULARY

The teacher can choose to present the words to students individually or in groups as necessary. Working with individual students orally may provide the strongest indicators of understanding due to the decreased emphasis on writing skills necessary to successfully complete the task. The words are presented to students one at a time and the students respond either by telling the teacher the definition of the word, acting it out, or writing the definition on a response sheet. The students are then asked to use the word in a sentence that is contextually accurate, demonstrating the meaning of the word.

STEP 3   ## SCORING THE RESPONSES

Responses are scored on a scale ranging from 0 to 3 points with 3 being the high end of the scale, indicating a complete understanding of the definition of the word. The ability to use the word in context is scored on the same scale with a score of 3 indicating the ability to use the word correctly in a contextual setting. See figure 43.1 for vocabulary rating system scoring instructions.

FIGURE 43.1 Scoring standards for vocabulary rating system.

WORD DEFINITIONS:

3-Point Response	**Examples**
Prereading: An accurate, precise definition of the word (*if a definition is given that differs from the way the word is used in the passage, a teacher may ask students if they know another definition of the word*)	*loyalty*—being faithful or showing allegiance to a person, idea, or country (*must include a full definition or a synonym*)
Postreading: An accurate, precise definition of the word as it is used in the passage read	*loyalty*—being faithful or showing allegiance to a country (*must include a full definition or a synonym*)

2-Point Response	
An example or description of the idea	*loyalty*—defending your friend's ideas

1-Point Response	
A more generalized viewpoint	*loyalty*—having a friend

0-Point Response	
No connection to actual meaning	*loyalty*—like kings and queens

USING THE WORD IN CONTEXT:

3-Point Response	**Examples**
Prereading: An accurate, precise use of the word (*if a use is given that differs from the way the word is contextualized in the passage, a teacher may ask students if they can use the word another way*)	*loyalty*—We show our love for our country and our willingness to defend it against our enemies by expressing our loyalty in reciting the Pledge of Allegiance.
Postreading: An accurate, precise use of the word as it is contextualized in the passage read	*loyalty*—Japanese Americans were put into special camps because the Americans doubted their willingness to help defend the country against our enemies. They doubted their loyalty to the United States.

2-Point Response	
A sentence containing a description rather than a definition	*loyalty*—We show our loyalty to America by reciting the Pledge of Allegiance.

1-Point Response	
Using the word in a more general way	*loyalty*—I'm always loyal to my friends.

0-Point Response	
Using the word incorrectly	*loyalty*—In England, the loyalty ride in fancy carriages.

APPLICATIONS AND EXAMPLES

Following Mr. Tulyathorn's vocabulary role-play lesson (described in chapter 5), he wants to determine the effectiveness of the strategy in assisting his students with the vocabulary contained in the text. He makes a list of the selected key words in the text he is using, those words that he emphasized and role played in the course of the presentation to students. Then he calls the students up individually to review the meanings of the words. Each student is asked to define or role play the words on his list. Mr. Tulyathorn relates the words to the textual experience by asking the questions in terms of the way the words were used within the text.

He said, "Toby, in our story today, the beautiful horses were prancing. Can you tell me what *prancing* means?"

The students are allowed to respond verbally or by acting out their understanding of the words. Toby responds, "That means the horses are jumping around and holding their heads up high, like this." And Toby proceeds to demonstrate what prancing looks like.

"Great," says Mr. T. "Can you make up a sentence with that word in it?"

Toby looks a bit bewildered, but then smiles and says, "The boys and girls fell off the horses, because they were prancing too much."

See File 43 of the accompanying CD for an example of vocabulary rating used in a seventh grade literature lesson.

Mr. T follows this procedure for several other important words with Toby and all the other students in the class, individually. By using the scoring guide described in this chapter and in figure 50.1, Mr. T. has a clearer understanding of the level of vocabulary understanding achieved by the students in his class following his vocabulary role-play activity. This helps him identify those students who need further development activities to internalize the words.

CONCLUSION

The use of a scoring rubric, such as the sample presented in this chapter, allows the teacher to more clearly see the vocabulary that students are having difficulty understanding. In addition, it offers a guide to the teacher as to the depth of a student's understanding. It identifies specific words that will require a different approach to establish clearly defined conceptualization of the text. Teachers must remember that contextual understanding of the definitions of words is a major element in comprehending text for students. That emphasizes the importance of multiple approaches to vocabulary building (see chapter 6) and the equal importance of multiple exposures for students to establish *extended mapping,* or the deeper understanding of particular words, especially those with multiple meanings.

REFERENCES

Jordan, M., & Herrell, A. (in preparation). *Assessing emerging vocabulary knowledge: The key to early intervention.*

44

RETELLING FOR ASSESSMENT

Using Free Recall to Determine Depth of Understanding

Although the use of prepared questions to determine students' comprehension of a reading passage is the most common strategy for assessment, much information is gained by simply asking students to retell the story they read. The examiner asks students to retell the story in their own words. The examiner takes notes as students retell the story. The notes can be taken on a blank sheet of paper or on a prepared retelling form. See figure 44.1 for an example of a story retelling form.

The story retelling assessment strategy actually consists of three stages (Barr, Blachowicz, & Wogman-Sadow, 1995). In the first stage, free recall, the student is asked to retell the story. This stage provides information about the parts of the story that the student sees as most important. In the second stage, prompted recall, the examiner asks questions about the parts of the story that the student left out in the free recall stage. These questions help the examiner to determine whether the omissions are related to memory or lack of understanding. In the third stage, IAA questioning (inference, analysis, application), the examiner asks questions that require higher level thinking. Questions that require inference (drawing conclusions from implied information), analysis (making assumptions based on underlying philosophies), and application (using information in a new situation) of the information from the story are asked during this stage. The result of a retelling assessment is an understanding of the student's comprehension on several levels. The examiner gets information of the student's comprehension that can be used for choosing instructional strategies even though a standardized score is not obtained. When retelling is used periodically the examiner can compare subsequent results and make judgments related to the effectiveness of the instruction that is being used.

STEP BY STEP

The steps in using retelling as assessment are:

STEP 1   CHOOSING READING MATERIAL AND PREPARING QUESTIONS

The teacher chooses an appropriate passage for the student to read. In the primary grades the reading material is often a storybook that is written at the student's in-

FIGURE 44.1 Example of a retelling assessment form for narrative text.

Narrative Retelling Summary Sheet

Name _____ Date _____

Title _____

Prediction from illustration _____

Prediction from title _____

Familiarity with topic _____

Behaviors during reading _____

_____

1 POINT is scored for each item:	Unprompted	Prompted
SETTING		
Begins with introduction	_____	_____
Gives time and place	_____	_____
CHARACTERS		
Names main character	_____	_____
Identifies other characters	_____	_____
PROBLEM		
Identifies the story problem or conflict	_____	_____
ACTION		
Recalls major events	_____	_____
OUTCOME		
Identifies how problem was solved	_____	_____
Gives story ending	_____	_____
SEQUENCE		
Retells story in order	_____	_____
(2pts—correct, 1 pt—partial, 0—no evidence of sequence)		
TOTAL SCORE	_____	

Observations and Comments:

structional level. Older students are usually given a short story at their instructional level. The teacher/examiner prepares a retelling form if one is to be used. The teacher/examiner also prepares follow-up questions for stage three of the procedure. These questions should require use of higher-level thinking such as inference, analysis, and application. Because the preparation for retelling requires time and thought, many teachers prepare a protocol for a group of stories that they use for retelling and save those stories for use in assessment.

STEP 2 INTRODUCING THE TASK

The teacher/examiner calls one student aside and introduces the retelling task by saying, "I want you to read a story. Then I will ask you to retell the story in your own words and I will ask you some questions." The teacher/examiner then engages the student in preparing to read by looking at the cover of the book or illustration connected to the story and asking the student to predict what the story will be about. The teacher/examiner supports the student in reading the title of the story and again asks if the student has any ideas about what the story will be about. The teacher/examiner asks the student what he knows about the topic in order to determine the student's familiarity with basic concepts. The student is then asked to read the story

FIGURE 44.2   Example of a retelling assessment form for informational text.

Informational Retelling Summary Sheet

Name _____ Date _____

Title _____

Prediction from illustration _____

Prediction from title _____

Familiarity with topic _____

Behaviors during reading _____

_____

_____

1 POINT is scored for each item:	Unprompted	Prompted
INTRODUCTION		
Identifies topic	_____	_____
Gives some purpose or focus	_____	_____
MAIN IDEAS (List Responses)		

_____

_____

_____

Number given _____   Actual number _____   Total Points _____

6 pts. all correct   **4 pts.** 2/3 correct   **2 pts.** 1/3 correct   **0 pts.** none correct

SEQUENCE OF IDEAS

   Gives ideas in correct order   _____   _____

   (2pts—correct, 1 pt—partial, 0—no evidence of sequence)

               TOTAL SCORE   _____

<u>Observations and Comments:</u>

silently. The teacher/examiner makes notes about the student's approach to the task, predictions, and familiarity with the topic.

STEP 3   CONDUCTING THE ASSESSMENT

After the student reads the passage, the teacher/examiner asks him to retell the story in his own words. The teacher/examiner makes notes to document the retelling. See figure 44.2 for an example of a retelling assessment form for informational text.

If anything is left out of the retelling, the teacher/examiner asks about those items by saying something like, "After the wolf blew down the first little pig's house, what did he do next?" The stage-two questions are simply to determine if the student understood the sequence of events in the story. Stage-three questions are used to determine the student's level of comprehension and instructional needs.

STEP 4   USING THE RESULTS

The teacher analyzes the results of the retelling assessment by contemplating several questions.

How complete was the initial retelling?

What was left out of the initial retelling? What story elements were missing?

Could the student respond to stage-two questions and fill in the pieces missing in the initial retelling?

Could the student supply inferential information?

Could the student answer analytic questions?

Could the student apply information from the story to new situations?

Were there any instances of misunderstanding? If so, what were they?

Were the causes of misunderstanding evident? If so, what were they?

Once the teacher/examiner reviews the retelling and questions, the information obtained is used to prepare an instructional plan. The areas of misunderstanding must be addressed. The breakdown in comprehension processing is evaluated by asking more questions.

Did the student misinterpret vocabulary?

Did the student fail to make correct connections among sentences?

Was the student able to draw on his past experiences?

Did the student understand the big picture, the holistic meaning of the story?

Was the student aware of any difficulty he had with the reading or retelling of the story?

Once the teacher/examiner decides which strategies the student needs from examining the answers to these questions, the teacher plans instruction for the student related to the areas of misunderstanding.

STEP 5   REPEATING THE PROCESS

After the teacher has implemented the instructional plan and the student has been given time to practice the prescribed strategies, the teacher repeats the retelling assessment to determine the success of the instructional plan and to identify any additional instructional needs.

APPLICATIONS AND EXAMPLES

Miss Newsome is assessing her students' reading to determine their instructional reading levels and their strengths and needs for instruction in comprehension. She wants to keep the assessment rather informal, so she decides to use retelling as the assessment tool. She chooses reading passages at several different levels that will span the abilities of the students in her class and prepares questions that she will use during the retelling task. She runs copies of the generic retelling format provided by her school district (see figure 44.1) and adds a page of questions for each passage she selects.

The first student she assesses is Jessica. She asks Jessica to join her at the reading table while the other students are engaged in literacy centers and begins the assessment by saying, "I want you to read a story. I will ask you to retell the story in your own words and then I will ask you some questions."

Miss Newsome and Jessica look at the picture at the top of the copy of the story and Miss Newsome says, "Look at the picture, Jessica. What do you think this story will be about?"

"Two girls," replies Jessica.

"Yes, there is a nice picture of two girls there. Would you read the title of the story to me?"

Jessica responds, "'Being Friends.' So these two girls must be friends!"

"That could be," says Miss Newsome, "and what does it mean when people are friends, Jessica?"

"Well, that means they share things, and they like to do the same things, and they like to be around each other, and stuff," Jessica answers.

"OK," Miss Newsome responds, "and now I would like you to read this story. When you are finished, we will talk about it a little."

Jessica reads the story silently and Miss Newsome takes some notes on her physical actions while reading (eye sweep, signs of tension, fidgeting, facial expression, vocalization, etc.). Here is the story Jessica is given to read:

Being Friends

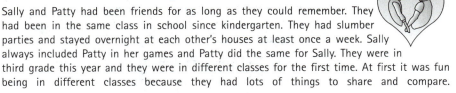

Sally and Patty had been friends for as long as they could remember. They had been in the same class in school since kindergarten. They had slumber parties and stayed overnight at each other's houses at least once a week. Sally always included Patty in her games and Patty did the same for Sally. They were in third grade this year and they were in different classes for the first time. At first it was fun being in different classes because they had lots of things to share and compare.

"You'll never believe what Miss Thomas did today," said Sally, one beautiful fall day.

"What did she do?" asked Patty.

"She gave us a big spelling test! She said each class was going to have one person represent the class in the schoolwide spelling bee. She's going to grade the test tonight and tomorrow she will tell us who is going to represent our class."

"We did the same thing in our class today!" replied Patty. "The words were really hard. I don't know if I did very well."

"You're a great speller, Patty," said Sally. "I'll bet you win in your class and I win in mine. Wouldn't that be great?"

The next day the girls waited and waited to hear who would represent their classes in the school spelling bee. At lunch Sally asked Patty, "Have you heard yet?"

"No," responded Patty. "Have you?"

"No," replied Sally. "I wish they'd tell us who the winners are. This waiting is hard."

By the end of the day, the two friends had almost given up. Nothing had been said about the spelling bee all day. At the very last minute, Mr. Jones, the principal, came on the intercom and made the big announcement. He named the spelling bee representatives for each of the classes in the school. The girls couldn't wait to see each other after school! They were both representing their classes in the school spelling bee!

"OK, Patty," said Sally. "We really have to study now. Those words in the schoolwide spelling bee are really hard. Let's get together every afternoon and help each other. One of us is going to win this spelling bee!"

At that moment the girls realized something very important. They had been so excited they had forgotten something. If one of them won the spelling bee that meant that the other one . . . would lose. The girls looked at each other with big round eyes.

"One of us can win. But, the other one will lose," said Patty sadly. "What will we do? We've got to study hard and do our best. We've got to help each other." The friends walked home, hand in hand, silently, with their heads down. What would they do now?

Jessica looks up at Miss Newsome when she finishes reading. Miss Newsome says, "Thank you, Jessica. Now will you tell the story in your own words?" Jessica begins telling the story, and Miss Newsome takes notes on the story retelling form.

Jessica begins, "It's about these two girls, Patty and Sally. They were really good friends. They had always been in the same class together until third grade. In third grade they were in different classes and they both got to be in the school spelling bee 'cause they were good spellers."

"Very good, Jessica," says Miss Newsome, pausing for a minute to see if Jessica is going to continue. Once Miss Newsome realizes that Jessica is finished with her retelling of the story, she begins to prompt her for more information.

"What was the order of events in the story?" asks Miss Newsome.

"Well," Jessica responds, "they were friends. They were in different classes. They both took spelling tests to try to be in the schoolwide spelling bee. They waited all day to hear the results. They both got picked. They were going to study together. They walked home together."

"Was there a problem in the story?" asks Miss Newsome.

"Yes, they would be competing against each other," replies Jessica.

"Was the problem solved?" Miss Newsome queries.

"No, it ended without telling how the problem was solved, but they were going to study together."

Miss Newsome then asks, "Were there any words or phrases in the story that were especially hard for you?"

"Well, I didn't know the word *intercom* but I sounded it out," replies Jessica.

"Very good," says Miss Newsome. "I have a few more questions." As she moves into the inference, analysis, and application questions, she continues to note Jessica's responses.

She then asks Jessica a series of questions that require higher-order thinking. See figure 44.3 for the questions and a record of Jessica's responses on the entire retelling assessment.

"You did a very good job with that, Jessica," says Miss Newsome as she sends her back to the literacy centers and calls another student for assessment. Later in the day she reviews the assessments given that day and plans appropriate instruction for the students.

For an example of how to use retelling as an assessment with informational text in high school, see File 44 of the CD that accompanies this text.

FIGURE 44.3 Example of scoring of Jessica's retelling assessment form for narrative text.

Jessica's Prompted Retelling:

Teacher: What was the order of events in the story?

Jessica: *They were friends. They were in different classes. They both took a spelling test to try to be in the schoolwide spelling bee. They waited all day to hear the results. They both got picked. They were going to study together. They walked home together.*

Teacher: Was there a problem in the story?

Jessisca: *Yes, they would be competing against each other.*

Teacher: Was the problem solved?

Jessica: *No, it ended without telling how the problem was solved, but they were going to study together.*

Teacher: Were there any words or phrases that were especially hard for you? (metacognition)

Jessica: *I didn't know the word "intercom," but I sounded it out.*

Jessica's responses to inferential, analysis, and application questions

Teacher: How did the girls feel about being in the spelling bee? (inferential)

Jessica: *They were happy and excited about it.*

Teacher: What was the main problem or conflict? (inferential)

Jessica: *They couldn't both win.*

Teacher: Why were they worried about both of them being in the spelling bee? (analysis)

Jessica: *Because they were afraid they wouldn't be friends any more.*

Teacher: What would you do if you were one of the girls? (application)

Jessica: *Make a contract to stay friends no matter who won, and study together and help each other.*

ANALYSIS: Jessica's unprompted retelling is sketchy but she was able to fill in details with prompting. She needs more practice in retelling with emphasis on events sequence. Her use of comprehension processes seems balanced.

FIGURE 44.3 Example of scoring of Jessica's retelling assessment form for narrative text.

Narrative Retelling Summary Sheet

Name _____ *Jessica* _____ Date _____

Title _____ *Being Friends* _____

Prediction from Illustration *It's about two girls* _____

Prediction from Title _____ *These two girls must be friends* _____

Familiarity with Topic _____ *Strong! Share things, like to do same things and be around each other*

Behaviors during reading *Little movement. Seems relaxed. Twists hair with one finger.*
Smiles occasionally.

1 POINT is scored for each item:	Unprompted	Prompted
SETTING		
Begins with introduction	*1*	
Gives time and place	*1*	
CHARACTERS		
Names main character	*1*	
Identifies other characters	*1*	
PROBLEM		
Identifies the story problem or conflict		*1*
ACTION		
Recalls major events		*1*
OUTCOME		
Identifies how problem was solved		*1*
Gives story ending		*1*
SEQUENCE		
Retells story in order		*1*
(2pts—correct, 1 pt—partial, 0—no evidence of sequence)		
TOTAL SCORE	*8*	

Observations and Comments:
Seems confident. Obviously enjoys reading.

CONCLUSION

Retelling assessments reveal a lot of valuable information about the student's comprehension of text. Preparing to use retellings takes some time, but the teacher builds a repertoire of retelling protocols once the strategy is implemented. The generic retelling form is used for the first part of the strategy. The first round of questions must be based upon the student's initial retelling, prompting the elements that the student omits in the initial retelling. The inference, analysis, and application questions are prepared in advance and related to the story being used. These same questions can be used for all students who are reading the same story.

The teacher examines the results, notes areas of concern, and develops an instructional plan based on the findings. The strategies contained in the first five sections of this book are appropriate for use in the instructional plans according to the individual needs identified through the assessment.

REFERENCES

Barr, R., Blachowicz, C., & Wogman-Sadow, M. (1995). *Reading diagnosis for teachers: An instructional approach*. White Plains. NY: Longman.

45

COMPREHENSION STYLE ASSESSMENT

How Does the Reader Construct Meaning?

Comprehension style is defined as the reader's approach to the text—his or her willingness to take risks, make and modify predictions, and use background knowledge to construct meaning. The research on the comprehension styles of "good comprehenders" (Wade, 1990) identifies a sequence of events that these efficient readers employ to construct meaning. Good readers generally read part of the text until they find out enough to formulate a hypothesis. As they read on, they evaluate the information they are reading and decide whether or not it fits their original hypothesis. They begin to make predictions about what will come next in the text and begin to make a series of predictions that are subsequently confirmed or adapted according to the information they are reading. If their predictions are not confirmed, good readers self-monitor and use strategies for rereading and reevaluating their predictions, adapting them almost constantly to determine whether or not their past experiences, predictions, and overall understanding of the reading are making sense.

Readers fit into general categories of comprehension style according to their use of predictions and self-monitoring (Wade, 1990). When teachers are aware of the comprehension styles of their students, they can prepare much more individual instructional plans to support students' reading comprehension.

The comprehension styles identified by Wade (1990) are as follows:

Good comprehenders interact with the text, constructing meaning and monitoring their own understanding. They draw on background knowledge and make reasonable inferences. They recognize when more information is needed to confirm hypotheses and adapt and confirm ideas as they read.

Non-risk takers rely heavily on the text and fail to go beyond the words on the page to make predictions. Non-risk takers do not use past experiences to infer but refer to exact words from the story when asked questions. If they can be tempted to make a guess, it usually is verbalized as a tentative question.

Nonintegrators draw on clues from the text and also from past experiences but don't integrate them. They tend to make new predictions for each section of the text without relating the new predictions to anything that has come before. Because nonintegrators do not accumulate understanding as they read additional sections of text, they cannot move beyond the text to create a holistic understanding of the reading passage.

Schema imposers make an initial prediction or hypothesis and then try to make the meaning of the text fit that first impression. These readers literally try to defend the initial hypothesis in spite of overwhelming evidence that the text does not support it. They are rigid and do not monitor the clues being read to make sure they fit the predictions they make.

Storytellers are extremely dependent on prior knowledge and experiences. Rather than answering questions related to the information in the text, storytellers relate the questions to their own experiences.

The information obtained through comprehension style assessment is important in planning future instruction. Understanding the role of background knowledge and self-monitoring if the student's construction of meaning is important is choosing strategies to teach to improve individual student comprehension. Because effective readers (good comprehenders) use a balance of prior experiences and text-based information to construct meaning as they self-monitor constantly, instructional plans based on comprehension styles assessment should focus on the weakness in these areas demonstrated during the assessment procedures.

STEP BY STEP

The steps in assessing comprehension style are:

STEP 1   CHOOSING AND PREPARING THE TEXT

The teacher chooses a short passage at the student's instructional reading level (the level at which the student misreads no more than 10 percent of the words). She should prepare a number of passages for use with students so she can choose passages of interest to each individual. The passage is rearranged so the topic sentence is last and no title appears. The student is asked to make a series of predictions, so the topic of the passage should not be revealed to the reader until the last sentence. The sentences are printed on the page so they can be covered and unveiled one at a time. See figure 45.1 for an example of how to adapt a text for comprehension style assessment.

FIGURE 45.1 Adapting a reading passage for comprehension style assessment.

Original Passage

> Ballet dancing is a very demanding profession. Many people watch it done and think it is beautiful. They often admire the way the bodies are used to form moving visual formations and images. But the years of training and discipline necessary to become outstanding are not obvious. They make it look so easy. This profession is so demanding of the human body that dancers often retire to teach in their early thirties.

Reformatted Passage

> Many people watch it done and think it is beautiful.
>
> They often admire the way the bodies are used to form moving visual formations and images.
>
> But the years of training and discipline necessary to become outstanding are not obvious.
>
> They make it look so easy.
>
> This profession is so demanding of the human body that dancers often retire to teach in their early thirties.
>
> Ballet dancing is a very demanding profession.

STEP 2 ADMINISTERING THE ASSESSMENT

The teacher has the student read the first sentence and then predict what she thinks the passage is about. After the student reads the sentence, the teacher asks, "What do you think this sentence is about?" After the student predicts, the teacher asks, "What clues in the sentence helped you?" This procedure is followed until all the sentences in the passage have been read and the student has verbalized ideas about the meaning of each sentence. The teacher then asks the student to read the entire passage and tell, in her own words, what it is about. The teacher, of course, notes the student's responses to each of the questions.

STEP 3 ANALYZING THE RESULTS

The teacher analyzes the transcript of the assessment, asking these questions.

Did the student:

Hypothesize?

Support the hypothesis with information from the passage?

Relate information in the text to background knowledge?

Integrate new information as it is read?

Adapt or modify predictions when the information doesn't fit?

Realize what the passage was about (a) almost immediately? (b) from a resonable number of clues? Or (c) not until the whole passage was read?

Use strategies to figure out unfamiliar words? Which strategies were used?

Seem confident that her hypothesis was correct?

Use any additional strategies? Visualization? Rereading? Cross-checking?

STEP 4 PLANNING FUTURE INSTRUCTION

After the teacher analyzes the results of the assessment, she identifies the comprehension strategies the student is using and the ones that need to be taught or reviewed. The teacher looks at the overall approach the student uses in constructing meaning and identifies the general comprehension style category that best describes the student's approach to text. These categories are only important in helping the teacher understand the types of strategies the student is overusing and identifying the strategies that must be reviewed to bring the student's strategy use into balance.

APPLICATIONS AND EXAMPLES

Mr. Bowen is interested in assessing his students' comprehension styles because he has been working with them on using a balance of strategies to support their understanding. His seventh graders started the year with low placement-test scores in both vocabulary and reading comprehension. He is eager to determine whether the instruction he has been doing has been effective. He also knows that comprehension style assessment will identify areas of strength and areas where he still needs to focus.

Mr. Bowen designs a series of brief reading passages based on some topics that he knows will be of interest to his students. He gradually gives more information in the passages so that the students can hypothesize and provide him with some information related to their use of text, experiences, and other factors as they verbalize their thoughts.

The first student Mr. Bowen tests is Leo, a boy who started the year with a poor self-concept and a limited vocabulary. Mr. Bowen has been implementing a strong vocabulary study theme all year. He is anxious to see how well Leo can combine strategies to unlock the meaning of the reading passage.

Mr. Bowen makes Leo comfortable and explains, "I am going to ask you to do something a little different today. I want you to read this paragraph aloud, sentence by sentence. After you read each sentence, you are going to tell me what you are thinking about the sentence. Try to see if you can figure out what the paragraph is about. Think out loud so I can follow. Tell me the clues you are using to figure out the problem."

Mr. Bowen uncovers the first sentence of the paragraph: "The man stops and listens carefully."

Leo reads the sentence aloud and then says, "I think he thinks someone is following him. You know, sometimes you're walking along and you think you hear footsteps behind you. This guy stopped. I think he was walking and he stopped to listen for footsteps. I've done that lots of times."

"OK, Leo, now read the next sentence," encourages Mr. Bowen as he uncovers the next sentence and quickly finishes making his notes.

"'He looks from side to side with a quizzical look on his face,'" reads Leo.

"Now he's trying to see if he sees anybody. I still think he's being followed."

"What does the word *quizzical* mean?" asks Mr. Bowen.

"It's he looks like he wants to ask a question. He has a question, he just doesn't have anyone to ask," replies Leo.

"How do you know the meaning of that word?" asks Mr. Bowen.

"I read it in a story the other day," says Leo. "But even if I hadn't, the part that says *quiz* would have told me it was like a question."

"Good thinking," says Mr. Bowen, as he scribbles more notes and unveils the next sentence.

"'He could have sworn he had heard the sound of a train whistle,'" reads Leo.

"Oh, I guess the man is really hearing things," he says. "First he hears someone walking behind him and now he hears a train."

"What makes you think he's hearing things?" asks Mr. Bowen.

"Well, he's probably scared. He thinks someone's walking behind him and he can't see anyone and sometimes when you're really scared, you hear things."

"'He looks from side to side once more and inches the car forward,'" reads Leo. "Now I'm really confused. First he's walking and now he's driving. He has to be driving 'cause it says he inches the car forward. Why is he driving so slow?"

Mr. Bowen says, "Can you think of anything you can do to help yourself understand this?"

"Yeah, I can go back to the beginning and read it again," says Leo. He reads, "'The man stops and listens carefully. He looks from side to side with a quizzical look on his face. He could have sworn he had heard the sound of a train whistle. He looks from side to side once more and inches the car forward.' Oh! Now I get it. He's been in the car the whole time. He hears a train and doesn't want to pull in front of it," says Leo enthusiastically.

Mr. Bowen adds notes to his paper as he uncovers the last sentence in the paragraph.

"'The man knows there have been a number of accidents at this railroad crossing in the past few weeks,'" reads Leo. "I get it now. I wish it had said something about the car in the first sentence. I needed that clue. I really got confused there for awhile."

"Well, remember all the things we've been talking about. The minute you realize you aren't understanding, you need to use one of your strategies."

"Thanks, Mr. Bowen, I'll remember," says Leo as he stands up to go to his seat.

Mr. Bowen marks at the bottom of the protocol sheet: "Using context clues and past experiences. Holds onto his predictions once they are made. Needs to be reminded to use metacognitive strategies. Vocabulary improving. Some tendencies to nonintegration and schema imposing. Work on periodic paraphrasing, predictions, and adaptions. Continue to work on vocabulary."

See File 45 of the accompanying CD to see how to use comprehension style assessment with beginning readers.

CONCLUSION

Assessing students' comprehension styles gives the teacher an opportunity to look into the thought processes and the strategy use of students while they are in the act of processing text and constructing meaning. This assessment, when done at the beginning of the year, gives the teacher important information about the students and the type of comprehension instruction they need to increase their understanding of the texts they read. Adapting the instruction to the needs of the students saves time and allows the teacher to work with small strategy-based groups while the rest of the class is engaged in reading extended text, another vital element in a strong, balanced, comprehensive reading program. Periodic assessment style checks help the teacher to evaluate the effectiveness of the comprehension instruction and to plan future lessons to meet the ever-changing needs of students. These assessments are valuable because they are directly related to the strategies being taught and provide an opportunity to set goals with students and to celebrate their growth and accomplishments in becoming more effective readers who monitor their own understanding.

REFERENCES

Wade, S. (1990). Using think alouds to assess comprehension. *The Reading Teacher, 3*, 442–451.

CLOZE ASSESSMENT

Evaluating the Use of Comprehension Processes

Focus on English Learners

Using cloze assessment with English learners will often help the teacher to identify areas where additional instruction is needed.

Cloze tests (Blachowicz, 1977) are reading passages in which words have been left out. The student is asked to supply appropriate words to place in the blanks in the passage so that the passage makes sense. Because this activity requires the student to use context to anticipate words, it can be modified to test the student's use of contextual clues at the sentence, paragraph, and macroprocessing (whole text) levels (Barr, Blachowicz, & Wogman-Sadow, 1995). A task entitled *modified cloze* allows the teacher to go back to sentences in which the student has misread a word, cover the word up and test the student's ability to fill in the blank with an appropriate word. By revealing just the beginning letter or letters of the word, the teacher can then assess the student's ability to combine phonics and context clues to supply the word. Cloze has many possibilities as an assessment strategy, but teachers need to be clear about what they are testing before they decide which words to leave out of the passage to be used. See figure 46.1 for examples of the different types of cloze passages.

Cloze passages can also be used for instruction in the various levels of comprehension strategies. Teachers need only identify the strategies to be taught or tested and then leave blanks in reading passages in the appropriate places. If students can supply appropriate words in cloze passages but don't use contextual clues in reading, then the teacher knows that the problem is one of application rather than knowledge and can remind the student to use the context while reading. As with all good assessments, cloze is only valuable as an assessment tool when the teacher uses the results to plan appropriate instruction.

STEP BY STEP

The steps in using cloze assessment are:

STEP 1   DECIDING THE PURPOSE OF TESTING

The teacher decides the purpose of the assessment to be given. If cloze passages are to be used for an entire class, then passages of text for the different reading levels within the class must be chosen. If one reading strategy is being tested, the teacher

222

FIGURE 46.1   Examples of cloze passages to test comprehension.

Sentence-level cloze passage	Words are left out of individual sentences but enough information is available in the sentence to allow the student to determine an appropriate word to be entered in the blank.	The boy was walking _____ down the street.
Anaphoric cloze passage	Several sentences are given that contain pronoun referents. The student must recognize the anaphoric relationships in the sentences to determine the missing words.	The boy was walking down the street. _____ was going to the store to buy some dog food for _____ dog.
Connective cloze activity	The sentences have connective words left out. The student must employ knowledge of connectives to choose an appropriate word.	The boy was going to the store _____ he needed to buy some dog food.
Paragraph-level cloze	The blanks are placed in strategic places in the paragraph so that the student must use the context to choose appropriate words to maintain the meaning of the paragraph.	The boy was _____ down the street to buy some dog food. _____ stopped and looked _____. On the _____ was a ten-dollar bill. He _____ it up and _____ to the store where he _____ a lot of _____.
Whole-text (macro) cloze	The sentences relate to the main ideas in the passage. The student must supply words in the blanks to demonstrate understanding of the passage.	The story is about a _____ who goes to the _____ to buy _____ for his _____. On the way to the _____, the boy finds a _____ on the _____. Instead of buying the _____ he intended to buy, he buys a lot of _____ instead.

reformats the reading passages by leaving out words in the appropriate places. See figure 42.1 for examples of the types of words to be omitted for specific purposes. A series of cloze passages can be used to test comprehension at different levels: sentence, paragraph, and whole text. In the same way, a series of passages similar to those in figure 42.1 can be designed to identify the students' knowledge of the various comprehension processes.

STEP 2   INTRODUCING THE TASK

The teacher tells the class, group, or student to be assessed that they will be asked to supply some missing words in reading passages. Some practice items are administered to make sure that the student(s) know what is expected. The teacher emphasizes that, since there are no words in the blanks, any word that makes sense in the blank is acceptable. In partial-cloze passages where the first letter or letters of the word are included, this fact is noted and the task and instructions change accordingly.

STEP 3   ADMINISTERING THE ASSESSMENT

If a whole class or group is to be tested, the teacher distributes the passages and the students simply fill in the blanks. The teacher will gain more information if he asks the students questions about how they decided which words to use; this may be done individually at a later time or as the students complete the task. If an individual is assessed, the teacher gives the student the cloze passages one at a time. The student completes them, reading and thinking aloud. (See chapter 19 on think-alouds.) The teacher asks questions of the student to determine the thought process the student is using and which resources the student is drawing upon. For example: What made you decide that he was buying dog food? How did you know to use that particular word? What other words would make sense there?

STEP 4   USING THE RESULTS

The teacher evaluates the responses given by the students. Depending on the type of cloze passages used, the teacher might plan instruction in particular areas of comprehension. See other sections of this book for suggestions of strategies to be taught. If the student has supplied appropriate words in the cloze passages but is not using context clues when reading, then the teacher knows the student understands the comprehension processes but is simply not applying them. In this case, the teacher plans activities in which the student must use and document his use of context clues. This can be done using think-alouds or sticky notes where the student must identify a strategy to use whenever he encounters a difficult word.

STEP 5   SETTING GOALS WITH THE STUDENTS

Depending upon the ages of the students, the teacher might choose to discuss the results of the assessment with them. By looking at the responses the students gave and meeting briefly with each student, the teacher and students can jointly set some goals for improving the use of comprehension strategies and ultimately the students' reading comprehension. Sharing assessment results often helps students to see the areas in which they need to work. Setting goals jointly provides the students with some ownership of the instructional plan.

APPLICATIONS AND EXAMPLES

Mrs. Frolli is teaching the use of various comprehension processes in her second-grade class. As she completes a comprehension focus activity, she uses cloze passages to determine whether the students are employing the process that was taught. She prepares a series of passages to be used for testing comprehension process use by her students. To do this, she takes one piece of text and reformats it by leaving blanks in strategic places within the text. See figure 46.2 for some examples.

After Mrs. Frolli completes an instructional unit on anaphoric relationships (associations where one word or phrase is substituted for another), she explains the upcoming assessment activity to her class. "Today I will be calling you up to the reading table individually during literacy center time. I will be asking you to read a short passage about two friends. The passage has some blanks in it and you will have to think of words that make sense to put in the blanks. I think you will all enjoy this activity." Mrs. Frolli gets the students started working at the literacy centers and calls the first student, Gina, up to the reading table. She gives Gina the cloze passage and asks her to fill in the blanks. When Gina completes the activity, Mrs. Frolli looks at her completed cloze passage, and asks some questions:

Being Friends

Sally and Patty had been friends for as long as __they__ could remember. __They__ had been in the same class in school since kindergarten. __They__ had slumber parties and stayed over night at each other's houses at least once a week. Sally always included Patty in __fun__ games and Patty did the same for __Sally__. __They__ were in third grade this year and __they__ were in different classes for the first time. At first __it__ was fun being in different classes because __they__ had lots of things to share and compare.

"You've done a good job figuring out the words to put in the blanks, Gina," says Mrs. Frolli. "There is just one sentence I'd like for you to read aloud. Start here where it says, 'Sally always included Patty' and read this sentence to me."

FIGURE 46.2 The
original passage, "Being
Friends," with cloze
passages.

Being Friends

Sally and Patty had been friends for as long as they could remember. They had been in the same class in school since kindergarten. They had slumber parties and stayed over night at each other's houses at least once a week. Sally always included Patty in her games and Patty did the same for Sally. They were in third grade this year and they were in different classes for the first time. At first it was fun being in different classes because they had lots of things to share and compare.

"You'll never believe what Miss Thomas did today," said Sally, one beautiful fall day.

"What did she do?" asked Patty.

"She gave us a great big spelling test. She said each class was going to have one person represent the class in the schoolwide spelling bee. She's going to grade the test tonight and tell us who will be the class representative tomorrow."

"We did the same thing in our class today!" replied Patty. "The words were really hard. I don't know if I did very well."

"You're a great speller, Patty. I bet you win in your class and I win in my class," said Sally.

The next day the girls waited and waited to hear who would represent their classes in the school spelling bee. At lunch Sally asked Patty, "Have you heard yet?"

"No," responded Patty. "Have you?"

"No," replied Sally. "I wish they'd tell us who the representatives are. This waiting is hard."

By the end of the day, the two friends had almost given up. Nothing had been said about the spelling bee all day. At the very last minute, Mr. Jones, the principal came on the intercom and made the big announcement. He named the spelling bee representatives for each of the classes in the school. The girls couldn't wait to see each other after school! They were both representing their classes in the school spelling bee!

"OK, Patty," said Sally. "We really have to study now. Those words in the school spelling bee are really hard. We can get together every afternoon and help each other. One of us is going to win this spelling bee!"

At that moment the girls realized something very important. They had been so excited they forgot something. If one of them won the spelling bee that meant that the other one . . . would lose. The girls looked at each other with big round eyes. "One of us can win. But, the other one will lose," said Patty sadly. "What will we do? We've got to study hard and do our best. We've got to help each other." The friends walked home silently with their heads down. They were lost in their own thoughts.

Cloze passage for assessing anaphoric relationship use

Sally and Patty had been friends for as long as _____ could remember. _____ had been in the same class in school since kindergarten. _____ had slumber parties and stayed over night at each other's houses at least once a week. Sally always included Patty in _____ games and Patty did the same for _____. _____ were in third grade this year and _____ were in different classes for the first time. At first _____ was fun being in different classes because _____ had lots of things to share and compare.

Note: All pronouns are removed.

Cloze passage for assessing connectives

Sally and Patty had been friends for _____ they could remember. They had been in the same class in school _____ kindergarten. They had slumber parties and stayed over night _____ each other's houses _____ once a week. Sally _____ included Patty in her games and Patty _____ Sally. They were in third grade this year and they were in different classes _____ time. _____ it was fun being in different classes _____ they had lots of things to share and compare.

Note: All connectives are removed. Students must be told that some of the blanks can be filled with phrases.

Gina reads the sentence aloud and then Mrs. Frolli says, "Now read it again and this time put pronouns in the blanks."

Gina reads, "'Sally always included Patty in her games and Patty did the same for her.'"

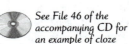

See File 46 of the accompanying CD for an example of cloze assessment in a seventh grade literature class.

"Oh, I get it!" Gina adds. "What I wrote makes sense, though."

"Yes, you did a good job with this. What you wrote did make sense. You really understand pronouns. I want to see you using what you have learned about pronouns in your writing now."

"I will. I see how they make the sentences more interesting to read," says Gina, a precocious 8-year-old.

CONCLUSION

Cloze passages have great potential for both instruction and assessment in comprehension strategy use. They are fairly simple to design when teachers have a clear understanding of their purpose and power. Teachers can use reading materials from various sources, both narrative and informational, to create appropriate level cloze passages for both teaching the comprehension processes and assessing their use. Brief student/teacher conferences following the cloze assessments are effective in engaging students in basic goal setting.

REFERENCES

Barr, R., Blachowicz, C., & Wogman-Sadow, M. (1995). *Reading diagnosis for teachers: An instructional approach*. White Plains, NY: Longman.

Blachowicz, C. (1977). Cloze activities for primary readers. *The Reading Teacher, 31*, 300–302.

47

THINK-ALOUD

Assessing Comprehension Strategy Use

The think-aloud procedure (Lytle, 1982) involves asking students to think out loud before, during, and after reading to verbalize the thought and decoding processes they are employing. This is especially important when a student is having difficulty with comprehension and the teacher needs to be able to pinpoint areas of concern. The teacher asks students to reflect on what is going on in their heads as the text is revealed and read line by line. Students are to comment on:

What they understand (*signaling understanding*)

What is causing them problems (*monitoring doubts*)

How they analyze appropriate parts of the text (*analyzing*)

How they reason as they try to solve problems (*reasoning*)

Which past experiences they call upon to help understand the text (*elaborating*)

What they know personally about the topic (*elaborating*)

How they evaluate the author's message and style (*judging*)

The result of using this protocol in assessing students' comprehension is that the teacher has a glimpse into students' thought processing, knowledge, and strategy use. Once the teacher understands the comprehension strategies students use, she can plan and implement instruction to support the students' use of a broader range of strategies or more effective use of the strategies with which they are familiar.

STEP BY STEP

The steps in implementing think-aloud assessments are:

STEP 1 INTRODUCING AND MODELING THE CATEGORIES FOR THINK-ALOUD

The teacher talks about the strategies she uses before, during, and after reading. The teacher chooses a short reading passage and begins by modeling prereading strategies, verbalizing as she predicts from the cover and title, and tells about whatever background knowledge she has about the topic of the book, the author, and illustrator. The teacher reads a short passage aloud, stopping periodically to think out loud about the processing that is going on in her head. As the teacher models a strategy, she identifies the strategy and adds it to a chart of think-aloud strategies to help the students remember them. This chart is posted in a prominent place in the classroom and used in subsequent steps in teaching and practicing think-alouds.

STEP 2   GUIDING THE PRACTICE OF THINK-ALOUD

The teacher chooses a short reading passage, reformats it so each sentence is written on a separate line or two, and displays it on the overhead projector, revealing only the illustration and title at first. She asks one student to predict what the story will be about from the illustration. After the student shares a prediction, the teacher asks the student to verbalize (think aloud) what went through his head as he was looking at the illustration and thinking of what to say. This procedure is repeated with another student predicting from the title and thinking aloud to demonstrate the thoughts she processed while contemplating a prediction. A third student is asked to talk about his knowledge of the topic of the passage to be read. Each time students share their thoughts, the teacher relates the thoughts to one of the categories posted on the think-aloud chart. The remainder of the reading passage is revealed one line/sentence at a time, and different students are asked to think aloud and share the processing of the sentence. After the passage is read, students are asked to think aloud again and talk about what they have learned by reading this particular passage, how it relates to prior knowledge they have, and what types of misunderstandings they were able to correct by reading and discussing the text.

STEP 3   RELATING THINK-ALOUD TO MONITORING YOUR OWN UNDERSTANDING

The teacher talks about the importance of monitoring your own understanding as you read. The chart of think-aloud categories is reviewed, and the teacher relates them to the strategies used by good readers. The students are instructed to think about the strategies whenever they have difficulty understanding something they are reading. The teacher discusses the relation of the strategies to the interactions readers practice as they try to make meaning from text.

STEP 4   INTRODUCING THINK-ALOUD AS AN ASSESSMENT STRATEGY

The teacher explains that she will be asking students to read and think aloud as a way of assessing the strategies they are using when they read. The procedure to be used is thoroughly discussed so that students know what to expect when they are asked to think aloud before, during, and after they read. The teacher explains how this information will help her to plan reading instruction and will help each of them to become better readers.

STEP 5   USING THINK-ALOUD AS AN ASSESSMENT STRATEGY

The teacher chooses a reading passage at an appropriate level for each student and asks the individual student to read the passage aloud, stopping at appropriate junctures to think aloud. It is important to think aloud before, during, and after reading to obtain the most comprehensive knowledge about students' strategy use. The think-aloud assessment protocol in figure 47.1 will be helpful in recording the responses of students as they are engaged in this assessment process.

FIGURE 47.1 Protocol form for think-aloud assessments.

Prediction from illustration/cover _____

_____

_____

Prediction from title _____

_____

_____

Exploration of prior knowledge _____

_____

_____

Strategies:	Comments and Teaching Points:
Signaling understanding	
Monitoring doubts	
Analyzing	
Reasoning	
Elaborating	
Judging	

Note: Tally uses of each strategy. Document instruction needed under comments and teaching points.

APPLICATIONS AND EXAMPLES

Mr. Samian is working with a group of 10th graders who are experiencing difficulty in reading. He decides to teach the think-aloud strategy to his students so that he can use the procedure to identify the strategies students are using and plan for instruction. He chooses a passage from the book *River Through the Ages* (Steele, 1994) because he plans to use the book in a social studies unit later in the semester. He wants to know how much prior knowledge the students have about the topic and whether or not they will be able to read and comprehend the book. He begins the lesson by demonstrating think-aloud, predicting from the illustration and asking a student to predict from the title and talk about her thoughts.

Mr. Samian has prepared a poster that lists the strategies used in think-alouds. As he and the students use one of the strategies in the demonstration lesson, he points to the chart and reviews its meaning. He guides the class through the reading and thought verbalization of one section of the book and then explains that he will be calling one student at a time up to read another passage to him and go through the think-aloud process with him. "I know this is not an easy thing to do. Thinking out loud makes you wonder if you're sounding silly or if your thoughts make sense to anyone else. I am only listening in order to determine the strategies that you use when you read. I will be able to plan lessons to help you improve your comprehension if I know which strategies you use and can determine the ones you need to learn."

Mr. Samian gives the students an assignment to do independently while he calls the students up one at a time to have them read a passage one sentence at a time and determine the strategies they know how to use and the ones they need to be taught.

See File 47 of the accompanying CD for an example of how to use Think-Aloud for assessment in primary grades.

CONCLUSION

Think-aloud as an assessment tool provides a powerful look into the students' thoughts as they read. This strategy is not easy to administer, however, because many students find it difficult to verbalize their thinking processes. It is extremely vital that the students see the procedure modeled and have an opportunity to practice thinking aloud before the strategy is used for assessment. The results that are obtained should be immediately discussed with readers to relieve them of anxieties. Many students are sensitive about their oral reading abilities, and it is important that think-alouds be done in a setting that provides a quiet, private atmosphere. Think-alouds may be done in a secluded area of the classroom, but other students should be thoroughly engaged in other work. The student being assessed should be working with the teacher in an area of the classroom that provides a sense of personal comfort and privacy. This especially applies when working with older students. Too often, teachers make assumptions not only about students' ability to read, but about their ability to comprehend what they are reading as well. It is the teacher's responsibility to make every effort to have as clear an understanding as possible of each student's ability to process and use information provided through textual means.

REFERENCES

Lytle, S. L. (1982). *Exploring comprehension style: A study of twelfth grade readers' transactions with text*. Unpublished dissertation. University of Pennsylvania.

Steele, P. (1994). *River through the ages*. New York: Troll.

48

PROCESS QUESTIONS

Identifying Metacognitive Strategies

Focus on English Learners

It is especially vital for the teacher to identify the processes being used by English learners. This knowledge also identifies processes needing more instruction.

The importance of identifying what processes students are using to make meaning of text is an important underlying element in diagnosing and prescribing for reading comprehension instruction. The introduction of *process questions* as an ongoing assessment tool provides the teacher and students an opportunity to examine the use of metacognitive strategies in gaining meaning from text (Irwin, 1991). These process questions rely on eliciting information related to the way students are interacting with text rather than the more traditional product questions, which simply elicit relevant facts and information from the text being read. Asking questions that merely call for pulling information from the text is not helpful to the teacher in determining how students are processing the text to obtain this information. In searching for processing cues, a teacher may find that students answer the same question in different ways, indicating a wide variation in the way students process textual information. Continually identifying these processing mechanisms is a great challenge to the teacher and often provides the key to understanding and assisting students in increasing their comprehension.

STEP BY STEP

The steps in implementing process question assessments are:

STEP 1   EXAMINING THE READING MATERIAL FOR KEY VOCABULARY AND CONCEPTS

The teacher reads the material that students will be reading to identify key vocabulary and concepts that the students must understand in order to make meaning from the text. In addition to key vocabulary and concepts, the teacher needs to identify experiences that students may have had that would relate to the reading material and strengthen their understandings of the text. These experiences may include other books or studies that have taken place during the school year and activities in which the students have participated.

Step 2   Engaging the Students in Dialogue Related to Key Vocabulary and Concepts

Once the material has been read, the teacher engages students in discussions of the key vocabulary and concepts encountered in the reading. The best approach to this stage of the assessment process is to have individual discussions with each student so that the teacher can determine exactly what each student understands of the key vocabulary and concepts. The process can be adapted to work with small groups of students but the teacher must keep records of the reponses of each student so that the process questions to be asked in the next stage are adapted to individual responses. The teacher probes to find the level of understanding using such open-ended probes as "Tell me more about that."

Step 3   Questioning the Students' Use of Comprehension Processes

The questions that the teacher uses to follow the discussion relate to the process that the student uses to obtain information or to process text. These questions help the teacher and the student to identify the comprehension processes being employed by the student. In the interchange of questions and responses, the student also becomes more aware of additional processes that might increase comprehension. Examples of the types of questions that may be asked are included in figure 48.1.

FIGURE 48.1 Examples of comprehension process questions.

Sentence-Level Comprehension	
Vocabulary	How did you know the meaning of this word?
	Have you seen this word used in a different way?
Sentence Meaning	How did you know what this meant?
	What other information did you need in order to understand this sentence?
Fluency & Expression	How do you think this character would have said this?
Paragraph-Level Comprehension	
Pronouns	Who is the word *he* referring to here?
Connectives	What does the word *however* imply?
Integration of Background Knowledge	
Prior Experiences	Have you ever had an experience like this?
Prediction	What have you done in the past that helped you to predict what was going to happen?
	What other books have you read that helped you to predict the outcome in this one?
Intertextual Knowledge	Do you remember another book where this happened?
Whole-Text Comprehension	
Main Idea	Can you find one sentence that states the main idea?
	Which parts of the story should be included in the summary?
Theme	Do you see any theme or thread of similar ideas throughout this passage?
Self-Monitoring Strategies	
Selection of Strategies	What can you do to help yourself understand this part?
Self-Monitoring	Can you tell this in your own words?

STEP 4   *PLANNING INSTRUCTION BASED ON THE STUDENTS' COMPREHENSION PROCESSING CUES*

Once the teacher and student have examined the comprehension processes that the student is using, the teacher plans lessons to support the student's expanded use of comprehension processing. The types of activities that can be included in these lessons are included in other chapters in this book. Students who need further instruction in the use of comprehension processing can be grouped for instruction. Their level of reading is not as important in this type of grouping as is their need for process instruction. The individuals within each group can be taught to employ comprehension processes using instructional reading materials at the appropriate level.

APPLICATIONS AND EXAMPLES

Mr. Jenkins' eighth-grade social science class is studying World War II. He notices that many of his students have difficulty using inference to identify unstated concepts in the materials they are reading. He selects a passage from Joy Hakim's *The History of US: War, Peace, and All That Jazz* (1995) that is rich with implied information. The first part of the passage is as follows:

A Little Boy

The men of the 509th Composite Group of the 313th Wing of the 21st Bombing Command of the 20th Air Force have been carefully chosen from a group of ace pilots. All have volunteered for a special mission. No one tells them what the mission will be. But whatever it is, they know they will be flying B-29s, the big workhorse bombers that are known as superfortresses.

Right away, there is something strange about the training they get at an airfield in Utah. Instead of flying planes loaded with huge bombs, they train with a single bomb of moderate size. And they are trained to worry about storms, especially electrical storms. Then, when they are sent to the Pacific, to the island of Tinian in the Marianas group of islands, they just sit around. It is frustrating. From Tinian it is an easy flight to Japan. The other airmen on the island are flying B-29s and dropping big bomb loads on Japan's cities. The 509th is sent on training flights—over and over again. Sometimes they are allowed to drop one bomb. It isn't long before the other pilots on Tinian begin making fun of the 509th. Someone even wrote a poem about them. Its last lines are:

Take it from one who knows the score,

The 509th is winning the war.

That is cruel. Everyone knows the 509th isn't winning the war; it isn't doing anything.

Meanwhile, in Washington, President Truman has come to a decision. He has called on two teams of experts: a team of scientists and a team of civilians and soldiers. They are to help him decide about the new superweapon. Will it be used? Can anything be used in its place? Both teams agree: the weapon should be used. They believe it will bring the war to an end. Without it, the war could continue for 10 or more years. Military chiefs, who don't know about the secret weapon, are pressing Truman to let them invade Japan. If that happens, America can expect a million casualties; Japan might have 10 times that number.

After the students have an opportunity to read the passage, Mr. Jenkins asks them to write a brief list of the information they gained from the text. He calls one student, Wally, aside while the others are writing. Wally has shown a great deal of difficulty with inference in his reading. Mr. Jenkins begins the conversation by saying to Wally, "Tell me the important parts of the passage you just read."

"Well," begins Wally, "it's about this group of pilots who are training on an island. They are frustrated because they aren't getting much chance to win the war. But it's kind of confusing, 'cause it's also about President Truman and some people trying to decide whether to bomb Japan. I guess the pilots are waiting for President Truman's orders."

"OK," responds Mr. Jenkins. "What do you know about the pilots?"

"Well, they volunteered for this mission but they didn't know what the mission was."

"Do you know how the group was formed?" asks Mr. Jenkins.

"No," responds Wally slowly, looking at the text in front of him.

"Read the first sentence aloud," urges Mr. Jenkins.

"The men of the 509th Composite Group of the 313th Wing of the 21st Bombing Command of the 20th Air Force have been carefully chosen from a group of ace pilots," reads Wally.

"What does the word *composite* mean?" asks Mr. Jenkins.

"I don't know," states Wally.

"Think about it . . . *composite* . . . Have you ever heard that word before?" asks Mr. Jenkins.

"Well, I remember the other day we read a novel that said that the characters were a composite of the people the author had known in his hometown. We said that it meant that the characters weren't based on individual people. They were pieces and parts of many different people. I just don't see how pilots could be pieces and parts of different people," replies Wally.

"You are right," says Mr. Jenkins. "The pilots can't be pieces and parts of different people. But, the sentence says that the 509th was a Composite Group of the 313th Wing."

"Oh! I get it. They are part of the 313th Wing but they have been chosen from different companies."

"That's good," responds Mr. Jenkins. "How did you figure it out?"

"My dad was in the Air Force. I know about companies and wings and commands," replies Wally. "Now it makes sense. They were chosen for this group from different companies. It says they were ace pilots. That means they were good. So, I guess they were chosen for this special mission because they were good. It must be an important mission."

"Now, think about what we've been studying. What do you think they are training for?"

"Oh, now I get it. These are the pilots who will be dropping the A-bombs over Japan. That's why the name of the article is 'A Little Boy.' I saw a movie about this. The bomb was little so it was called Little Boy. OK, now I understand why it also talks about President Truman. The pilots are waiting for the word to drop the bomb. That's why they are not doing much and why they have to study all about storms, so they don't get caught in a storm and drop the bomb somewhere besides Japan."

"Do you see how that movie you saw helped you to figure it out?" asks Mr. Jenkins. "Everything you know, everything you read, everything you see on TV or in the movies may help you out when you are reading."

"Yeah, and I remembered the word *composite* from another book we read," replies Wally with a smile.

Mr. Jenkins takes a minute to write a note in his planbook. He will spend some time with Wally asking process questions and teaching him to tap into his background knowledge to help him to actively engage in problem solving when he doesn't understand what he is reading. Since he has only explored vocabulary knowledge and background experiences as strategies, Mr. Jenkins wants to begin his work with Wally in those two areas.

 For an example of process questioning in grade three, see File 48 of the accompanying CD.

CONCLUSION

Teachers need to understand the processes students are employing to gain meaning from text. When students have difficulty comprehending what they are reading, questions related to their use of processes support the teacher in understanding exactly what kind of instruction is needed to improve their comprehension. It takes a few minutes of individual interaction with the student for the teacher to gain this important information, but it saves time for both the teacher and student eventually because it allows the teacher to focus instruction in the areas that will provide the most successful results.

This type of questioning can be employed whenever the teacher discusses the meaning of reading with students. It doesn't have to be a formal testing situation. Instead of always asking questions related to the content of the reading passage, process questions could be interspersed into the interactions. This helps the students to connect the answers they give and the strategy they used to obtain the answer. This reinforces the student's self-monitoring and supports active engagement with the text and the use of metacognitive strategies in an ongoing way.

REFERENCES

Hakim, J. (1995). *A history of US: War, peace, and all that jazz.* New York: Oxford Press.

Irwin, J. (1991). *Teaching comprehension processes* (2nd ed.) Needham Heights, MD: Allyn and Bacon.

QUESTION-ANSWER RELATIONSHIPS

Identifying Question Types and Locating Answers

Focus on English Learners

This chapter provides several models that are useful in assisting English learners as they progress from literal interpretations of text into higher-level thinking and analysis.

Question-answer relationships, better known as QARs, are a way of making sure that the questions the teacher uses to assess students' comprehension represent the various levels of questions commonly thought to represent higher-level thinking. In Bloom's taxonomy of the cognitive domain (Bloom, Engelhart, Furst, Hill, & Krathwohl, 1956), he identifies a range of questions that ask the student to process information and give responses in increasingly more complex ways. The lowest level of question asks the student to recall information that is directly stated in the text. The questions move from level to level, progressively asking the student to perform more cognitively demanding tasks in relation to the reading material. QARs consist of a taxonomy of questions similar to Bloom's taxonomy that the teacher uses to construct questions related to a specific reading passage.

In QARs the students are asked to answer questions that require progressively more demanding cognitive interactions with the information contained in the passage, including:

- **literal questions,** in which they simply recall information from the text
- **comprehension questions,** in which they are asked to interpret ideas contained in the text
- **application questions,** in which they must use information from the text to solve real-life problems
- **analysis questions,** in which they are asked to break the information they gained by reading the text into simpler parts and explain the connections among the parts
- **synthesis questions,** in which students must integrate the new information they have processed into their existing schema and use it in some practical way
- **evaluation questions,** in which they judge the merits of the ideas contained in the reading against a standard (Reutzel & Cooter, 2000)

In a slightly simplified version of the QAR, Pearson and Johnson (1978) classify their questions in relation to the source of the information needed to respond to the question. Their classifications include:

Textually explicit information—information directly stated in the text

Textually implicit information—information that is implied in the text

Scriptually implicit information—information that is already in the mind of the reader (*script* refers to schema and prior knowledge)

Using this model, the teacher again designs questions that require three different types of information. Some of the questions relate to information that is directly stated in the reading material. Some questions require the use of inference and some require students to process their prior knowledge in relation to the material that is read.

If the teacher is specifically interested in the comprehension processes that students are using effectively and the processes for which they need further instruction, the questions for the QAR can be structured to yield that type of information. The questioning taxonomy would require questions such as:

- Textually explicit questions that ask students to define vocabulary, state main ideas, and summarize events
- Textually implicit questions that require students to infer anaphoric relationships, implied connectives, and unstated details
- Scriptually implicit questions that require students to relate their background experiences and knowledge to the text (Irwin, 1991)

Examples of questions related to these three different taxonomies are shown in figure 49.1.

FIGURE 49.1 Examples of three models of question-answer relationships related to *Johnny Appleseed* (1990) by R. Lindbergh.

QAR Model 1: Questions Based on Bloom's taxonomy

Literal question: What was Johnny Appleseed's real name?

Comprehension question: Why was Johnny Appleseed well known?

Application question: What could you do as a personal project that would be similar to what Johnny Appleseed did?

Analysis question: What was happening at this time in history that encouraged Johnny Appleseed to do what he did?

Synthesis question: What other things must have happened in order for Johnny's seeds to grow into apple trees?

Evaluative question: Which parts of this story do you think may be factual?

QAR Model 2: Text-Explicit and Text-Implicit Questions

Text-explicit question: What was Johnny Appleseed's real name?

Text-implicit question: Did Johnny Appleseed have a wife and family?

Scriptually implicit question: Why was this man nicknamed Johnny Appleseed?

QAR Model 3: Text/Comprehension Process-Based Questions

Text-explicit questions

   Microprocesses: What does the word *frontier* mean?

   Macroprocesses: What was Johnny Appleseed's main contribution to the settlement of the west?

Text-implicit questions

   Integrative processes: When the text refers to Johnny Appleseed, who is it really talking about?

   Elaborative processes: Why was Johnny Appleseed described as "long and lean"?

Scriptually implicit questions

   How long would it take to walk across the entire United States?

   What did it mean when it said, "apples sharp and sweet"?

Having the choice of three taxonomies of questions available enables the teacher to formulate questions that will provide the type of information she needs to assess the knowledge students have gained from the instruction that has been provided. It also allows the teacher to identify areas of comprehension for which students require more instruction and guided practice.

Step by Step

The steps in implementing QARs to assess student comprehension are:

Step 1   Choosing the QAR Model to Be Used

The teacher chooses from the three models of QAR to give the type of information needed to plan future lessons and/or monitor the student's understanding of concepts that have been recently taught.

Step 2   Preparing the Questions

Using the taxonomies described in figure 49.1, the teacher prepares questions related to a specific reading passage. The teacher prepares a QAR protocol sheet listing the questions and leaving space for the students' responses and additional notes. See figure 49.2 for a sample QAR protocol sheet.

Step 3   Administering the QARs

The teacher works with individual students to administer the QARs. The teacher asks the student to sit beside her and says, "I want you to read this passage to yourself. I will ask you some questions when you have finished reading. Let's read the title together."

"What do you think this story is going to be about?" the teacher asks. She listens to the student's response and notes it on the protocol sheet.

"Do you know anything about this topic?" she asks, and records the response.

Finally she asks, "Would you say you are very familiar, somewhat familiar, or unfamiliar with this topic?"

The teacher gives the student time to read the passage silently and then asks the questions, recording the student's responses. After the reading and questioning is complete, the teacher may choose to discuss the responses with the student and ask him to clarify any areas needing explanation or expansion.

Step 4   Analyzing the Responses

The teacher looks over the protocol sheet, marking correct responses and noting areas needing further attention. If there appears to be an area of concern, the teacher notes it and prepares an observation note reminding herself to observe the student in future reading lessons to determine what, if any, additional instruction is needed in that particular area.

Step 5   Planning Future Comprehension Instruction

After the group or class has been assessed, the teacher uses the results to group the students for further instruction. Lessons are planned related to the areas of weakness identified by the QARs. The broad types of comprehension instruction that comprise the sections of this text can be used as a basis for planning instruction. The individual strategies described in this text can be used to teach or reteach the comprehension processes in which the students need further support.

FIGURE 49.2 Sample QAR protocol sheet.

Student's Name _____ Date _____

Name of Book _____*Johnny Appleseed*_____

Prediction Based on Title _____

Background Knowledge _____

Very Familiar _____ Somewhat Familiar _____ Unfamiliar _____

Instructions: I want you to read this passage to yourself. I will ask you some questions when you have finished reading.

Let's read the title together. (Read the title with the student.)

What do you think this story is going to be about? Student response: _____
_____
_____

Do you know anything about this topic? Student response: _____
_____
_____

Would you say you are very familiar, somewhat familiar, or unfamiliar with this topic? Student response: _____
_____
_____

Give the student time to read the passage silently and then ask the following questions, recording the student's responses.

Text-explicit questions

Microprocesses: What does the word *frontier* mean? _____
_____

Macroprocesses: What was Johnny Appleseed's main contribution to the settlement of the west?
_____
_____

Text-implicit questions

Integrative processes: When the text refers to Johnny Appleseed, who is it really talking about?
_____
_____

Elaborative processes: Why was Johnny Appleseed described as "long and lean"? _____
_____

Scriptually implicit questions

How long would it take to walk across the entire United States? _____
_____

What did it mean when it said, "apples sharp and sweet"? _____
_____

APPLICATIONS AND EXAMPLES

Miss Kinion has been working with her third graders to help them to use their past experiences to understand the books they are reading. She is preparing a QAR protocol for the book *Thank You, Mr. Falker* (Polacco, 1998), which one of her reading groups has just completed. She wants to assess their use of all the comprehension processes, but she is especially interested in their use of the elaborative process, which focuses on their ability to relate their own experiences to the text.

FIGURE 49.3   QAR protocol sheet for *Thank You, Mr. Falker.*

Student's Name _____   Date _____

Name of Book _____*Thank You, Mr. Falker*_____

Instructions: We have just read this book. I want to ask you some questions about some of the things you read. Do the best you can.

Microprocesses: What does the word *miracle* mean? Can you use it in a sentence?

What does the word *stumbled* mean? Can you use it in a sentence?

Macroprocesses: Read the page where Trisha and her grandma are pointing to the stars. After you read it to yourself, tell me what it is about, in your own words.

Integrative Processes: Listen to this sentence, "Are all of you so perfect that you can look at another person and find fault with her?"

　Whom was speaking?

　Who did he mean when he said "all of you"?

Elaborative Processes: Have you ever felt like Trisha did in the first part of this story?

Tell me about it. Did you think of that while you were reading this story?

Have you ever had a teacher like Mr. Falker? Tell me about how they are alike.

See File 49 of the accompanying CD for an example of QAR use in a middle school social studies class.

Miss Kinion designs the QAR questions to sample the students' uses of vocabulary knowledge, making connections between pronouns and referents, and paraphrasing all strategies they have been practicing. She designs several approaches to tap into their use of personal experiences, though, since they don't seem to use this strategy as much as they should.

Miss Kinion looks for several words in the text that she will ask the students to define and use in sentences. She looks for a section they can read silently and then paraphrase, and she looks for a section with a number of anaphoric relationships that she can probe. She intends to ask the students to relate several of the incidents in the book to their own experiences. She carefully chooses her words to make the questions clear to the students and then reviews the protocol sheet. See figure 49.3 to review the protocol sheet she designs for *Thank You, Mr. Falker*.

Once the protocol sheet is complete, Miss Kinion calls the students in the group up to the reading table one at a time and administers the QARs. Because she has designed the protocol herself, based on the instruction she gave during the reading of the book, she has information that gives her the teaching points she needs to pursue with each of the students once the assessment is complete. In addition, she has a good idea which of the strategies she teaches are being understood and used by her students.

CONCLUSION

QARs are a particularly effective approach to assessing students' abilities to comprehend text. Because the questions are prepared by the teacher for the specific reading material appropriate for the readers, the assessment provides vital information related to students' processing of text. The teacher chooses the sequence of questions to be asked according to the instruction that has been given, so the question protocol is also specific to the approach the student has experienced. The teacher gets information related to the effectiveness of the comprehension instruction and the individual abilities of the students.

REFERENCES

Bloom, B. S., Engelhart, M. D., Furst, E., Hill, W. H., & Krathwohl, D. R. (1956). *Taxonomy of educational objectives. The classification of educational goals. Handbook 1: Cognitive domain.* New York: Longman, Green.

Irwin, J.W. (1991). *Teaching reading comprehension processes* (2nd ed.). Boston: Allyn & Bacon.

Lindbergh, R. (1990). *Johnny Appleseed.* Boston: Little, Brown & Company.

Pearson, P., & Johnson, D. (1978). *Teaching reading comprehension.* New York: Holt, Rinehart & Winston.

Polacco, P. (1998). *Thank you, Mr. Falker.* New York: Philomel Books.

Reutzel, D. & Cooter, R. (2000). *Teaching children to read: Putting the pieces together.* (3rd ed.). Upper Saddle River, NJ: Merrill/Prentice Hall.

SUGGESTED READING

Mesmer, H., Hutchins, E. (2002), Using QARs with charts and graphs. *The Reading Teacher*, 56, 21–27.

ELEMENT INTERVIEWS

Engaging Students in Interactions Centered on Story Elements

The use of element interviews is an approach to assessment that requires the student to engage actively in a verbal interaction that demonstrates understanding of various story elements. Depending on the story element being evaluated, the teacher may:

1. ask the student to respond to a series of questions by taking the point of view of a character in the text,
2. ask the student to take the interviewer on a tour of the setting, or
3. ask the student to engage in a debate with another student with each student supporting a different side of the story problem or conflict.

The teacher prepares a list of interview questions related to the story element to be assessed and conducts the interviews with individual students. The level of the questions varies according to the age of the students, but there is always a gradual increase in the difficulty of the questions as the interview progresses. The point of this approach is to assess students' knowledge of story elements and their comprehension of the story. A set of sample protocols for the various element interviews is shown in figure 50.1.

STEP BY STEP

The steps in conducting element interviews are:

STEP 1   INTRODUCING THE TASK

The teacher models the interview process with the whole class or small group using a familiar story. One student asks the questions as the interviewer and the teacher or a volunteer student answers the questions. The teacher reminds the students that they are to pretend to be the character or tour guide, depending on the task being taught, and must give all their responses in character.

STEP 2   PREPARING PROTOCOL FORMS

The teacher plans the questions to be asked and prepares a protocol form on which the questions are listed with blanks where student responses are written.

FIGURE 50.1 Sample questions for element interviews.

FIGURE 50.1 Sample questions for element interviews.

Character Interview of Ira from <u>Ira Sleeps Over</u>

<u>Instructions</u>:

"You are to pretend to be Ira. Answer the questions I ask you as if you are Ira telling your story."

<u>Sample Questions</u>:

Tell me about your family.

What was the problem?

What advice did you get from your mother? Father? Sister?

Did you take your Teddy Bear?

How was the problem solved?

Take a Tour: Setting Interview for <u>Ira Sleeps Over</u>

<u>Instructions</u>:

"Here is a picture of the floor plans of Ira's and Reggie's houses. Pretend I never saw the houses before and take me on a tour showing me where all the important action in the story took place."

Conflict Interview

<u>Instructions</u>:

"Pretend you are Ira. You are having a very hard time trying to make a decision. Think aloud and tell all the things you are thinking about as you try to decide what to do."

<u>OR</u>:

Select two students and have one play Ira and the other play his sister and have them discuss the conflict in the story, taking sides.

STEP 3   ASSESSING INDIVIDUAL STUDENTS

The teacher provides the class with an assignment so that he can call one student at a time to the interview. The teacher gives the instructions and conducts the interview, writing down the student's responses and any other pertinent notes related to the student's behavior during testing.

STEP 4   ANALYZING AND USING THE STUDENT RESPONSES

The teacher notes the question that the student was able to answer and lists teaching points related to the questions that reveal confusion or misunderstanding. The teacher carefully notes the points to be reviewed and the points at which the student was not able to "stay in character." Comprehension scores should not be confused with students' lack of acting ability. The students who show difficulty in staying in character may, however, need more exposure to dramatic reenactment activities.

APPLICATIONS AND EXAMPLES

Mrs. Garabedian's second graders are reading the picture books nominated for the Young Reader's Favorite Book competition. All elementary school classes in the state are invited to read the nominated books and vote for their favorite each year. Because Mrs. G. recognizes that the books are more difficult than the regular books that her students usually read, she wants to check their comprehension of the stories. She introduces the class to element interviews gradually as she teaches the various elements.

Once she has spent time helping students to understand the ways in which characters are developed, she focuses on building characters in her writing lessons. She also discusses the characters at length whenever she reads a book aloud to her students.

Mrs. Garabedian decides to teach character interviews using a favorite book, *Ira Sleeps Over* (Waber, 1972). Because she has read *Ira* aloud to the class and many of the students have read the book individually, she knows the plot of the story is familiar to students. She introduces the concept of character interviews by saying, "Today we are going to do something different. I am going to ask one of you to come up and pretend to be Ira. You'll have to do some good acting. I'll ask you some questions about the story we just reread. The person who is being interviewed will answer the questions aloud, but I want each of you to think about how you would answer the questions if you were Ira. You can write your answers down as you listen to the interview. Jacob, why don't you come up and play Ira?"

Jacob comes up to the front of the class and sits down in a chair facing Mrs. G. "How many of you have seen interviews on television?" Mrs. G. asks. All the students raise their hands. "OK, so you know how this works. I'm the TV reporter and I ask questions. Jacob is pretending to be Ira so he has to think about the story we read and answer the questions."

Mrs. G. has prepared a protocol sheet on which she has listed the questions she wants to ask. She has left room on the protocol sheet to add other questions that she might want to use to clarify the responses to the basic questions.

"Ira, tell me about your family," she begins.

Jacob smiles. "Well, I have a mother and father and one sister."

"How old is your sister?" Mrs. G. asks.

"I'm 7 and she's 9," Jacob/Ira replies. "Is that OK, Mrs. G.? The story didn't tell us how old they were. I think the sister was older, though."

"That's fine," says Mrs. G. "If it's in the story, you have to answer the way the author wrote it, though. Now, tell us more about your family. What do they like to do? What are they like?"

"Well, my dad likes to read the paper and watch TV, and my mother likes to knit. My sister just likes to bug me."

"Now, tell us about the time you were invited over to spend the night with your friend, Reggie. What was the problem?" asks Mrs. G.

"Oh, that was embarrassing," says Jacob/Ira. "I had never slept without my Teddy Bear. I didn't know whether to take him to Reggie's house or not. My mom and dad said to take him, but my dumb sister said that Reggie would laugh at me."

"Did you take your Teddy Bear?" asks Mrs. G.

"Well, yes and no. I couldn't make up my mind. My mother and dad kept saying, 'Take him,' and my sister kept saying, 'He'll laugh!' So, I didn't take him but I ended up coming back for him later."

"How did you feel about that?" asks Mrs. G.

"I was really confused. I kept changing my mind. I didn't want Reggie to laugh but I didn't want to sleep without him, either," replies Jacob/Ira.

"How was the problem solved?" asks Mrs. G.

"Well, Reggie has a Teddy Bear, too. His has a silly name like mine does, too. Once I found out that Reggie has a Teddy, I went home to get mine. As usual, my dumb sister was wrong!"

"Very good!" says Mrs. Garabedian. "You really were a great Ira!"

"How many of you were able to answer all the questions as if you were Ira?" she asks the class. Many hands go up. "Well, I'm going to interview some of the rest of you today. Instead of being Ira though, you'll be Grandpa from *Grandpa's Teeth* (Clement, 1997). Won't that be fun?"

"Oh, Mrs. G." says Randy. "That's going to be hard. Do we have to talk the way Grandpa talks without his teeth?"

"I think you can do it," says Mrs. G. with a smile. Mrs. G. gets the students started on their reading workshop and sets up a table at the back of the room. She sits behind the table so she can see the class and puts a chair across the table from her chair so the person being interviewed won't be distracted by the other students.

FIGURE 50.2 Protocol sheet for character interviews for *Grandpa's Teeth*.

Character Interviews: Character _____ Student _____

Title of Book _____ Date _____

Instructions:

"I want you to pretend to be the character, Grandpa. Now, I will ask you some questions about the time you lost your teeth, Grandpa. Don't forget to pretend you are Grandpa as you answer the questions."

Tell me about your family. _____

What was the problem? _____

How did you feel about having lost your teeth? _____

Was your family helpful? _____

Who else was helpful? _____

It must have been hard, going so long without your teeth. Tell us about some of the things that worried you. _____

How did it all turn out? _____

How did you feel at the end? _____

_____

_____

_____

_____

She has prepared a protocol sheet for the interviews and is anxious to find out how well the students understand the new story. See figure 50.2 for the protocol sheet for *Grandpa's Teeth*.

Mrs. Garabedian plans to interview four students each day so that she can complete the interviews in one week. She will use the results she gets from the interviews to plan future lessons in comprehension strategies. She will also ask each of the students to follow up their interview session by writing a paragraph about how Grandpa felt when his teeth were lost. After everyone has been interviewed, she will use this writing assignment to further discuss character development and help the students to learn to put themselves in the place of the characters in the books they are reading.

See File 50 of the accompanying CD for an example of element interviews in a high school literature class.

CONCLUSION

Element interviews are a slightly different approach to gaining access to the students' thought processes after they have read a book. The focus of the interview will change depending upon the book that's been read. The interview approach gives the teacher the opportunity to assess the students' knowledge of the story, setting, characters, and plot in any story with simple adaptations of the questions. Although no standard score is obtained through this type of testing, the teacher gains valuable knowledge related to the students' comprehension of the story and also of their comprehension of basic story elements. This assessment strategy can be adapted to serve as a writing connection to literature by having students design the questions, thinking about the story elements of setting, problem, character, cause and effect, events, and sequence as they compose the questions. Several students playing different characters can be interviewed in a talk show format as a class activity.

REFERENCES

Clement, R. (1997). *Grandpa's teeth*. Sydney, Australia: Harper Collins.

Waber, B. (1972). *Ira sleeps over*. Boston: Houghton Mifflin.